# Scones for the Heart

# SCONES *for the* HEART

184 inspiring morsels
of wit and wisdom
to warm your soul

by
George D. Durrant

BONNEVILLE BOOKS™
Springville, Utah

ISBN: 1-55517-593-7
v.2

Published by Bonneville Books
Imprint of Cedar Fort Inc.
www.cedarfort.com

Distributed by:

Typeset by Kristin Nelson
Cover design by Adam Ford


Printed in the United States of America
10 9 8 7 6 5 4 3 2 1

Printed on acid-free paper

Library of Congress Cataloging-in-Publication Data

Durrant, George D.
Scones for the heart : 184 inspiring morsels of wit and wisdom to warm your soul / by George D. Durrant.
p. cm.
ISBN 1-55517-593-7 (pbk. : alk. paper)
1. Christian life--Church of Jesus Christ of Latter-day Saints authors. 2. Durrant, George D. I. Title.
BX8656 .D87 2002
242--dc21

2001006190

# TABLE OF CONTENTS

## SCONES FOR THE HEART



## SCONES FOR THE FAMILY

**PRIESTHOOD SCONES**



**SCONES OF COMMUNICATION**



**TEACHING SCONES**

**MISSIONARY SCONES**

**TESTIMONY SCONES**



**THE SCONES OF REPENTANCE**

**SELF ESTEEM SCONES**



**FAMILY HOME EVENING SCONES**



**HOLIDAY SCONES**



**TEMPLE SCONES**

**GOSPEL LIVING SCONES**

**THE SCONES OF SACRIFICE AND SERVICE**

# SCONES FOR THE HEART

## The Joy Of Giving And Receiving Scones

I would often come crying to my mother about the persecution heaped upon me by my older brothers and their friends. She would then say to them, "You kids should quit teasing George. He's not the one that acts like a baby. You kids are the babies." When she would say that I would stick my head out from behind her skirt and say, "That's right!"

Once when I was playing with them they told me to go in the house because I was too little to play the games they were playing. Heartbroken, I ran as quickly as I could to my mother. She heard my sobs and listened to my account of their evil deeds. However on this day she was making bread and she didn't use her normal tactic of calling the others in for a rebuke. Instead she took pieces of dough and molded each into small flat pieces. Soon she placed each small piece of dough in a frying pan filled with sizzling grease. She was making scones, and scones are good.

The sight and smell of the browning scones was enough to make me quit crying. I wondered why she was making so many. I knew that I couldn't eat but a small portion of them. She seemed to be making dozens. Finally she handed me the pan heaped to overflowing and said: "Take these scones and go back outside and see if those other kids will play with you now."

I went back outside and suddenly my whole world was changed. I had instant friends. I heard remarks such as: "Could I have a scone?" "What do you want to play now?" "Give me another one." "You can be the captain." "Can I have another scone?" "You can play any position you want." "How about one more?"

That day I learned that every one is always hungry for a scone. Giving scones to others is the key to popularity. Carry a pan full of scones where ever you go and everyone will be your friend. Sadly, however, keeping a pan of scones to serve to others is not possible. Either they get eaten too quickly or they soon become cold and greasy and undesirable.

But there is another place to carry an even more delicious kind of scones. That place is in your heart. You can carry a never-ending supply of these scones and the more you give away the more which will still be there. The ingredients of these scones are kind, encouraging, positive words and helpful, generous deeds. These scones are always fresh, warm, delicious and desirable. The hunger for such scones is found in every person you meet. The stories in this book are about giving and receiving the scones of the heart.

## Eating Scones at Home With The Family Is Like Being In Heaven

We had a late Sacrament Meeting and as we walked home I asked Sister Durrant, "Could we have scones tonight?"

She replied, "Making scones is so much work."

I answered, "I know. I was thinking about it during Church. I analyzed it completely and came to the conclusion that making scones is just barely within the Sabbath Day laws. But I know it's a lot of work so let's not do it."

She replied as I hoped she would by saying, "Well, if you all helped we could do it."

Soon she made some dough. Out daughter Kathryn fried some eggs without even turning them over. The milk in the fridge was so cold that it was almost frozen. As the eggs fried,

Marilyn placed the scone dough in the frying pan and as they sizzled they changed from white to a nice brown.

Joyfully we surrounded our table. I humorously announced, "We will now call upon our most popular, most intelligent, and our best looking family member to lead us in prayer."

Each of the children, feeling that I was describing him or her, responded, "I gave the prayer last time."

Then I named one of the children and the others replied, "It did not sound like you were talking bout him."

We are not a very rich family, but we had enough money so that each member of the family had a different colored drinking glass. We prayed and then we started to eat. The margarine was dripping off the hot scones as we dipped them in the eggs and took numerous gulps of delicious cold milk. We talked, laughed and loved.

Then it was as though there was a pounding on the window. We open the window and it was as if our whole house was flooded with blessings.

## Have A Scone For Everyone

I went home teaching one night shortly after I was ordained an elder. Because I was now an Elder, I thought I ought to say something during the visit, which thing I had never done before. But I was still a junior companion and my old seminary teacher, Raymond Bailey, was doing almost all the talking. I did come in with two or three inspiring comments on the good weather.

The little old lady we were visiting was afflicted with arthritis and she couldn't stand up from her chair. She was listening and she would respond with comments which inspired me. As I was sitting there I was so thrilled to be home teaching and feeling love for this sister.

When we were preparing to leave, she said something that threw me into a panic. She said, "Could the two of you give me a blessing?"

I started to pray. And my prayers were answered because nobody had any oil. I didn't know how to give anybody a blessing. My seminary teacher said, "We'll go home and get some oil and we'll be right back."

On the way to get the oil I said, "I can't help you, Brother Bailey."

He asked, "Why not?"

I said, "I don't know how."

He then explained to me what I was to do. He then said, "You can do that, can't you?"

I replied, "Yeah, I can do that."

We came back to her home and I anointed her head with the oil. Then Brother Bailey's hands joined mine on her head and he gave her a mighty blessing. My soul was tingling with spiritual sensations. Finally he said, "Amen." We each took a step backwards and looked down at this dear sister. To my surprise she stood up. With tears in her eyes, she took my hand in both of hers and said, "I'm so thrilled that you're the kind of young man who can come and give me a blessing."

I had to break away from her, I couldn't take it. I left Brother Bailey to say good-night. I went out on the front walk and looked up at the stars over American Fork and thought, "I've found what I want to do with my life. I'm just going to go around giving people blessings."

I had found my "pan of scones." I wanted to give people blessings.

# SCONES FOR THE FAMILY

## Being With Family Is Better Than Being in Disneyland

*A father told me this story:*

Two months ago we had a most amazing thing happen in our family. For years we had wanted to go to Disneyland. This was the year we were to go. We had saved for this trip for several months. Now we had the money and the vacation time to go. Three weeks before we were to depart, we were sitting at the dinner table. There was a feeling of real gloom in our home. I tried to cheer everybody up, but I could not. We ate in that silence that sometimes falls upon families.

Finally my oldest son, seventeen years old, asked, "Why do we have to go to Disneyland?"

Almost in anger, I said, "Now, just what do you mean by that? Have you and your friends planned something? You are getting so that nothing in the family is as important as being with your friends."

"No, it's not that," he said softly.

Again silence returned. Then my daughter said, "I know what he means, and I don't want to go to Disneyland either."

I was shocked. We had planned this trip for years.

I almost shouted as I said in a commanding voice, "Well, whether you want to or not, we are all going to Disneyland."

My wife put her hand gently on my hand and said, "Your brother phoned today and told us his children really felt bad that we were going to miss Kenley Creek this year to go to Disneyland. And I think that is what is troubling the children."

Then, almost in chorus, the children said, "We want to see our cousins. That is why we don't want to go to Disneyland."

I said, "Hey, look, I want to see the family too. But I only get so much vacation time, and we all decided it would be Disneyland. The family goes to Kenley Creek every year. We went there last year, and we'll go there next year, but this year we decided on Disneyland. Of course, if you all want to change the plans, well . . . I'd sooner see my brothers and sisters. But I thought this time we would do what you wanted to do."

My oldest son, who is known for his tough-guy attitude, seemed near tears as he asked, "Can we change, Dad?"

So we changed plans. I phoned my brother, and while we were talking I told him that we had decided to go to Kenley Creek. I could hear him shouting to his children, "Your cousins are coming to Kenley Creek!"

Our children were happy again.

*Then this father told me the story of Kenley Creek.*

When my father and mother were young we did not have much money. We couldn't go on vacation to any place that cost a lot. So every year Mom and Dad would pack the wooden grub box with all kinds of food. We'd tie the old canvas tent to the top of the 1947 Ford. All us children would pile in like sardines in a can, and off we would go to the mountains and to Kenley Creek.

We did that every year. Finally my older brother got married. His wife was sort of a fancy, rich girl. She had been all over the country on vacations. We didn't think that she would go with us to Kenley Creek, but she did and she had the time of her life.

One by one we all got married, and every summer at a certain time we would all come home and drive up to Kenley Creek.

The year after Dad died, we wondered if we should go. But Mom said that Dad would want us to go and that he'd be there with us. And so we all went.

As the years passed, each of us brothers and sisters had children of our own. My brother could play the accordion, and each night under the moonlight of the Kenley Creek sky he played polkas and all the kids would dance with their cousins.

Finally Mom died. But every year at Kenley Creek, in the quiet of the mountain evening, it seemed like Mom and Dad would come back and sit by the campfire with all of us. With the eyes of our hearts we could see them smile as they watched the grandkids dance and eat the watermelon that had been cooled by the cold waters of the stream. We brothers and sisters would talk of the times gone by, and Mom and Dad would just listen.

We all were a family, and we loved each other more and more as the years passed by.

When we decided to go to Disneyland, I guess I just didn't know how much these family ties meant to the children. We knew how much it meant to us but not to them.

So we changed our mind and went to Kenley Creek. We did so because being with our family meant more than all the Disneylands in the world.

## No Trip Is Too Long If It Takes You To Your Family

After my Saturday evening address, which concluded at nine o'clock, I jumped in my rental car and headed from Missouri to Indiana to visit my daughter's family, whom I had not seen in nearly nine months. I drove until midnight and sang all the way. I couldn't help singing for joy, because every minute of the journey I could see little five-year-old Lexie, three-year-old Ben, and little six-month-old Tyler in my mind and in my heart. With such a vision I did not want to stop, but wisdom dictated that I get a motel and sleep for a few hours.

At four in the morning, I was on the road again. I passed by the big arch at St. Louis and crossed the bridge that spanned the Mississippi. Now I was on a highway that led directly to Jeffersonville, Indiana, where my wonderful family anxiously awaited the arrival of Grandpa.

As I whizzed along I took great pleasure in seeing the signs which indicated how far it was to Jeffersonville. One hundred miles, then sixty-five, then forty, then twenty. By now I could not restrain my joy. I sang and whistled and talked out loud. Soon I was less than one-half hour away from pure happiness. Finally I was at the exit, then on the river road, then at the turnoff. Then I could see the house. A few minutes later I was greeted at the door by that wonderful salutation, "Grandpa. Grandpa! Grandpa!" I was with people that I love more than life itself. I cannot begin to say how much joy my presence brought to that little family who were so starved for family and for home and for Grandpa.

I could only stay the afternoon and the evening. At four in the morning I'd head up the road that I had come down—back to St. Louis to catch a flight home and to get back to my teaching post.

When it was bedtime I went to the children's room to tell them stories. But before the stories Lexie and Ben began to jump up and down on Lexie's bed. Their mother scolded them and told them to stop. So I decided to take everything into my own hands and to make everything all right. Soon I was standing on the bed beside the two little ones, and seconds later I was jumping up and down with them. Neither they nor I could stop laughing, even though my daughter tried to act exasperated. Then, she too gave up and joined in the fun.

The next morning, I quietly arose so as to not wake any of them. I went to the children's room. They were fast asleep. I kissed Ben on the cheek and then little Tyler and finally Princess Lexie. It was as if I were kissing angels. I turned away and was soon out the door and in my car. I could not hold back the tears that are so much a part of saying sweet good-byes.

## The Best Thing I've Done As Mission President Is To Build My Kids A Swing

I knew that in order to preside effectively in the mission, I must first preside well at home. I spent much time with my family, knowing they were the only ones who would still be mine at the end of my mission. If they felt secure and happy in the early days of our mission, things would go from good to better.

One of the first orders of business was to throw a big rope over a high limb on the huge ash tree that towered over our front yard. An acrobatic elder climbed the rope and tied it to the limb. Thus the giant mission home swing was born. With the swing came instant neighborhood friends for our younger children.

A few months after our arrival, we attended a mission presidents' seminar. Each president was asked what he felt was his best idea so far. Each reported on some program which he felt had enhanced the work. When my turn came, I said, "The best thing I've done so far is to build a swing." Everyone laughed.

President S. Dilworth Young was amazed and asked, "What?" I described the swing and explained that my major goal was to be a good father. I told of a young wife who had visited me just a few days before and had said, "My experience as a mission president's daughter was a nightmare from which

I shall never recover." I felt the Lord had sent her to me to teach me to look first to my family and then to the mission duties. The swing became my symbol of this setting of priorities. Later came a basketball standard and a sand pile. Our yard became a park where I spent much time with my children and where they settled for three happy years. I believe they will forever remember with joy their time in Kentucky and Tennessee.

## Being At An Amusement Park With Your Family Is Church Work

While I was mission president, I would quite often resolve that it was again time for some more high-priority Church work. Then we would all go to an amusement park called Opryland in Nashville, Tennessee. It is a beautiful park where groups perform country-western music. I know of few more pleasant places. I just walked around the park with a smile on my face, holding hands with my children, eating all the cotton candy I could stand.

Once in a while, a thought would enter my mind: "Hey, you're the mission president. You'd better get back to the office." But then I'd smile again and say to myself, "Well, I'm doing my Church work here. I'm with my children and my wife. We're having a fun day and tonight I'll be able to write in my journal that I did six hours of glorious Church work today." I'd eat a little more cotton candy and let the children lead me wherever they wanted to go.

## Husband, Father And Priesthood Are The Greatest Honors

As I think of the honor of fatherhood, I recall that at work I was once asked to fill out a questionnaire. One of the questions was "What honors have you received?" I thought as I read the question, "I'll leave that one and come back to it." I filled in all the other blanks and then again looked at the words "What honors have you received?" I could think of none. I'd never been all-state in anything nor had I been elected to any office. I felt a little unimportant as I left the item blank. I folded the paper and placed it in the envelope for mailing. But before I sealed it, I paused. I took the paper out of the envelope and smoothed it on the table.

I picked up my pen. In response to the question, "What honors have you received?" I wrote the glorious words, "The Melchizedek Priesthood." My soul was stirred as I considered again the honor and thrill of being an elder. But having written that, I now knew that I must write more. I then recorded another honor—I wrote the word "Husband." It's such a joy to be a husband and to strive to be worthy of the honor of having a woman love and respect you. Having listed these two supreme honors, "The Melchizedek Priesthood" and "Husband," I was now inspired to list my final and greatest honor. I wrote with reverence the sacred word "Father."

So my honors were listed: Melchizedek Priesthood, husband, and father.

Such honors when seen with eyes that really see make the honors of men shrink and hide in the wings.

## No Great Men But Only Great Challenges

I recall a story that came out of World War II and which I saw depicted in an old movie. In the story a navy pilot during the early days of the Pacific campaign had been quickly elevated in rank due to the fact that many of his superiors were killed in the intense struggle. Finally this young officer became aware that he would soon be asked to become a commander of many other pilots. He knew that in that role he would have the almost unbearable responsibility of directing men to places from which they would never return.

He was called before the admiral, knowing what he would be asked to do. He decided to refuse the command. As he had suspected, the orders were that he take the assignment. In response he quickly refused on the grounds that he was not qualified. The admiral arose from his chair, came around the desk, and put his hand on the young man's shoulders. Looking into his eyes, the admiral said, "What do you want me to do—find a great man for this terrible responsibility? Well, let me tell you something. There aren't any great men. There are only great responsibilities. When ordinary men like you and me meet a great responsibility, and fulfill it, then a great man is born."

## I'd Come To The Delivery Room But I'm Reading This Sports Illustrated

Our second son was our third child. At the time I was teaching seminary in Brigham City, Utah. It was my birthday. I was called to the phone. Marilyn, who was close to the time of delivery, said, "I believe I have a special birthday present for you. Come home and let's go to the hospital to get the gift."

I excitedly told the students, "Teach yourselves," and away I went. Soon we were at the hospital. She went to the room where mothers go to have babies and I went to the room where fathers go to wait. Later I was reading a magazine when the doctor interrupted me by asking, "Would you like to come into the delivery room?"

I replied, "Well, I would, but I'm reading this Sports Illustrated magazine."

He replied, "Maybe you could read that later."

"I'm right in the middle of an article." I then told him that I sort of got a bit queasy in such circumstances. He told me that he was sure I'd be all right.

In kindness he said, "Come on in. Marilyn would like you to and I'm sure you'll do just fine."

I was out of excuses, and so I followed along.

The kind doctor explained to me all that was happening. Soon the room where we were seemed to be a holy place. A place very much connected to another holy place. I've felt close to Our Heavenly Father at certain sacred times in my life but never had I felt this close.

I stood in spiritual awe as the baby was born. I don't know just when his spirit came down from heaven to give him life, but I knew that he had very recently come to us from God. The doctor held him by his ankles and for a few seconds there was silence and then the baby cried. I cried too. I've never been part of such a miracle.

## President, You Are Not As Great As My Father

The mission president and his wife are looking up at him from their seats. He starts to speak. His voice breaks with emotion as he looks into the eyes of the mission president and says: "President, you're a great man, and I love you. But I want to tell you something. You're not as great a man as my father. My father is the greatest man I've ever known."

The elder pauses. His emotions make it difficult for him to continue, because he has just made a statement that came right from the bottom of his heart.

As a mission president, whenever I heard an elder refer to his father in such a way I knew that there wasn't going to be any difficulty working with that elder. I knew that when a missionary thought of his father in that way he was in a state of mind that would make him valiant.

Now let's just have a look at this Elder's father, this father whom we have just been told is a great man. You might say, "I'll bet he's a stake president." Well, he isn't. You might say, "He must be a bishop." But he isn't. You might say, "I'll bet he's a great speaker and teacher in the Church." He isn't. If we could see this father, we might even wonder why the elder said what he did. He might not look that impressive at all. He might be a most ordinary looking man. He might not be anything great in the business world. He might have a job which seems quite unimportant. Now, this doesn't mean for sure he isn't a stake president—he might be, of course. It doesn't mean for sure he isn't a bishop. It doesn't mean he isn't a dynamic man. But these are not the things the elder is talking about.

You see, the elder is away from home; he has forgotten some of the faults his father has, and all he can see are those glorious traits that make his father his father. And that's why this statement, spoken with all the sincerity of his soul, coming from the bottom of his heart, thrills the souls of all those who hear it. This statement uttered about a father (and the same thing holds true for a mother) by a son or daughter tells us much about that son or daughter. If you could make such a statement about your parents right now, it could change your whole life.

## Fathers Know More Than We Think That They Do

I know of one young man who wanted to get advice from his Church leader, advice about his girl friend and his prospective marriage and a number of other personal matters. He particularly admired this leader, so he went to him and asked for advice.

The leader's advice was, "Go home and talk it over with your father."

The young man became quite irritated at this. "My father

wouldn't understand this," he said. "I don't talk to him about such things."

When he saw this leader some time later he told him what had happened. "I was most upset with your counsel at the time," he said, "but some days later I was hauling hay with my father. As we worked together I got to thinking about what you had said, and I decided to ask his advice as you had suggested."

He continued, "We sat down on a bale of hay and talked. I was amazed at my dad's response. I didn't think he understood about such things. But he told me about how he met Mom and about their courtship. Suddenly I found myself enthralled with what he was saying. I asked him more and more searching questions about things. The answers he gave me seemed to ring loud and clear and true to me. I took my dad's advice. It turned out to be exactly the right thing for me to do."

## I Wish My Dad Was Crazy

Once I gave some of my children a ride to school. I was in a particularly jolly mood and made many remarks that the children felt were funny. I even sang a little for them. (They also thought this was funny, although I hadn't intended it to be.) We had a ball as we rode along.

Later, one of my children reported that after they had all left the car another child had said to him, "Your dad is crazy." Then, after a pause, he had continued, "I sure wish my dad was crazy."

## When I Taught My Family I Felt Like A Real Father

Some years ago, while pursuing a graduate degree, I conducted a study on the subject of family home evening and its influence on children. To carry out the research, I located a number of families who had seldom, if ever, held family home evenings. I visited these families, who were less active in the Church, and asked them if they would conduct a family home evening each week for a period of three months. I advised them that I felt that by doing so it would help their children have more self-confidence. To measure the effects of the home evenings on the children, I asked the parents for permission to give their children a "self-image test" both before and after the three months.

One man didn't seem enthusiastic at all about my request that he and his family hold family home evenings each week for three months. He attempted to escape involvement by saying, with some embarrassment, "I can't teach." I assured him that if he would call the family together and do his best, the teaching part would work out all right; I think he only agreed because he lacked the courage to tell me he wouldn't do it. As I left his house, he had little to say and I felt he wished that I had never called on him.

Three months later, I returned, by appointment, to call on him and his family. As I left my car and closed the door, his front door opened and he come out onto the well-lit porch to greet me. I've never met a friendlier man or experienced a warmer welcome.

He immediately called his family of five children together. He, his wife, and the children sat on a stone bench that ran from the fireplace to the other side of the room. I took a seat in front of them and after some conversation I asked him for a report. The children, ranging in age from teenagers to a five-year-old, burst in before he could respond and each one expressed enthusiasm for what had happened in the family home evenings.

Then the wife spoke. "It has been a wonderful experience

for us," she said, and then with considerable emotion she added, "and the very best lessons we had were those Jerry taught."

I thought that Jerry was one of the children. I smiled and said, "That's quite a compliment for you, Jerry." I then asked, "Now, which one of you children is Jerry?"

The wife quickly replied, "Oh no, Jerry isn't one of the children; Jerry is my husband."

I was a bit embarrassed at my error and my eyes quickly focused on the father. He was looking down and for a time he remained silent. In a quiet and humble tone he spoke, "Aw, I didn't do so good."

His wife was forceful and sincere as she replied, "Jerry, when you taught us it just seemed so powerful. It just seemed as if we were a family. We'll never forget the things you said."

Jerry was deeply touched by these heartfelt words. He looked up and into my eyes and spoke, "I guess I did do pretty good." After a pause he said, "You know, I've always been kind of the black sheep of my family. Growing up, I felt that the others in the family were better than me. So I guess I sort of rebelled and didn't do much in the Church. I got so I just didn't even go."

I listened intently as he continued. "I didn't want to have these family home evenings because I knew they were part of the Church, and besides, I just didn't feel I could do it. But one night after my wife had taught a lesson one week and my daughter another week, I decided I'd try one."

His eyes grew moist as he said: "I'll never forget the feeling I had in my heart as I talked about good things with my family. It just seemed that I was for the first time the father that I was supposed to be. I felt so good about what I'd done that the next Sunday morning I decided to go over to the church. I've been going over there every Sunday since then and I've never been so happy in all my life."

## Could We Count the Night That We Went To The Temple?

While doing my dissertation I asked families who were not doing so to begin to have family home evenings each Monday night for at least twelve weeks.

I shall forever remember one family's experience.

When I went to this family to make my original request, I found a ruggedly handsome father, a beautiful wife, and five young children. The home was lovely and well kept. Upon my arrival in the home, the father put his smoking pipe aside and talked to us in a most cordial way. A can of beer was open near the side of his chair. As we spoke of several subjects, I learned that he refereed high school basketball games. Thus we had a common interest—sports.

Finally I told him the purpose of my visit. I made the request, and he accepted, saying that he would faithfully conduct a family home evening each week. His wife and family seemed pleased at his response. I gave them a few guidelines to follow, administered the self-image test to their children and told them that I'd visit them again in three months.

Winter had turned to spring before I saw them again. I called them by phone and made an appointment to come to their home. As I was greeted by this family; I felt almost overwhelmed by their welcome. We visited for a time and then I asked, "Well, did you do it? Did you have a home evening every week for the past three months as you said you would?"

The father looked at me intently and said, "I'm not sure. Most weeks we did, but there was one week we aren't sure if what we did was a family home evening or not."

I was pleased at their faithfulness and said, "Well, if you had one every week but one, that's pretty good."

The mother then said, "I think we could even count what

we did that week. Anyway, we wanted to ask you if what we did would count."

I said, "Tell me what you did and we'll see."

The father replied, "That's the week we went to the temple to be sealed together forever as a family." His eyes were moist with tears as he asked, "Can we count that?"

I was caught off-guard by this unexpected response and I could hardly speak because of emotion. I softly replied, "Yes, I believe we could count that."

The mother's eyes and face shone as she said, "We went to the temple on my birthday."

He quickly added, "I couldn't even get her much of a present. Since we started paying tithing, there's not much money left over for presents."

Tears fell freely from his wife's face as she looked into his eyes and said, "When you took me to the temple, that was the best present that I've ever received because that's what I wanted more than anything else in the world."

By now the children all wanted to tell me about the temple and what going there meant to them. After listening to their happy reports, I asked the father, "What happened to cause this mighty change?"

His simple reply was, "Well, I did what you said. Each week I'd call my family together and we'd have family home evening. After a few weeks, I saw the children sitting there real close to me and their mother. We all felt so good and so happy. I just decided it was time we started changing things. We talked about going to the temple so that we could be together forever. We talked to our home teachers and then to the bishop. And in a few weeks we felt we were worthy to go to the temple."

The father then asked, "Do you think we could count that as a family home evening?"

I thought for a moment and then said, "Yeah, let's count it."

## My Father Told Me He Loved Me In His Own Way

My own father had a hard time saying "I love you." As a matter of fact, I do not recall that I ever heard him say that to anyone. He was good to me and because of all that he did for me I was very suspicious that he loved me; I really knew he did, but he never would say it.

He had been a miner in the silver mines and later he became a poultry-man. He was a rough outdoorsman and had expertise in hunting and fishing. He was really a man's man and to me he was a great father. But he never said, "George, I love you." One day he did come close to telling me he loved me.

I was about to depart on my mission to England. I was nearly twenty-two years old. (Missionaries didn't go at age nineteen then.) It was in the middle of November and there was snow on the ground. I was to depart in three days. Since I was the youngest of nine children, when I departed all the children would be gone from home. My father must have felt a bit saddened by this. He and I were alone in our big kitchen where we seemed to live our lives (seldom did we go in the front room). He stood looking out the window that was the upper portion of our back door. He suddenly said, "George, come over here." I went to his side and looked out. About a hundred yards beyond our barn was a thicket of brush and trees. There in the snow on the edge of the brush was a beautiful Chinese pheasant. My father spoke again, "George, get the gun."

I replied, "Dad, the season ended over a week ago."

I'll never forget what he said next because it was the most loving thing he ever spoke to me. He said, "I know that. You go get the gun and go out there and shoot that pheasant. And while you're doing it, I'll call the cops and they'll come and arrest you and you won't have to go."

I was by this time much taller than he. I looked down at him and he looked away. I put my hand on his shoulder and then pulled him close to me. Together we cried. My dad, my dear dad, had for the first time said in the best words he could muster, and in the best way he knew how, what I had longed to hear for twenty-two years. He had said, "George, my son, I love you."

## A Dad And A Son On A Log

We can say "I love you" in a number of ways. When my son Dwight was six years old, I took him from Salt Lake City to Provo one day. While I worked at BYU he played with friends in the neighborhood where we had once lived. At the day's end I picked him up and we drove toward home. We stopped for a snack; we took our order from the cafe and walked about twenty-five yards to the bank of the Provo River. There, sitting on a log, we ate. I looked at the river and then at my son on the opposite end of the log.

I spoke, "I've got a better hamburger than you."

He answered, "Mine's just like yours."

I added, "My milkshake is better than yours."

He replied, "Mine's the same flavor as yours."

"My fries are better," I said.

"I've got ones just like yours," he replied convincingly.

After a pause I looked at him and said, "I've got one thing that you haven't got."

He was certain that I didn't have and asked with a challenge, "What?"

"I've got a son that I call Crow. And I'm sitting on a log with him and I love him with all my heart. And you don't have that."

Crow didn't answer. He just looked at me for a few seconds, then bit into his hamburger and with his other hand threw a rock in the river. I had bested him and he knew it.

## Better To Be Father Than To Be King

If I had lived in the days of King Arthur I would have been one of the simple folks in the kingdom. My family and I would have lived in a little village about three miles south of the castle.

One day King Arthur, returning from a battle came riding by on a white horse, accompanied by several knights. As these great men rode past our thatched covered cottage the king looked over and watched us. We were playing basketball on a dirt court that we had smoothed out near our little garden. Our ball was one your mother had knitted and filled with straw. Our hoop was a fruit basket whose bottom had been worn through. All you kids were laughing and shouting, “Daddy! Daddy! Throw it to me.”

King Arthur reined up his horse, pause and watched us for a long time. The knights finally grew impatient and said, “Let’s go King.”

Arthur replied as if he was in a different world, “Just a minute. Just a minute.” And then looking back he slowly rode forward. He was on his way toward a great battle. But in his heart, as he went along in silence, he remembered me. In his mind he could see Marilyn looking on admiringly at me and you children laughing and playing and calling me, “Dad.”

He, the mighty king, was jealous of me-one of the simple folks. As he moved silently toward making history, he asked his knights, “Who was that man back there with those children?”

They replied, “Who cares?”

He answered softly, “That woman and those children seem to care.”

## Go Forward. Do Your Best.
## Love Your Family.

Some years ago I was serving as a bishop. At the same time I was working on a doctor's degree at a university and holding a full time job. My children felt I was spending too much time away from them. I was under some strain, fearing that because of my desire to succeed in so many areas I was really failing as a man.

One Sunday evening all the members of my ward had gone home. I had stayed on for a while to complete some work. I walked into the chapel to turn off the lights before departing for home. I felt lonely in the empty chapel. As I stood there I felt that my back would not bear for another day the heavy burdens which I was carrying.

I fell to my knees near the pulpit and cried to the Lord. I told him, as one friend would another, my deepest concerns. I poured out the feelings of my soul to him and described in detail my seemingly insurmountable tasks. When I finished I remained kneeling. And as I did I heard him speak to me in my heart. The answer he gave me was all I needed, for he said just three things:

Go forward.

Do your best.

Love your family.

I arose a new man. My burdens had been made light. I'd keep going. I would spend less time on the unimportant things in the ward, and I might not get "A" grades in school, but I'd keep going. I'd do my best, and that would be success. And most of all, I'd love my family. Oh, how I'd love them! I'd love my wife and I'd tell her so. I'd spend time with my children, and I'd know that such is the highest form of Church work.

And so I say to you, to all who, with me, are honored with the calling of *father*, let us:

Go forward.

Do our best.

And love our families.

## My Mother Probably Saved My Life

I was a senior in high school at the time. You know, that's about the age when you think you can make your own decisions. I told Mom that I was going to Las Vegas with my buddies. She calmly asked me what we were going down for, how long we would be gone, and so on. I gave her what I thought were good answers. I was polite and kind and considerate.

She didn't say much more about it, and finally it came time for us to go. I had a little bag packed; and as I walked out toward the car my mother followed me out. "George," she said, "come back just a minute, will you?"

I said, "Sure, Mom," and stepped back into the house.

"George," she said, "don't go."

"Gee, Mom," I protested, "they're waiting for me. I promised to go. I want to go. It'll be a good little vacation for me, and I've got the money to go."

"George, don't go," she repeated.

"But why, Mom?" I asked.

"I don't know why," she replied, "but please don't go."

"Mom, I've got to go," I insisted.

Yet again she said, "Don't go."

Now a strange feeling began to come over me. "Mom, why?"

This time she said, "I just know you shouldn't go."

The feeling had now become so overwhelming that I just walked out of the house and said to my friends, "I can't go."

They began to get upset. "Why not?" they asked.

I replied, "Because my mom says I shouldn't go."

Of course, they tried to persuade me, then finally to taunt me into going. "Ah, come on. What are you, some kind of a mama's boy?"

I simply said, "No, I'm not a mama's boy, but she said I shouldn't go and I'm not going."

They finally gave up on me and drove away in some degree of disgust.

Two days later I learned that my friends' car had turned over several times as they were traveling down the highway late at night and that all four of those fellows had been thrown out. Not one of them had been seriously injured; one was knocked unconscious for a time, but he was revived and he had no after-effects. The police officer said it was a miracle someone hadn't been killed. I've always wondered what would have happened if there had been five fellows in that car. I wonder if five would have been as lucky as four. I guess I'll never know. But I do know that my mom knew I shouldn't go; and I know now, as I knew then, that she was right.

## An Angel Or A Mother

Devin, like many athletes, was highly recruited by many universities who desired him to play on their team. One night just before the big decision had to be made, Devin was sleeping in his basement bedroom. Suddenly he was awakened by someone standing at this bedside. It was Marilyn, his mother. She couldn't sleep because of her concern for him. She was dressed in a white nightgown. Without any formal or informal introduction, she simply said, "Devin, you're going to go to BYU." Then she departed as quickly as she had come. The next day when Devin awoke and came to breakfast, he said, "Father, last night something strange happened. I don't know if it was the angel Moroni or someone else. All I know is that somebody appeared at my bedside and told me I had to go to BYU." Marilyn, who was stirring pancake batter, stirred even faster.

## Mothers Know How Other Mothers Feel

I recall a five-year-old Indian boy whom I knew in Brigham City. He had danced the eagle dance in the Peach Days parade and had delighted each of the thousands who watched from the roadside.

He lived in an apartment near the center of Brigham City, and he didn't even have a dog. (I shouldn't put such sad things in a book.)

While the boy was visiting an uncle in Perry, a small town south of Brigham City, a man recognized him as the boy who had danced in the parade. The man asked, "Would you dance for me?"

The boy replied, "No."

The man said, "Come and see what I've got behind my house."

The boy followed and saw a mother dog and three tiny puppies. The man said, "If you'll dance for me, I'll give you something." And as he said this, he looked at the dogs. The boy looked at the dogs and then at the man. The boy and the man understood each other.

Did the boy dance? Of course he did. You would have too. Any boy would have. How do we know? Because we were once five years old and we know how he felt. What was he thinking while he danced? We know what he was thinking. We don't have to be a psychologist to know. He was thinking, "Which puppy will be mine?"

The boy danced as he had never danced before, and when he finished the man clapped and said, "Because you danced so well, the mother dog and all three of these puppies are yours. Take them home." The boy felt unsurpassed joy.

An hour or so later he and the four dogs arrived at the family's apartment. The mother came to the door. She saw the dogs. She heard the story. And she thought... What did she think? How did she feel? Go ask your mother how she felt. She'll know.

## When Mom Cried, I Decided Not To Quit And That Made All The Difference

In those days, as I said in an earlier chapter, my mother kind of meddled in all my affairs. She was so glad that I was going to college, and she said she could tell it was making me into a better person. Because of that I knew I had to run this idea of quitting past her. I didn't exactly relish the idea of doing that, because I sure didn't like disappointing her. But I felt I couldn't keep up something that demanded as much as school demanded.

I finally mustered up my courage, and one evening, after doing the dinner dishes so that she wouldn't have to, I said, "Ma, I've got something to tell you."

She was really excited that I was going to tell her something, because I didn't talk to her or Dad much about anything that mattered. I sort of stammered as I said, "Ma, I've decided to quit school."

Wiping away a tear from her eye with her apron, she said: "George, you can't quit. You just can't."

"Ma," I said, in a voice that was hampered by the fact that I was about to cry, "I'm not doing any good at school. It's just too hard for me. You saw my grades. I'm doing terrible in school."

"I know that," she said. "But you just can't quit."

"Why?" I asked in sort of desperation.

"Because what you are going to do in life you need to go to school to do."

"What am I going to do in life?"

"I don't know. All I know is that you have to keep going to school so that you can do it."

"I'm quittin'," I said, with all the determination I could muster. And at that her tears began to flow.

Seeing how I had disappointed her, I blurted out, "Ma, I was just kidding. I won't quit." And so I didn't, and that changed everything for me.

## After Mom Said That, I Never Did It Again

During my last year of high school I felt I'd like to be sort of true to the faith but at the same time I wanted to enjoy a bit of the world. Usually each day when I came home from school my mother would make me a peanut butter sandwich so that I would be able to last until supper. But one day I came home and discovered that she and a bunch of sisters from the Relief Society were in our front room making a quilt. This upset me quite a bit, because I had to make my own peanut butter sandwich, and they never did taste right when I made them.

The door that separated our kitchen from the front room was closed, but I could still hear the ladies in there talking. I wasn't too interested in what they were saying until I heard them start in on how the kids at the high school were all going to the dogs. To hear the details of what they were saying, I pulled my chair over close to the door. One lady after another spoke up to declare what she had heard the kids up at the high school were doing that was not right. As a group, the ladies were able to compile quite an accurate list of our misbehaviors.

Up to this point my mother had not spoken. Then finally I heard her voice as she spoke louder than all the rest. I listened intently to see what she would add to the list. But she added nothing to the list. Instead she said: "You might be right about the bad things the kids up at the school are doing, but I know this—my son George is not doing any of those things."

Hearing that, I said to myself, "I'm going to stop doing those things."

Nobody in their right mind would ever want to disappoint somebody who loved them as much as my mother loved me.

## I Knew My Mother Was Right

As I mentioned, all throughout my school days, when I'd arrive home from school my mother would make me a peanut butter sandwich. Sometimes my brothers and sisters would say, "Let him make his own sandwich."

But she would say, "Never mind. I like to do it for him."

Then when just Mother and I were alone, I'd say, "The reason that I like you to make sandwiches for me is that when you make them they taste better."

And she'd say, "I like to do it for you, George.

As I arrived in junior high school I came to know many feelings of insecurity. And in senior high those feelings had increased. In my younger years my mother would hold me on her lap and I'd feel better. But now that I was in high school I felt a little embarrassed about sitting on her lap. For that reason I wouldn't do so until I had pulled the drapes so that no one could look in. She would run her fingers through my hair and she'd say, "George, you are special." That would make me feel so good; because I felt deep down in my heart that she was right.

But at the same time I wondered why no one else seemed to know that I was special. I wondered why the girls didn't know. I was never overburdened with invitations to Girls' Day dances and things like that. I wondered why my classmates didn't know I was special and elect me to at least a minor student body office. I wondered why the teachers didn't know and give me better grades. And I wondered why the basketball coach didn't know and put me in the game before the very end.

But most of all I wondered why I knew I was special, yet on the other hand I couldn't really seem to act and feel special. I wondered why I couldn't have more confidence; why I couldn't have a better personality; why I couldn't do things better. I felt deep down in my mind that I really did have something to offer but I didn't know how to let it loose.

## A Merciful Mother

The old Chevrolet made it beyond the Point of the Mountain, but as we passed the Utah state prison it sputtered some. Nothing worked very well in the motor of the ten-year-old four-door, but at least it ran. That was more than could be said for the heater. It didn't work at all. That had been all right in the summer and fall, and even in the early winter. But the bitterly cold January temperatures made travel painful with only cold air surging up through the floorboard cracks.

We surely wouldn't have made such a journey on winter's coldest day unless we had to. How else could we join the navy than by going to the naval recruiting office at Fort Douglas?

As we rode along, I kept wondering if I was doing a wise thing. I said to myself, "The navy—four years." That thought seemed as cold to me as the toes in my leather shoes. But what was the alternative—college? I'd tried that and I seemed to be going downhill there. Besides, if I didn't join the navy, I'd be drafted into the army. It seemed to me that the navy was better because the sailors' uniforms seemed more appealing to me than those of the soldiers. That sound reasoning added to my conviction that I was indeed doing the right thing.

Dutson was driving because it was his car. He had warned us about the heater and said that if we complained we could get out and walk. Berry had wanted to be in the navy since high school. He had sort of been the recruiting officer who had put this sea-going idea in our heads. Beano was in the National Guard already, but that was at home, and he wanted to see a little more of the world than American Fork, Lehi, and Pleasant Grove. Bago was my best friend and wanted no part of the infantry. Fraught was the athlete and was ready for any new adventure.

As the cold air turned our ears blue, we all tried to say funny things to keep our minds off our suffering. I didn't say much, because this whole idea still seemed to me a bit less than magnificent. That's why I hadn't discussed it with Mom and Dad. I had just announced it to them as I went out of the door. Before they could question me, I was in Dutson's waiting car. I could tell it hurt Mom a lot.

Mom always had these ideas of what I was going to be. Never even in the corner of her visions had she seen me on a ship or in a navy suit. That bothered me, but I'd sort of gotten used to disappointing her—and also disappointing myself.

I'm sure the idea of the navy would have been all right if I'd talked it over with my parents and others and if I'd really decided that that was what I wanted. But to take such a step on a twenty-four-hour whim unsettled my soul.

But the others seemed happy about our purposeful journey, so I tried to stay in step.

At last we were in South Salt Lake and were traveling east

toward Fort Douglas. It appeared that we would make it with only minor frostbite. Just seeing the military barracks and other buildings gave me an even more uneasy feeling. Could I leave Mom and her cooking and my room to live away from home for four years? I couldn't bear the thought. Yet I couldn't turn back. What would my friends say? What would I say? "I didn't follow through on this either." I'd said that enough already.

Now we were seated inside, filling out what seemed like thousands of papers. We were told to prepare for our physicals. At the first station I heard one of the medics say to another, "We've got to fail some of these guys. The higher command says we are too lenient."

An hour later as we all sat waiting for further word, a medic entered the room. "Men," he said, "I've got some bad news. Three of you didn't pass the physical. Durrant, your leg needs attention; Bago, you don't weigh enough to match your height; and Beano, you are too heavy to meet navy standards."

Berry, Fraught, and Dutson had made it. They tried to contain their joy. The other three of us attempted to conceal our disappointment. In doing that, all succeeded quite well.

On the journey home, we three who had failed were told by the jovial three who had made it, "You guys will end up in the infantry while we are out sailing the seven seas." I'd never in my life felt like such a failure. I hadn't wanted to go into the navy, but to be rejected by them seemed like the last straw.

When the battered Chevrolet rolled to a stop out in front of our old adobe house, I slowly crawled out. I surely wasn't coming home as a war hero. I felt what I thought must have been the feelings of a coward.

Mom, having heard the car pull up, opened the front door of our home. I entered and took off my heavy coat. I wanted to stand by the coal stove and get warm, but more than that I wanted to be alone. I walked quickly across the large kitchen toward my bedroom.

"When do you leave for the navy?" Mom asked with a fearful tone.

"I don't leave to go nowhere," I said with a voice that was just one degree short of tears.

"Why?"

"Cause. They don't want me." With that I closed the door and climbed into bed with my clothes still on.

I didn't pray in the usual manner, but my very breath seemed like a petition of desperation to both heaven and earth.

The bedroom door slowly opened and Mom entered. She sat down beside where I lay. For quite a while she sat in silence. Finally she spoke, "George, I want you to go back to school."

"School? I tried that. I don't know what I want to be. So what good is school? I don't know anything. What's the use anyway?"

"I've got some money. I'll get some more. I'll help and so will Dad. You'll do better. You could learn to be an artist or a writer."

I didn't answer. Why didn't Mom ever give up? I'd given up. Why couldn't she? Oh, how I loved her! She was always there. But never had her presence been so vital as it was now.

Finally I spoke, "Spring quarter starts in about two months. I could earn some money by then. I could join the National Guard. That's what Beano wants me to do." With each word I spoke, and each tearful nod of Mom's approval, hope was pushing out my despair.

"Supper's ready, George. Why don't you come and eat?"

I didn't answer, but it sure did seem like a good idea. I'd need a lot of strength for the good things that lay ahead.

As I ate with Mom and Dad, I got that deep-down feeling that this was my best day so far, and I could tell Mom and Dad felt the same way.

I guess it's easy for mothers to show mercy. They get to do a lot of that when they have a child like you or me. They tell me that mother's milk is good for a baby. I can tell you first-hand that mother's mercy is essential for teenagers. The world seems to have a multitude of methods of smacking us with justice. I suppose that is why the Lord was so generous in filling mothers with mercy.

# MARRIAGE SCONES

## Both Physical And Spiritual Attraction Make A Good Marriage

I was interviewed near the end of my mission by Elder Spencer W. Kimball. Of that experience I recall:

He asked me, "Elder Durrant, how do you feel about yourself and your mission? Do you have any special concerns that you would like to discuss with me?"

I did not reply for several seconds. Then I spoke, "There is one concern. There is a sister missionary serving in our district. She has been here her entire mission, as have I. I have seen her often. She now serves in Scarborough. She has brought many to the truth. I have seen her teach, and I've felt the power of her testimony."

I paused and then continued, "I have such great respect for her. I really feel I am falling in love with her."

I said no more. He asked, "Is it Sister Burnham?"

I looked into his eyes and answered softly, "Yes, it is."

He smiled and replied, "I don't blame you for feeling as you do. I just interviewed her, and she is impressive."

I smiled and nodded my head in agreement.

He leaned forward and said, "Elder Durrant, you have fallen in love spiritually. That's all you can do on a mission. But that is not enough to allow you to know what the future will bring. So now you must put this matter aside and lock your heart until your mission is concluded. Then when you return home, you can determine if you not only love her spiritually but also physically. Because, you see, love must be both of those ways, both spiritual and physical. Neither the physical side of love and marriage nor the spiritual side can be complete without the other."

I did as he advised me and put the matter aside.

A month later, Sister Burnham—whose first name, I later learned, was Marilyn—finished her greatly successful mission and returned home. Four months later, I did also.

As the dome-liner train made the final leg of its journey from New York to Utah, it wound its way through the Colorado Rockies. I sat in silence considering the future. Two hours later, the train slowed and then stopped at the Provo, Utah, station. I was home.

As I climbed down the two stairs to the platform, I saw my mother. I took her in my arms and felt inexpressible joy, love, and gratitude. Because of her teachings and her profound sacrifices, I had found my own soul.

After greeting other family members, I saw Sister Burnham. My heart leaped within me. Seeing that I had greeted all the others, she walked to me and we shook hands in a most electrifying manner.

A few days later, I did as the Apostle had counseled. I began gathering information that would help us determine if our love was more than spiritual. We found that it surely was.

Based on the abundance of heartfelt data, on Christmas Eve 1955 I presented to Sister Burnham—by now I called her Marilyn—a small diamond, one of the smallest to ever come out of Africa, but to her it seemed the size of a marble. She quickly accepted my offer.

Because marriage plans take time, we were not married until the following year—January 19, 1956.

The advice I received on the banks of the murky Humber River has been profoundly important to me. The feeling that I felt there and what I learned caused those everflowing waters of the Humber to be the most beautiful of all rivers to me.

## Tell Her That You Love Her And Ask Her To Marry You

I had a fellow come to see me once. He had been in my ward while I served as bishop of a BYU ward. When he came to the ward, he had already served a mission in Europe. I was transferred to Salt Lake City and was then released as bishop. About six months later he came to see me. He came into my office and said, "How are you doing, Bishop?"

I replied, "Fine."

And he said, "I haven't got time to just pass the time of day. I'm here on business."

I asked, "What's your business?"

He said, "I just got out of the temple."

I said, "That's good. I'm glad you were there."

"Yes, but I went there for a special reason. I've been fasting and praying for two days. I've been to the temple because I wanted to know if I should marry her. I've been to the temple and prayed in the temple and the only answer was to come and see you. Here I am. What should I do?"

I said, "Tell me about her."

"She's a beautiful girl. She's just a wonderful person. She loves the Lord and she loves me. I don't know what to do. I get that close to asking her to marry me, and then I can't do it. I don't know why I can't do it, but I can't. I just get thinking about it and I can't do it. I came here to ask you what I should do."

"How do you feel about her?"

He said, "I think I love her. But I don't know for sure.

I asked, "And she loves you?"

"Yes."

"And she's really a tremendous person?"

He said, "She sure is."

I thought for a moment, said a silent prayer, and replied, “Well, okay. You came here to ask me what to do. Here’s what you should do. Say goodbye to me and go out get in your car. Drive back to Provo as fast as you can. Go find her. Ask her if you can go some place where the two of you can be alone.”

He listened intently as I continued, “When you get where you and she are alone, hold her hand, look into her eyes and say, “Honey, I love you, and I want to marry you.”

I had said what I felt impressed to say and so I was now silent. He didn’t say anything for a few seconds. Finally he said, “Is that what I should do?”

And I said, “That’s what you should do.”

He said, “I’ll see you later, Bishop.”

I didn’t see him for six months. Then I saw both of them. He said, “This is Bishop Durrant. And Bishop Durrant, this is my wife.”

She gasped and said, “You are Bishop Durrant?”

And I said, “Yes.”

“Oh, Bishop Durrant, I’ll love you forever.”

## Then You Will Know

Here is one criteria you might use, especially if you’re a guy. Get a date, preferably on a hot summer day. Right now you’d have to wait a while for hot weather, so maybe you better move ahead earlier than that. Anyway, take her for a walk up on the mountain. Advise her that you’ve got the lunch and you tell her not to worry about anything. You say, “There’s a spring up there and you will be able to drink some cool water up near the top. When you get to the spring, which is dry, apologize and explain that you didn’t know it would be dried up. You thought you would be able to get a drink there. Then keep hiking up the mountain further than she wants to go. Kind of drag her across a log and skin her knee. Finally, sit down at the picnic and say, "Oh no, I forgot the drinks!" Then see if she's ornery.

This is a good test because you'll put her through a lot more than that after you're married. If she's ornery at such a punch-less picnic, then you can imagine how she will be under some of the stress you and she will endure. Maybe after the picnic you won't want to proceed and maybe she won't either. So it works both ways

You see, when you get married and you want to go to Alaska to work in a bank, and you say, "Honey, we're going to Alaska."

And she says, "Oh, but mother lives in Springville."

And you say, "I know that, but let's go."

So she replies, "I just thought I'd remind you where mother lives. But I'm glad to go to Alaska."

Later she sends a message out by dog sled which says, "Mother, we're up in Alaska and we're going to have a baby."

And mother says, "Come home."

She replies, "Mother, I am home. I'm with him!"

## You Won't Starve

It's good to be married to somebody from Idaho because just before you starve to death, Dad will bring you a sack of potatoes. It always happens.

People come to me and say, "We're not going to get married because we can't afford it now and so we're going to get married in a year."

I reply, "Oh, let's move it up."

They say, "We can't move it up. We'll starve."

I say, "Get the BYU paper. Let's look through it."

They ask, "What for?"

"We'll see if we can find anyone on campus who has starved."

They say, "There's nobody in the paper like that."

And I say, "You feel that you will be the first ones?"

## Marry Her.
## She Is A Tough One

There was an Elder who served where I was president. He was one of the most outstanding Elders I have ever known. He came to see me after his mission when I had an office in the Joseph Smith building. He could never quite decide about this certain girl. I'd see them together on campus. She was one of the sweetest girls I'd ever met, but to me she did not seem to be the girl that could lead him to his destiny. There was another girl who I felt was the one for him. When I'd talk to the elder I'd show favoritism toward this second girl.

One day a knock came on my office door. Sitting at my desk I shouted, "Come in."

The girl I discussed first entered. I waited for the young man to follow her in but I soon discovered that he was not with her. Without speaking or smiling she quickly took a seat. She sat up straight and leaned forward.

She immediately took over by saying, "I did not come here to get advice. I came here to set you straight on a few things. I know he means a lot to you and he listens to every thing that you say. I know you want him to marry the other girl. But you are wrong. I'm the girl for him. I don't care what you think. I am going to marry him and you just as well get used to the idea. I want you to know that I'm the kind of woman who can make him amount to everything he's suppose to because that man has great potential, and I'm the one who's going to help him fulfill that potential. And I'm getting tired of him putting me off and you encouraging him to consider the other girl."

She was speaking faster and more firmly with each sentence. She continued, "I've prayed to the Lord and I know this is right, and I'm going to have him, and you just as well know that." And she said, "If you want to tell him what I said, you go right ahead and tell him because I don't care."

As suddenly as she had begun, she finished. There was no more talking because I had nothing to say. She then arose and after a quick goodbye, opened the door, closed it with a bang, and was gone.

An hour or so later he came in. He slumped down in the chair and started talking and said, "I still don't know what to do. What do you think?"

I knew exactly what I thought. This time I sat up straight and leaned forward and said with enthusiasm, "She is a tiger. If you let her go, you're a fool. I've never talked to anybody with such power. There is a woman! But it's up to you. You do what you want, but what a mistake to ever lose her."

He leaned forward and said, "Do you really feel that way?"

I replied, "I sure do. She is tough. Men need a tough woman. There is not a man who doesn't need to be shaped up and a woman can do it and what a blessing it is when it happens."

After a short engagement they were married, and what a glorious wife and mother she has been.

## It Is Possible To Be Married And To Be Happier Than You Have Ever Dreamed

While I was teaching at Brigham Young University, a girl from my class came to my office to talk to me privately. She asked me if I thought she could get into the movies. I said, "I think so, if you have enough money for a ticket." We both laughed because we knew her question was not about watching a movie but about being an actress. She had been in many productions at BYU, and was beautiful, and very talented.

As we spoke more seriously, I told her I thought she had an excellent chance of being an actress if that was what she wanted. She said, "But do you think if I was an actress I would be able to hold to the standards of the Church?"

I looked into her eyes and thought for a few seconds, and then felt impressed to say, "Oh, yes, you could."

Then tears came to her eyes and she could scarcely speak. Finally gaining her composure, she said, "I don't really want to be an actress. What I really want to be is a wife and a mother. But," she continued, "I'm scared. I have seen heartbreak in my own home and I was just wondering if it was possible to get married and be happy."

The spirit in the room was such that my eyes were moistened with tears also. I slowly said, "I want you to know it is possible to get married and be happier than you've ever even dreamed."

We then sat in silence for a few seconds, until she finally said, "That's what I wanted to know, Brother Durrant. My real goal in life is to get married and become a mother and be happy."

## You've Created The Exact Image Of Your Wife

In those early, pre-children days, I was majoring in art at Brigham Young University. In my sculpturing class, I had an assignment to create a figure out of a large piece of wood. I set my heart on carving something from a log. We had no car at the time, and so I couldn't really get to the woods to get such a log. I walked around the neighborhood in hopes that I'd find one in someone's yard.

It was on a day when I was feeling a little sorry for myself anyway. I felt frustrated that I didn't have a log. Then I decided the reason I couldn't get a log was because we didn't have a car. I concluded that the reason we didn't have a car was because we didn't have any money. "Why do we have to be so poor?" I asked myself.

I decided to lie down on the bed and feel sorry for myself. You asked me what was wrong. I gave my usual answer, "Nothing." You persisted. Finally I said, "I need a log to carve for my sculpture class. And we don't have a car so I can't get one so I guess I'll fail the class and fail college and fail everything else in life."

Instead of giving me the sympathy I thought I needed, you put on your coat and walked out on me. A half hour later you opened the front door and entered, dragging a log behind you. You never told me then or since where you got that log. It was really a beauty—the very log I had envisioned in my mind that I needed.

When you laid it at my feet I was completely choked with emotion. I wanted to reach out and pull you close and tell you of my love. So often I want to do that because of what you do for me. But so often I don't seem to be able to say or convey to you how deeply grateful I am to you. I try—but words just won't do it.

I took the log to the art class. I began to chip away the outer bark and finally the wood itself. I carved almost unconsciously. Finally, a figure of a woman emerged from wood. The teacher came to me, and as we both backed away to have a general look, he put his hand on my shoulder and surprised me by saying, "George, you have carved the exact image of your wife."

It was then that I realized that my heart and not my head had directed my hands. I had indeed followed an inward pattern of my love, and the final product was Marilyn.

## Of Course He Does Not Understand

A girl called me and she said, "I want to come and see you. It's about one of your missionaries. He's the cause of all my problems. I want to come in and tell you what is going on in our marriage. I'm bringing him in with me."

They came in. She said, "I don't know what to do. I am just so sad. I don't think I can live another day under the kind of arrangement we've got. He's responsible for the problems. He's going to school and works at night and he comes home and is too tired to talk to me. He never talks to me and I don't talk to anyone all day. We've got three little ones and we're going to have another one. None of them can carry on an intelligent conversation. I am not close to any of the neighbors and my mother lives back east. I've had it up to here. I can't go on. Besides, I don't feel good. The problem is he doesn't understand. Do you?"

And he meekly answered, "I try to."

Then she said, "Well, you don't. And I want your mission president to know you don't."

He wanted to disappear. You can imagine. After a few seconds of silence I spoke, "Can I just tell you a little bit? Can I tell you what a splendid missionary your husband was? I've never seen a better one. He is a fantastic man. Here he is working as hard as he can. He just wants to get something that is the best for his family. I know he doesn't understand. What man is there that ever understood a woman who's going to have a baby. There's no way. A man has never been through it and never will go through it. He doesn't understand. I don't understand." I about came to tears. "How can we understand? But we try, and he's trying."

She said, "Oh, President Durrant. He's the grandest guy in the whole world. I love him with all my heart and soul. Honey, I'm sorry."

He said, "I'm the one who should be sorry. I try, and I'm going to try harder."

Then she said, "I know, but you go to school all day and you work, and naturally you're tired."

"I know," he replied. "But I could talk to you more. Maybe pretty soon I won't have to work so hard."

He started to cry and she started to cry, and I fought like the dickens not to. I'm telling you, marriage on some days is not a Cadillac ride. It is a handcart journey.

## He Survived Because Of Sister Mormon

Here is a sad story:

*"But behold, I, Mormon, began to be old; and knowing it to be the last struggle of my people...and it came to pass that they (the Lamanites) came to battle against us, and every soul was filled with terror because of the greatness of their numbers*

*"When they had gone through and hewn down all my people save it were twenty and four of us. (Among whom was my son Moroni)..."*

Mormon had a son! Therefore, we know that there was a Sister Mormon. That thrills me because when I know that, then the whole story that took place before this final scene takes on a different perspective. Can't you just see Mormon, as a young man, coming home from war? He's tired and discouraged. He walks up toward the house. There standing in the doorway is a lovely woman. She's standing in the door watching him come up the path and coming out the door on both sides of her is the smell of newly baked bread. Just oozing out from around her. She says, "Hi, honey, how ya doing?"

And he says, "Oh, I can't take this war. I'm so tired and beat and discouraged."

She could say, "Well, I've got a war here at home and you are always gone." That would be too much for Mormon to bear so she does not say that. Instead she says, "Come on in, my dear husband."

After a brief private greeting he says, "Hey, where's Moroni?"

She replies, "He's out back. I'll call him."

She goes to the back door and calls, "Moroni, Daddy's home!"

Moroni comes chugging in with a smile clear across his face. Mormon picks him up and holds him high about his head and says, "How's my boy?'

And little Moroni says, "Daddy, I'm so glad you're home. Can we play some games?"

This humble father says, "I've always got time to play games with you. Come on, let's go play."

I don't know what they played. I hope it was basketball or something equally as fun. That night little Moroni gets to stay up late because Daddy's home. He hasn't been home for a while. He's been out writing a book, fighting battles, and preaching to people who won't listen. But now he's home. He's really home. He's within the walls of all his happiness. With little Moroni in his lap, he rocks back and forth. The fire is just about to go out and Moroni falls asleep. Mormon takes his young son and gently puts him in his bed and covers him up and gives him a kiss. Then he comes back and says, "Honey, I can't do it. I can't go on."

She says, "You have to."

He says, "The people count on me to much. But maybe I can do it. I just wish that it was not so hard."

She smiles and he holds her close and life goes on.

# THE SCONES THAT COME FROM THE CHILDREN

## Don't Stop Having Children Until You Have Had Your Last One

As I entered BYU's Harold B. Lee Library, which houses a marvelous Family History Center, I was in a reflective mood. The year 1990 had come much sooner than I had thought it would back in 1956 when I had gazed into the future after Marilyn and I came out of the temple where we had just been married.

As part of my family history effort, I planned to review again the family record that we had already sent in as part of what was known in the 1960s and 1970s as the four-generation program.

Upon entering the center, I removed my overcoat and laid it on a nearby chair. I then found and opened the drawer that contained hundreds of small white boxes in which are the film copies of the four-generation family group records. My eyes swept the labels until I saw the box that contained the D's. I removed it from the drawer, turned, and headed toward the row of microfilm readers where I could view the magnified records.

I was not prepared for the emotional experience that was about to occur. I turned the film ahead until I was reading "Durrant" records. Then, suddenly, my eyes focused on a record wherein I, George Donald Durrant, was recorded as the father. Just below my name was the name Marilyn Kay Burnham. Thinking of the joy that our marriage had brought into my life, my heart softened, but I was still not quite prepared for what I was soon to see.

I slightly lowered my gaze. On the line for the first child was the name Matthew Burnham Durrant. Unbidden, my thoughts jumped back to 1957 to Fort Chaffee, Arkansas. And to the birth of our firstborn child.

Next was the name Kathryn Kay Durrant—our first daughter. I could see her as a baby and then as a radiantly beautiful woman, and tears welled up in my eyes. Next was Devin. Instantly I pictured myself in the Cooley Memorial Hospital in Brigham City witnessing his birth. Marinda, Dwight, and Warren were the next three names. I thought of each of them, and my heart overflowed with gratitude.

What happened next was among the three or four most penetrating emotional experiences of my life. You see, no more children were listed. I looked up to the date when we had submitted this record—1965. To myself I softly spoke, "When we compiled this record and sent it to the Church, we had only six children."

With that thought, a chill started across my shoulder and swept down my back as I asked myself, "What if that had indeed been the final number of our children? What if we had not had Sarah and Mark join our family?" I could scarcely bear the thought. Tears flooded my eyes as I considered all that would not have been part of my life—of our lives—if we had not had Sarah and Mark.

As I looked back at the record, I said silently but desperately, "This is not our family." For an instant I wanted to write on the film's reflected image the names *Sarah* and *Mark*. But that would do no good. So I just looked up and said, "Oh, dear God, thank you for Marilyn, Matt, Kathryn, Devin, Marinda, Dwight, Warren." And then I added with emphasis, "And Sarah and Mark—the last ones."

I removed the film from the reader, put it in its box, walked to the drawer, put the film away, put on my coat, and walked down the stairs and back into the world—the wonderful world where we live as a family. I pulled my coat up higher on my neck to protect myself from the cold, but my heart was warm because Marilyn and I had all of our children, including the last ones.

So what of birth control? Well, all I can say is that when you someday look at your family group record, don't see a blank space or two where the names of your last ones could have been listed.

Be sure, therefore, to have your first one or ones, and your middle one or ones, and . . . I get choked up as I say this, be sure, absolutely sure, that you don't stop until you have your last one.

But how will you know? Oh, you'll know, all right. You'll know. You and your spouse and the Lord will all know.

## Be Careful What You Put In The Baby's Crib

I heard of one man who took a ball and put it in the crib with his three-day-old baby. He wanted the little one to get used to the ball and make playing with balls the greatest priority in life.

It worked. His dream came true. This child became a super athlete. The problem was, when the time came he couldn't play for the school team because of poor grades and lousy citizenship.

The father later lamented that he wished he had put a good book in the crib.

## The Baby Looks Just Like His Father But Let's Keep Him Anyway

A few months after our wedding, I came home from my labors to assist my wife in preparing our evening meal. As I peeled the potatoes with a paring knife she was nearby opening a can of peas. The words she spoke on that great moment in history I shall never forget, for it was my single most fulfilling moment. She said, "I went to the doctor today. We are going to have a baby."

Her words almost put me into a state of shock. I had to quit peeling the potatoes—my hands trembled with such excitement that the task became too dangerous to continue. I sat down in the chair. Marilyn put her hand on my shoulder and told me that I would be all right. As the time for the baby's arrival came closer, I was drafted into the army and stationed in Arkansas. I had to live on the base while Marilyn lived in town some twelve miles away.

The army doctor told us that when she came to the base hospital to have the child I'd be notified so that I could be there. But on the night of the birth I was not notified. The next day I stood outside the army mess hall in a line waiting for the noon meal. Someone came to me and said, "Durrant, you are to call the hospital." I crossed the road to a phone booth and called.

The nurse announced to me via phone the long awaited magnificent message, "Private Durrant, you are the father of a fine baby son."

Tears of joy filled my eyes. I bounded out of the phone booth with the agility of a great athlete. I half ran and half jumped along as I shouted to my soldier friends who had known that the event was near, "I've got a son! I've got a son! I'm a father! I'm a father!" Even now as I recall these memories I feel excitement surging through my soul. My buddies cheered for me as I quickly ran the few blocks to the post hospital, my mind filled with thoughts of joy. I felt like pinching myself to make sure I wasn't involved in a dream. But I knew it wasn't a dream. It was true. I was indeed a father. I recall thinking, as I neared the hospital, "I'd like to light a new star in the sky to announce the arrival of my son." Nothing short of that seemed adequate to express how happy I was.

I dashed into the hospital and down the hall. As I went along I saw the glass windows of the newborn baby room. I stopped and looked in. There among the three or four little ones was a baby whose crib bore the name Durrant. As I looked my whole soul tingled with a spiritual thrill. This was my son. And I was his father.

I went to Marilyn's room. She seemed more beautiful than ever. As we talked of all the wonders of what had happened, I excitedly said, "That little boy—he looks just like me."

She squeezed my hand as she said, "I know that, but let's keep him anyway."

Thus our firstborn was delivered to us in an army hospital. The cost was just eight dollars.

As he grew into manhood I have often told him, "Matt you cost us eight dollars, but I want you to know that you have been worth it." He's been worth every cent of that—plus a billion dollars more.

## Just Be My Son

Many years ago Marilyn, my young sons Matt and Devin, and I went to a BYU football game. The sky was overcast; the air was cold. It was a wonderful game because BYU was winning (unusual in those days). Just as the second half began, a very wet mix of rain and snow blew in. We were wearing warm coats, but we didn't have any kind of plastic protection or anything like that. As the weather worsened, my greatest fear was that Devin would get wet and cold, lose all interest in the game, and begin a campaign to go home. I couldn't bear that. It had been so long since BYU had beaten the University of Utah that I had to be there until the end even if we all froze to death. To ensure that we would not have to leave, I sat on the north side of our family where I could take most of the moisture that was pounding in on us. I held Devin next to me, trying to shield him from the wet, cold snow. But even though I pulled my big overcoat up over his head and had him snuggled close to me, it was futile. I just couldn't completely protect him. To keep his mind off from the cold I talked constantly to him:

"Now, watch that man! He's going to throw the ball. See it fly through the snow. The other man will catch it and then run. Watch, see him run. Oh, they got him!"

Devin liked that kind of running narrative, but he was getting wet and cold. I'd wipe the water off his head with my handkerchief. Then I'd twist the soaked cloth to wring out the water. To my pleasant surprise, Devin didn't complain or ask to leave. Finally the storm was over. The sun came out. BYU was well ahead and victory was assured. I felt Devin move away from me and sit up straight in his own seat. Suddenly, he stood up and moved right in front of my knees. Facing me, he looked up and said, "Dad, you've done so much for me, isn't there something I can do for you?"

I had a hard time holding back the tears as I looked into his eyes. I replied, "Yeah, there is something you can do for me, Devin. You just be my son, just be my son." I sensed that he knew that I wanted him to go out in life and do good things. That moment with my family at a football game was a moment I will remember forever.

## How Many Other Guys On The Team Got A Kiss From Their Father Before They Came To Practice?

My son was on the high school basketball team. At one point the coach advised the team members that he didn't think they were all doing as much as they should to be ready for the forthcoming tournament. He asked them all to make some special sacrifice with that in mind.

My son and some of the others decided that their sacrifice would be to get up early each morning and go over to school and practice basketball before school started. One morning while he was in the midst of this program I got up as early as he did so as to cook him breakfast. (His mother had had a broken sleep, and since it was now very early she remained in bed.)

We happened to have some bacon in the fridge. I cooked a lot more of it than I would have been able to had his mother been up. I fried him a few eggs. I made him some toast. I made him a drink by mixing some ice, some milk, some chocolate and a little ice cream. It was kind of a "good morning" milk shake. I had my son sit down at the table, then I served it all to him as if he were a king.

As he ate we talked. The only time my children have ever really talked to me is when I've been with them. He was most gracious as we talked, and we had a choice time together—just a father and son in that kitchen. When the food was all gone (and that wasn't long, the way he ate), it was time for him to go. He announced, "I've got to go quick, Pops." (That's what he calls me.)

"Couldn't you just stay for a minute longer?" I asked. "Just long enough for you and me to kneel down and have a word of prayer?"

He could have said, "No, I've got to hurry," or he could have been ornery about it. But instead he quickly said, "Sure, Pops. There's always time for that."

He knelt down, and I knelt as close as I could to him. I acted as the voice for our prayer. I told Heavenly Father how grateful I was to have such a son. And in my prayers I poured out quite a few sentimentalities as I told the Lord how deeply I appreciated the way this young man was living and the things he was doing. I said so many things that the prayer was a rather long one. But he was patient and didn't seem to be fidgety, so I prayed on and on until I finally said "Amen."

After the prayer we both stood up. The Spirit of the Lord

was present and my heart was filled with joy. I felt impressed to embrace my son and give him a kiss on the cheek. I don't do that often, but at that moment I just felt compelled to do it. Sensing what was happening, he didn't quickly take a karate stance as he could have done. Instead he embraced me and allowed me to kiss him on the cheek. As I did so I said, "Sure love ya." He looked at me with kind of a grin on his face and he said, "Sure love you, Pops." Then he turned and went towards the door.

Just as he was about to close the door, he looked back and grinned again. He almost laughed as he good naturedly said, "Gee, Pops, I wonder how many other Provo High basketball players got a kiss from their dad before they went to school this morning?" I told him to get out of there or he would get something more than just a kiss—a kick in the pants. He laughed and hurried away. I watched him from the window until he was gone from sight. Oh, how I felt my love for him that morning!

## The Relationship Changed When I Became His Champion Rather Than His Critic

My son Warren was a large ninth-grader when we moved from Provo to Salt Lake City. Coaches in his new school were sure he'd be able to play because his brother Devin was a BYU star. Warren tried, but his gentle and remarkable talents weren't those of a smoothly coordinated athlete.

Warren really didn't have the intense interest or the desire needed to improve his game. The constant criticism of his coach took a toll on his self image. He wanted to give up high school athletics and pursue other matters. At the time, I couldn't understand that. I pressured him to at least try.

He did for a while, but he finally said, "I don't want to play any more." His mother supported him and emphasized,

"It's his decision." This hurt me greatly, but I learned to live with it.

After that he played for the church team. I became his coach. My whole tactic of coaching was to sit on the bench and shout, "Way to go, Warren!" "Good shot, Warren!" "Way to jump, Warren!" He'd look over at me on the side-line and smile. Warren was playing basketball the way it ought to be played on all levels. He was just plain having fun. He was doing his best, and I, his father, was praising his every move. After each game, I'd put my arm around him and say, "That was a great game, Warren." We—a dad, a boy, and a ball—established a relationship that I don't think we could have developed in any other way.

## Go To Korea, But While You Are Gone I'll Take Care Of Your Family

The darkest day of my life occurred while I was serving in the army at Fort Chaffee, Arkansas. I had just finished radio school and was awaiting my assignment to another post—a post that I hoped would be somewhere in the United States or in Europe, someplace where Marilyn and our soon-to-be-born baby could be with me. Our class of twenty graduates stood casually in the appointed place to await our orders. The sergeant, with papers in hand, approached quickly and called us to attention, then later to stand at ease. He began to read the first ten names. The names he read were each assigned to Germany. The next eight were assigned to various places in the United States. Only two of us remained. He paused, and then with some seeming sympathy he said, "Private Ryles and Private Durrant, you are assigned to Korea." I had dreaded such a command as one can only dread the most awful of life's circumstances. Those orders meant that for a year and a half I would not see Marilyn and the baby. My hopes and dreams were shattered. All seemed lost. I longed for it all to be a dream, a horrible nightmare. But it wasn't. An hour later Marilyn met me at the bus stop in Fort Smith. She looked at my forlorn expression, and without my telling her she knew. We joined hands and walked the several blocks home without speaking a word.

That night in our little house in Fort Smith, Arkansas, while we lay in bed, Marilyn, with her head on my shoulder, wet my shirt with her tears. She could scarcely conceive how she could, in her loneliness, care for our baby for so long. Our love bound us together in such a manner that to be separated was more painful than having a limb torn from our bodies.

Because my departure date was two months away, I decided that there was still time to have the orders changed. In desperation, I phoned the base commander. "Please, sir," I pleaded, "I know others who want to go but who are to stay in the States. Could you not intervene and change me with one of them so that I would not have to be separated from my wife and little child!"

He kindly replied, "Private Durrant, you should not have called me. There is a chain of command, you know." But he added compassionately, "I understand your feelings. Through the years of my service, I have at times been sent away from my family. I did not want to go. But what kind of an army would it be if none of us were willing to go where we are needed?"

I wrote to my congressman, who could not help.

Our evening, and morning, and a multitude of other silent prayers were powerful because of our pure and desperate motivation. We knew that our appeals were heard in heaven, but the answer we sought did not come. As the remaining days of our being together grew smaller in number, our despair gradually pushed aside all of our hope. During those days, our baby son Matthew was born. When he was one month old, the doctor advised us that he needed an operation for a herniated navel. This medical procedure was not serious, but it could not be scheduled until the day after my appointed departure, and that grieved me greatly.

The day before I was to leave and a few days before the baby's scheduled surgery, I called a friend with whom I had served a mission. Together, by the power of the priesthood and in the name of Jesus Christ, we blessed tiny Matthew Durrant.

As my friend anointed the baby, and as I spoke the words of the blessing, I felt a miracle was occurring. However, after we said amen, I looked at his navel and noticed that the obvious condition was the same. Again hope faded.

At Fort Lewis, I was delayed for three weeks awaiting my flight to Korea. After being there for five days, I received a letter that I sensed was of great importance. Instead of opening it immediately, I placed it in my shirt pocket, left the barracks, and walked down the road a mile or so and into a clump of pine trees. There, all alone, I opened the letter.

*Dear George,*

*I took the baby in for the operation, but the doctor examined his condition and said, "This baby doesn't need any surgery. As you can see for yourself his navel is perfectly normal."*

There was much more to the letter, but my emotions were such that for the moment I could read no more. I fell to my knees in gratitude. Then, in my mind, I heard my Heavenly Father say, "All your prayers have been heard, and this is your answer. Go to Korea, and while you are gone, I will care for your family."

My heart was flooded with hope. I could feel the words of the hymn, "All is well, all is well."

I went to Korea. Each night for more than a year of nights, I walked up on a slight hill that overlooked a pleasant valley of rice fields and picturesque homes. There on that high place, I silently prayed, "Dear Heavenly Father, you promised me you would care for my wife and son. I just wanted to remind you."

Then, though we were thousands of miles apart, it would be as though Marilyn would join me on the hill, and we would stand there together.

## Coming Home Made Me Feel Like I Had The Whole World In My Hands

Finally, I was aboard a troop ship headed home from Korea. After several days on the sea, I stood on the sunny deck and could see in the distance the United States' western shore. I could hear a song playing on a nearby radio. I had never heard the words before, even though I think it was an old song made recently popular. The words were, "He's got the whole world in his hands." I didn't know at the time that the words referred to our Heavenly Father, and I thought the message was strictly for me, for I truly felt that I did indeed have the whole world in my hands. I felt the sort of hope that filled my soul so full of light that my love was for a time perfect. I knew then that the world could be held in my hands. At least, the part of the world that was dear to me—the world of my family.

# PRIESTHOOD SCONES

## My Car Started Better Because It Knew I Was Getting More Authority

Don's Sweet Shop was a sweet shop owned by a guy named Don. Don was a smart guy. He not only had a place where you could get delicious hamburgers and milkshakes, but more important than that, he also hired the best-looking girls in all of American Fork. Needless to say, I enjoyed frequenting Don's wonderful place.

I'd never, to that time, been so happy as I was one night when I reached out to open the door and enter Don's Sweet Shop to have my favorite flavor of milkshake. I was dressed a little fancier than usual because I'd just had an interview with my stake president. So, of course, I was wearing a suit.

He had asked me several questions about my Church attendance, my habits, and my feelings. After I'd replied, he said, "George, we'd like you to be an elder. How would you like that?"

I replied with great joy, "I'd like that a lot, President."

He said, "You'll be a good elder, George. I've watched you for several years, and you've been a good boy. Now you are ready to do a lot of good things in your life. Things like college, a mission, and marriage."

Then he asked, "How do you feel about all that?"

I felt real good, so I replied, "I've never done much stuff, President. But lately I've been thinking a lot. Maybe I'll do better."

After I'd said good night to him, I headed right to Don's. I was wearing my navy blue suit—blue is my color. And, of course, because of what had happened in my stake president's office, I was feeling as good inside as I was looking on the outside.

As I entered I noticed that there were three girls working behind the counter. As they saw how good I was looking, they seemed to sort of push and shove each other in a race to get to the counter where I'd just sat down. Finally, the one who had won smiled and said, "Hi, George."

I smiled and lowered my voice an octave or so, so I'd sound as spiritual as an elder ought to sound.

"Hi," I replied.

"What would you like?" she asked.

"Well, I'd like a cherry chocolate milkshake with more cherry in it than chocolate," I answered.

"I know just how you like it, George," she said as she hurried away to her task.

As I waited for my treat, I looked around to see who else was there. I nodded a greeting to each. As people went toward the door, I would catch their eye and say, "See you later." Up until then I knew that I had a few friends. But now I felt as if I had a million friends in American Fork alone.

When people entered, even though I was timid, I greeted them with a warm smile, and they would respond in just the same way. I'd never until that time thought of myself as being popular, but now it seemed to me that people liked me—and I sure did like them.

"Here it is, George," the pretty waitress said as she set the overflowing, extra thick milkshake before me.

As I sat sipping the delicious cherry chocolate contents into my mouth, my mind went soaring. I was having a silent conversation with myself. Without speaking, I heard myself say, "I'll bet I could do stuff. I'll bet I could do college work and all that kind of stuff. I'll bet I could paint pictures and do all sorts of art stuff. And live good and pay tithing and do spiritual stuff, and love everybody and help people and do stuff like that. I'll bet I could even go on a mission. It would be hard for me because I sure feel timid about talking to people and that kind of stuff, but I'll bet I could. I'll bet I could really amount to something in life. I'll bet I could do a lot of stuff."

My thinking was suddenly interrupted by the noise milkshakes make when they are gone.

I called the girl over and gave her a dollar bill. She asked, "Was it good, George?"

"Yeah," I said. "It was real good. I enjoyed it a lot."

I paid the bill and said good-bye. I headed for home because I had some stuff to do.

It seemed to me that that night and other times when I get to thinking that I can do stuff that I look better, and feel kinder, and act friendlier, and walk better with the Lord.

## Better To Be A Priesthood Man Than A Harvard Man Or A Yale Man

In the "olden days," when our children were small, the pattern of the Church was that we would all go to church on Sunday morning for priesthood meeting and Sunday School, then we would go back in the early evening for sacrament meeting. One Sunday afternoon my young son, hoping I had had enough meetings for one day and would excuse the entire family from the evening meeting, asked, "Are you going to go to church again?"

I replied, "I sure am."

Saddened by my response, he asked, "Why?"

I wanted to give him a profound answer about the importance of sacrament meeting, so I paused to consider what to say. While I did so my little daughter Kathryn, who was younger than her brother, softly replied, "Because Dad is a priesthood man, that's why."

That answer—"Because Dad is a priesthood man"—has since that day been a guiding light in my life. In considering why or why not I should or should not do certain things the answer is: "Because I am a priesthood man. That is why."

## I Didn't Call The Bishop, He Just Came

Have you ever used a jackhammer to break up cement? For years I'd seen workers doing that on projects and I always wanted to give it a go. One day I got my chance. I found out that it was really fun for the first ten minutes, and then the pain starts to set in.

Many years ago we had decided to add a room onto the east side of our house. To accomplish this task, the first order of business was to rent a jackhammer and the compressor that makes it work. With this amazing tool I would knock out the concrete porch and steps that were in the way of the addition.

On that Saturday morning I could hardly wait to rent the machine and get going. I hooked everything up and with great noise and much jarring I knocked off one corner of the cement. My sons and their friends watching me have such fun wanted to take a turn, but I told them, "No, I can do this myself." That was a statement I would come to regret.

The longer I worked, the less fun it was. My arms, which were more used to holding papers than construction tools, were fast becoming weary of holding the heavy jackhammer. I longed for my sons to get involved, but they had by now departed.

I discovered that the job was bigger than it had at first appeared. As the cement was chipped away I had to hold the hammer up more to an angle where it would be effective. Soon

I was getting charley horses in my arm muscles. But I had no choice but to continue, as I had to take the machines back to the rental place at the end of the day.

I prayed for strength and was able to keep going. I determined that if I could just complete this job I would be willing to go all the rest of my life without ever again having the fun of using a jackhammer.

Now time was running out. Some weeks earlier, I had made a speaking appointment for the late afternoon of this day in a nearby town. Now it was nearly time to go to that appointment. I wondered what to do. I prayed that the Lord would soften the heart of the cement so that it would crumble at the next jar of the jackhammer.

In the moment of greatest distress someone tapped me on the shoulder. As I looked to see who it was I heard the words, "That looks fun. Could I have a turn."

I had never in my life been so glad to see my bishop as I was at that time. I stepped back and said: "Sure, Bishop. It is fun. Go ahead and try it." The hammer seemed to respond to his great strength. Large chunks began to fall away. I said, "Bishop, I have to go give a talk."

"Don't worry," he said. "You go, and I'll do what I can here."

Two hours later, returning home, I drove into my driveway. As my headlights shone ahead I could see that the equipment was gone and so was the cement porch. My bishop had left a note that read, "I finished the job and took the jackhammer back. Thanks for the fun."

I went in the house and Marilyn asked, "When did you call the bishop and ask him to come?"

Trying to hold back my emotions, I replied, "I did not call him. He just came."

"Why?" she asked.

"Because I had done all I could, and I told the Lord that. And so He sent the bishop."

## The Bishop Seemed To Think That I Was The Only One Who Could Give The Closing Prayer

In my youth I got a job at a service station which sometimes required that I work on Sunday. I'd go to church every time I could, but sometimes I would have to miss sacrament meeting. I didn't yet know for sure that the Church was true, but I really thought it was. I'd go to sacrament meeting and the bishop would meet me at the door and shake hands with me and tell me how glad he was to see me. I liked him.

He would say, "George, would you like to give the closing prayer?" It seemed that every time I went to church he would say that. I used to sit there and think, "I wonder if anyone else in the church knows how to give the closing prayer?" Finally the closing song would be near the end of the last verse and I would walk to the front. I'd bow my head and offer the closing prayer. I'd get a special feeling as I stood there talking to the Lord. After I had offered such a prayer, ward members would come up to me and say, "That sure was a good closing prayer," and I'd think to myself, "You know, that really was a good prayer." I felt a special kind of thrill doing something for the Lord. It was not like making a basket in a basketball game, but in a different way it was even better.

## I Want You To Get Active In The Church Because I Want You To Be My Bishop

In one home teaching assignment I visited the home of a man who was not true to the faith. He was an imposing man in appearance and in intellect. He was a weather forecaster. The weather has always been a favorite home teaching message of mine and so our visits to his home were easy. But one day my priesthood leader told me that I should be more bold in teaching this man. I offered some hesitation to my leader but to no avail. He assigned me to be bold.

So the next time when my young priest companion and I went to his home, I was quite nervous. I knew that on this evening we were not going there to discuss the weather.

Soon we were in this family's lovely home. At the right moment I took a deep breath, uttered a silent prayer for courage and said, "I have a special message for you tonight. I want you to become my bishop."

I could see the stunned look on his face. But before he could offer any rebuttal I continued. "I want you to be my bishop because I really love and respect you." I could see him soften a bit and my heart was now really into this.

"But," I continued, "before you can become my bishop, you have to quit smoking." I then paused and said, "In the name of the Lord, I tell you that you must quit smoking. Will you do that?"

Tears filled his eyes as he said, "Do you know how hard it is to quit smoking?"

He wanted no answer to his question and I offered none. I told him again of my love. Boldness leads to boldness, especially if it is immersed in love. I added, "Another thing you need to do to be my bishop is to start coming to church."

His reply was that he was not an active member. I told him that I had seen him walk around our block showing his two little girls flowers and birds and other of nature's marvels. I told him that the greatest calling in the Church was to be a good father and that he was fulfilling that calling as well as I had ever seen it done. "But now," I said, "it is time to bring those girls to church."

Amidst her tears his wife said, "Oh, honey. Let's do it. Let's go back to church."

But it was too hard for him at that time to come back.

Sometime later he did return. I believe it was because at that later time some other home teacher was able to help him more than I was. But I had tried, and the Lord made it so that I loved this man from that time on with a love that was a joy to me. And he returned my love. It is amazing to me that when we go out to rescue another it somehow takes us deeper and deeper into the center of the Church.

## The Custodian Leads The Superintendent

A high school building custodian worked five days a week under the direction of the high school principal. Because the principal served under the district superintendent, we could say that the custodian served under him also. The state superintendent of public instruction has some authority over all schools and so in a small sense he too was considered a boss of the custodian.

It happened that the custodian, the principal, and both the district and state superintendents all lived in the same ward. The custodian was the high priests group leader and the three school administrators were all high priests in his group.

Thus, once each month these three school officials came to the custodian, whom they directed at the school, to report to him in personal priesthood interviews their priesthood stewardships and to receive from him direction in their Church duties.

# SCONES OF COMMUNICATION

## Now Tell Your Brother What You Just Told Me

Once our family was on a month-long journey to Canada. We had been in the car for days and were together so much that the children began to get on each other's nerves. After the first week of the journey we stayed in a vacant house owned by a friend of ours. One morning I was shaving when my oldest son came in and announced, "I want to catch a bus home."

When I asked why, he replied, "I've looked forward to this trip for almost a year. But I didn't know then that I'd have to be around my brother so much. I just can't stand to be around him any more. He makes life miserable for me. I want to go home."

I felt like saying, "Don't be ridiculous; you can't go home. Why don't you grow up? It's probably more your fault than it is his. Now get out of here and forget going home. Just quit causing trouble."

This might have been the correct answer, but it wasn't the right time for the right answer and, for once, I didn't give the so-called right answer. Instead I said, "Okay, let me finish shaving and we'll talk about it."

In a half-hour I asked both of the boys to join me in an empty bedroom. We sat on the rug in the middle of the room.

I said, "Tell me again, son, what you told me before." He went through the same speech as before. The younger brother listened intently, and as he heard more and more it seemed his heart would break. He started to cry. When the opening remarks were concluded, I turned around and looked into the tear-filled eyes of the younger brother. I asked, "What do you have to say?"

He replied as best he could through his tears, "I know I bug you a lot, but it's just that whatever game we play or whatever we do you always win."

The older brother quickly replied, "Sure I win—I'm better than you."

The younger brother then added, "I know that. But every time you win, I lose. And I get so tired of losing I can't stand it." Then he sobbed.

The older brother's countenance changed as he said, "Just don't bug me so much and things will be better."

The younger boy replied, "I'll try not to."

We talked—that is, they did—and I listened. The spirit of love came among us. The boys now could understand each other. The older boy was ready to go on with us, and our vacation was saved. Listening had done in a feeling and voluntary way what a lecture might have done in a forceful and mandatory way.

## The Lord Did Not Bless Our Voices, He Blessed Our Ears

My friend and I were the only two members of the Church in our part of Korea. During our services, the Protestant chaplain, sitting in his nearby office, could hear us when we sang. The other fellow who met with me couldn't sing well either. We wanted to sound like the Tabernacle Choir so that the chaplain would be impressed. To get some help, we prayed. Our prayers were miraculously answered. After that, angelic tones lifted us to new heights of happiness.

Several months later, I crossed the ocean and came

home. I sat by my wife Marilyn in church. With my newfound confidence, I sang at the top of my voice. After one verse Marilyn whispered, "You still don't sing well."

My mind did some quick considering. I decided that when we had prayed and had asked the Lord to bless us so we'd sound better, he hadn't blessed our voices—he had blessed our ears.

## She Asked Me What Was Wrong With Her And I Told Her

While I was a bishop another girl came to my office. She too wondered why she felt so insecure and why she had so few friends and wasn't getting any dates at all. I had noticed her for a period of months and had felt that she wasn't keeping herself as neat as she could have. I'm not an expert in how girls should apply makeup or how they should comb their hair, but I could tell that her eyebrows and other parts of her face were improperly made up.

As we talked she expressed to me her feelings that no one cared about her, that only I, her bishop, had any sincere interest in her. She asked me a question. "What can I do, how can I improve?" As I thought about the question I felt impressed to reply, "Before I say what I'm going to say I want you to know that I do love you and that I do care. But there are some things that you need to hear."

I went on, "I don't think you're taking care of yourself properly. I don't think your hair is as lustrous and well kept as it might be. I feel that your makeup is being improperly applied. I feel that your dresses could be more lovely." She started to cry. I said, "Go ahead and cry, but you need to hear these things."

She continued to cry as I added, "I'm not going to leave

this matter by telling you what is wrong. I'm going to ask a girl in our ward who knows about beauty and charm to be your counselor. And I want you to go to her and follow her advice."

Amidst her tears she said, "I won't do it."

"Now, as your bishop, I call you to do that," I said firmly. After many more tears she agreed. I called the other girl in and the two of them got together. A few days later I moved from the town to another assignment.

It was about a year later that I returned to my former place of employment. As I was walking down the sidewalk on the campus a girl came toward me. I didn't notice her much at first, but it soon became obvious that she was on a collision course with me and she wasn't about to turn aside. I stopped and she reached out her hand and said, "Bishop, I'm so glad to see you!"

I was confused as to who she was and said, "Now let's see, do I know you?"

She said, "Bishop, don't you know who I am?" With a most warm smile she said her name. Then I remembered our experience together and I could see that it was the girl I had assigned to improve her appearance.

The only words I could think to say were, "You're beautiful!"

"And furthermore," she said, "I'm going to get married."

She had combed her hair in a way that was becoming to her, her makeup was just right for her face, and her dress was a color that somehow complemented her complexion. She had started to care about her appearance and was doing all she could to make herself beautiful. In so doing she had developed an inward pride and in her heart she had a more special feeling. I could tell a difference not only in her overall grooming but also in her countenance. She seemed to glow, and as I walked away I knew I had just had the joy of seeing a truly beautiful person.

## The Only Time Your Children Can Talk To You Is When You Are With Them

The greatest victory I ever won was on our home court. My oldest son, Matt, was in the ninth grade. He wanted with all his heart to be an athlete. He was pretty good at basketball, but he wasn't growing much. During that period of time he was pretty ornery. He would seldom talk to me, and when he did it was in an unpleasant tone. Yet I'd heard that over at school he was the most friendly and amiable boy on campus. I wanted him to talk to me because I felt that something was troubling him. My desires for such a conversation had not yet been rewarded.

One day we were out playing basketball before dinner, just the two of us. We were playing a good game of one-on-one. I'd score and then he'd score. While we were playing, I started talking to him. I asked him, "How did it go in school today?"

His only answer was an uncomfortable silence. I raised my voice and asked, "Did you hear me? How did it go at school today?"

Finally he answered, "Why do you ask such dumb questions?"

A bit surprised at his abrupt reply, I thought to myself, "I guess that was a dumb question." I decided to upgrade my queries. I asked, "What did you have for school lunch?"

He replied, "What does that matter? Every day we have the same dumb stuff."

I wasn't quite sure just what to ask him next. We shot a few more baskets. In my silence I was wishing he wasn't so unhappy. Then an inspired question came to me. I asked, "How did it go in gym today?"

His countenance brightened as he enthusiastically

replied, "Hey, in gym today I did pretty good." He started talking to me. We bounced the ball a little less and just stood around between baskets. As our conversation thickened, he spoke with some emotion. "Dad, I don't know if you ever wonder why I'm so ornery."

I replied, "Oh, no. I never wonder about that."

"Well, the reason is that I don't like the way I look."

I was silent for a few seconds. Then I said, "You look good. You look just like me." With that he kind of gulped with a slight indication of pain.

"No, Dad, you look all right but I don't. I'm not as big as I want to be and I wear glasses. When I look at myself in the mirror, I just don't look like an athlete."

I knew what he was talking about. As a youth, I'd had some of those same problems. He kept talking to me, and I didn't know what to say. I could have said, "Don't be silly. You look like an athlete. You'll grow one of these days so don't worry about it. You'll be a great athlete." But I didn't give those pat answers. I just listened and I thought and I cared.

Just then Marilyn called and told us to come to dinner. We left the basketball court and walked across the back lawn. As we passed under the big trees I put my arm around his shoulder. We climbed up the back stairs. There was a feeling of love and understanding between us. I hadn't answered any of his questions, but he'd had a chance to tell me, his dad, how he felt and that had helped him.

## When We Are Both Resurrected, We'll Play Again And I'll Thrash You

Not long ago I played one-on-one basketball against Mark, my youngest. When I could see that defeat was inevitable and that he was acting pretty smug, I called time out.

I looked up into his eyes and said, "Mark, let me tell you something. Let's put my athletic prowess into the proper perspective. You and I know that there will be a resurrection."

Mark is a religious young man, so he was interested. I continued, "When the resurrection occurs, our bodies will come back to life. Once again the strength we had when we were at our prime will return. When that happens and my full physical powers return, I'll meet you again on the court. I'll go one-on-one with you, just as we are doing today. Then, I assure you, my young son, my hook shot will hit dead center and I'll block every shot you put up. Then it will be *me* who will hit long shot after long shot. It will be *me* who will fake right and go left. It will be *me* who will soar high for each rebound. The results will then be much different than they are now."

I detected that Mark was trembling a bit, so I threw him the ball and we resumed the game.

## How Are You Doing, Pops?

When my son Devin was in junior high he used to call me down to his room every evening. "Pops, come on down to my room," he'd call out. I'd call back, "I'm too tired." And he'd say, "Pops, if you knew how much it meant to me, you'd come down."

Now, what other choice did I have when my son treated me like that? He wanted me to go down, so I did. I'd sit down and he'd say, "How did it go at work today, Pops? What happened?"

We'd look at each other and exchange grins, and sometimes I'd ask, "What do you want to know for?"

He'd reply, "Because I'm interested in you, Pops. I'm interested in your progress and how you're doing." So I'd start talking, telling him things that had gone on at work that day.

Then I'd ask, "How did it go with you?"

We'd more or less give each other a report, and then he'd say: "Okay, Pops, you can go. I just want to keep track of what you're doing."

Those were such special times for me. They were a priceless gift from my son.

# TEACHING SCONES

## What Will I Say?

I recall a film made for the seminaries. It shows a huge buck deer—a mighty stag—standing upon a high mountain viewing the panorama before him. Down on the highway he sees two young spike deer running and playing together. Instantaneously he can see in his mind's eye the scene of many years earlier when he had been frolicking on that same highway with another young deer. Around the corner had come a huge truck. He had been able to jump to safety just in time; his young friend hadn't been so fortunate and was hit by the truck and killed.

The stag now takes off, crashing through the timber as he runs down the mountain at great speed. He reaches the bottom, but as he approaches the two young deer two questions loom large in his mind: "What will I do? What will I say?"

## Someday He Will Get A Great Religion Teacher, And Then He Will Be All Right

At one point in time, one of my sons was a little doubtful as to whether or not he would serve a mission. I didn't know what to do. I couldn't twist his arm and say that he had to promise me that he would. But I did remember that he was only seventeen. Sometimes people who are seventeen are not like they're going to be when they're nineteen. I prayed about it a good deal and talked to him as much as I could without seeming to preach to him. I had a fretful heart as I considered that he might not go.

I knew my son intended to go to BYU, however, and I hoped that when he got there he would get a religion teacher who would teach him the gospel in a way that would motivate him to want to go on a mission. Lo and behold, just as he enrolled at BYU, that school's officials called me and asked me if I'd come there as a religion teacher. Yes, you've guessed it! On the first day of class I looked down, and there, sitting on the front row grinning up at me, was my own son.

## I Can Only Play The First Verse

One time, while I was teaching seminary, we really sang well. There was a particularly good spirit in the classroom and the song was keyed in such a way that the guys could reach the high notes. We sang with great gusto, and I was so impressed that I was looking up at the ceiling, enjoying myself in singing. It came time for the second verse, and I boomed out with the first few words. To my surprise and embarrassment, I found myself singing a solo.

I looked around the classroom and noticed that Robert, the young man who had been playing the piano, was no longer at the piano bench. He had returned to his seat on the front row. I looked down to where he sat and said, "Robert, we want to sing more of that song." With a broad grin he replied, "I'm sorry, Brother Durrant, but I only know how to play the first verse." I arose from my chair and went over to where Robert was. I struck him playfully on the arm, and then as I looked down at him I burst into great laughter. Oh, how I loved Robert! How could you help but love someone who could make such an announcement!

I feel that the Lord understood that moment and that perhaps he too was gently laughing at Robert. I believe that good humor is the kind wherein we feel that the Lord would laugh and humor in bad taste is the type that would make him want to cry. Robert was one of those who often "goofed off good." I wouldn't really know what to expect when I'd walk into the classroom each day. But when it came time to be serious, Robert's eyes would open wide and he would listen with all the intensity he could muster. Often, when we talked of the Savior and of the spiritual things of life, I could even perceive that there were tears in his eyes. Then, when we got through with the serious business, once again there would be some humor coming from Robert. He made the seminary class a joyous thing to be part of. Robert had the rare and almost perfect gift of knowing how to "goof off good." His humor was always kind. His words and deeds never hurt anyone's feelings. He never made light of sacred things.

Later Robert went on a mission. Shortly after he had returned home I had the good fortune of meeting his mission president. He asked me if I knew Robert and I said I did. The president said, "Robert, with his humorous ways, caused us all to love him so much that we all cried when he ended his mission." The president continued: "Because of his ability to make people laugh and then turn around and make them cry, he was one of the most influential missionaries we had during my entire mission."

## Going To See Your Teachers In Their Offices Can Teach You Things That Can't Be Learned In A Classroom

During college I once went to a teacher's office to see him. I wondered if I should quit school, because I had no real direction in my life. I didn't know whom to go to for help. But this teacher's name kept coming to me, and so I mustered all my courage and approached his door.

I knocked and heard him shout gruffly, "Come in!" I opened the door and looked in. When he saw me he smiled, stood up, shook my hand, and said, "Sit down, my friend."

We talked. After several moments, he put his feet up on another chair and we talked some more.

He didn't seem to want to talk about sociology—he just seemed to want to talk about me.

"What are you majoring in?" he asked.

"I'm not sure," I replied.

"Well, what are you good at?"

"Nothing, I guess."

"Come on, George," he said warmly. "A guy like you has to be good at a lot of things."

"Well," I said shyly and with a touch of humor, "when I was a little kid I could keep the Crayolas in the lines."

He laughed, then pulled his chair close to mine, looked into my eyes, and said, "Then why don't you major in art? You could do it. A guy like you can do anything you want to do. You've got what it takes."

To me that was the greatest lecture that he had ever given.

## The Student Teacher Is Entitled To Good Fortune

One day while I was serving as a student teacher of art three boys were grouped together in the back, and they had all left their papers white and untouched. I walked over to them and said, "Hey, guys, how about all of us getting busy? What do you say?" The two boys who were standing returned to their seats and were soon drawing, but the third, with whom the other two had been visiting, just sat staring out the window.

There was an empty seat by him and so I sat down.

"Jay," I said, "I hear that you can really throw the javelin."

He didn't respond.

"Is that right?" I asked.

"That's right," he said in a tone that indicated he didn't want to talk.

"Do you think the snow will be melted so they can hold the meet this Friday?" He didn't reply. I continued, "It looks like it. It's warm out today. If they hold the meet I'm coming to see you throw."

He still hadn't looked at me, and I sensed I should move on. I was disappointed he hadn't responded.

As I moved away I could see him begin to draw something on his paper.

The next day something happened that I shall never forget.

I called the roll, and when I was nearly finished a girl came in late. I gently said, "Welcome, Betty." She slammed her book down on her desk. I spoke again, "Betty, don't get too comfortable yet. You need to go to the office and get an admit slip."

"What for?" she said with disgust.

"Because you missed class yesterday, and you know you must get an admit slip."

With that she stood up and walked to the front. She stood close to me and almost shouted as she said, "I'll tell you what you can do with your admit slips." She proceeded to shout obscenities at me that I hadn't heard since my army days.

Betty was in a rage to the point that it twisted her otherwise beautiful face. I, of course, as her vocabulary at the time dwarfed mine, was speechless. I knew immediately that she was not having her best day so far and that she was bound and determined to keep me from having my best day too.

Having finished her tirade, she stormed out of the door and slammed it closed.

"Don't mind her," Herman said. "She explodes like an atom bomb every once in a while. It's not your fault."

The class seemed to be sobered by what had happened. Somehow I sensed her attack had caused them to feel closer to me. I felt a surge of love for them. It seems that as students and their teacher go through things together it can make them feel a common bond with each other.

After class I went down to the office and asked the secretary if the girl had come there.

"Oh yes, she did," the secretary answered. "She's got a lot of problems at home that she can't cope with, so once in a while she acts a bit berserk. I understand she shouted at you. If you want we'll put her in the class she was in before—that's where she should be, but it wasn't working out so well, and we thought we'd try art."

"No, I don't want her to leave. Maybe I can help. At least, I'd like to try."

"All right. Good luck."

Friday I went to the track meet. The spring snow had melted, and it was a beautiful day. I saw Jay throw the javelin.

The next Monday, after class had begun, I went back to where he sat. He surprised me by speaking to me first.

"Did you come to see me throw?" he asked.

I nodded my head up and down and sort of smiled a prideful smile as I said, "I was there, all right. I saw you run forward and then rear back and let it go. I watched that javelin sail up into the clear blue sky, and as I watched it fly farther and farther I said to myself, 'I don't think that thing will ever come down.'"

He looked into my eyes, and something went between us.

Something that can go between people. Something good that happens sometimes between students and teachers.

After a few seconds of silence Jay spoke again. “Look at this drawing of this house and fence and trees. It don’t look quite right. What can I do to make it better?”

“Well, my friend,” I replied, “the sky looks good. But right here in the foreground...”

Oh, back to the girl! She was there every day. She didn’t tell me she was sorry, but she didn’t swear at me anymore. Even if she had I’d still have wanted her in there. After all, there weren’t any signs on the wall saying Don’t Swear at the Teacher.

When my time was up and I told my students good-bye, she smiled at me. And to me, that was apology enough.

## Helping My Best Teacher Quit Teaching

“You’ve got to win by two,” I shouted as my more-than-worthy opponent scored on a lucky hook shot from the left side of the basket. It had been a grueling game to this point. We matched basket after basket. I was putting all I had into defense, and I knew that I must score on each possession or he’d win. The thought of his winning, more than my losing, gave me supreme motivation, for if he won I would have let down all the students.

I was in my last year of high school, and going down to defeat at the hands of a teacher—worse yet, a student teacher—was inexcusable. It would have disgraced the entire senior class.

After the teacher scored, he personally delivered the ball to me where the top of the key would have been painted had we not been playing on a dirt court at a campground. As he handed me the ball he crouched down in a defensive stance, and we looked deeply into each other's eyes with determination that defied description.

Suddenly I faked right, but he stayed firm. I went left, and quickly he was directly in my way. I knew my only hope was to jump and shoot. The ball was on line. If it went in, we'd be tied. I could tell he was tired by the way he was gasping for breath. I knew that if I could tie it now, I'd win.

Just as I celebrated in my mind, the ball hit the back of the rim and catapulted back toward me. I had to get the rebound, but it was just a fraction of an inch beyond my grasp. He had it.

I pressed him as closely as I could without fouling. He was breathing so hard I knew his accuracy on a long shot would be poor. I knew I must not let him get around me.

Suddenly he jumped and shot. The ball, to my relief, was way off course. I moved quickly to get the rebound. But there was no rebound. The ball careened off the old wooden backboard through the hoop. It was over. He had won.

He gasped, and then said, "Good job, George"—gasp—"you're a"—gasp—"good player."

The other students mumbled their disapproval of my performance as they headed to get their barbecued hamburgers. The lines for the food were long. Seeing that we would be last, my opponent and I sat down on a log near the creek and began to talk. First we spoke of where he went to high school and about the time he played varsity basketball. After several minutes of conversation, I asked him where he would be teaching seminary the next year. I was shocked at his reply.

He picked a stick up from the ground and, holding it in his right hand, tapped it gently into his left. I could tell he was in deep thought. Finally he spoke. "I was thinking about that today. You know, while I've been teaching your class, things haven't gone so well. I can't seem to keep you guys interested. I can tell you've personally been bored, because you spend most of your time sitting in the back talking to Val and Bob."

He was hitting his hand harder now as he continued, "I guess I'm just not cut out to be a teacher. So my wife and I decided today that I'd go into business with my brother."

He fell silent. I couldn't respond—it never occurred to me that he wouldn't be a teacher. To me he was the best there was. I could tell from the first day he came to our classroom that he liked me. He liked all of us. *Maybe that's why we took advantage of him*, I thought.

"Don't quit being a teacher," I pleaded. "You're the first teacher who ever played me one-on-one. I love your class. I know I talk a lot, but that doesn't mean I'm not listening." As we walked toward the food line I said, "I'm sorry. It's just—well, anyway, I like you. Don't quit." At that point someone called us to come eat, and so our talk ended.

But he did quit, this wonderful man whom I remember now some forty-five years later. A man whom I now recognize was a role model gave up teaching to go into business, and a lunkhead like me helped him to decide that. I'm not writing to criticize myself. I'm writing on behalf of all the lunkheads and all the duds (and I'm addressing myself) to you who could be great teachers. Don't quit because of supposed failure. We mature, we creatures who, as Christ's words indicate, need to be taught that we can be good human beings. Don't quit; we need you. Don't turn away. Not for money nor for an easier way. You know who you are. You feel it in your heart that you should be a teacher. Don't turn your back on us; don't turn your back on teaching.

## The Worst Class Becomes The Best

During my second year in Brigham City, in the early part of the winter, my dear friend Brother Horsley suddenly became ill. Two days later, he died. This great man had had many moments in which he was a master teacher. He could control rowdy students in a most effective manner. Meeting the needs of one rambunctious class required every one of his special skills. All of us on the faculty, knowing the makeup of this group, marveled that Brother Horsley was succeeding with them.

But now Brother Horsley was gone, and each of us agreed to teach one of his classes so that hiring a new teacher wouldn't be necessary and his wife could continue to receive his pay.

What I feared most happened. I was free fifth period, and that was when the infamous class met.

Brother Bowen, the newly appointed principal, gulped as he said, "George, you've been teaching the ninth graders, but now I see no choice but to invite you to step in and teach Brother Horsley's fifth period." He paused as if in pain for me, then continued, "Brother Horsley's fine class of juniors and seniors."

I knew I was about to "suffer long," not by choice, but by decree.

The next day I recalled a story I'd heard another teacher tell. He'd said, "When one of my classes would come over to the seminary from the high school, I'd watch them approach, and I'd be reminded of what Delilah told Samson. I'd say to myself, 'The Philistines are upon us.'"

It was fifth hour. I said good-bye to my fourth-hour ninth graders and walked the fifteen steps to the door of Brother Horsley's room. I paused, took a deep breath, and entered. My suffering was about to begin.

My anticipation of suffering was not an underestimate. I

did indeed suffer or struggle much during those fateful four months, but amid the suffering, as is always the case, I experienced much joy. Now, strangely, after many years have passed, all I really remember is the joy.

Thinking back, I recall that during the first several days with this class I had determined to be tough and not to allow a single ounce of tomfoolery. But these students knew what tough was, and they could tell that I wasn't it. Early confrontations with them did nothing more than cause me to lose all semblance of charity, and at the same time, my attitude and behavior caused them to be more determined than ever to destroy any environment in which positive learning could occur.,

In frustration I decided that by all indications I was losing. Having acknowledged that dismal truth, an idea entered my head, and I said to myself, *I can't conquer them, so I'll join them.*

Carrying out this new strategy, I'd reason with them about what was taking place in our class. We talked of why we needed things to change. I recall that one day, right after our song, prayer, and scripture, my heart was sick because they had mockingly carried out these sacred activities.

I told them of my deep disappointment and announced that thereafter we would not have a devotional at the beginning of class. I sincerely reasoned that such sacred things as prayer and scripture reading could not be done in a light-minded manner without in a sense mocking God.

The largest fellow in the class, who was nicknamed "Mr. Clean," objected, stating, "Come on, Brother Durrant. Don't make us stop having devotionals. We want to have a devotional."

I answered, "So do I. I want to have a devotional with all my heart. But we can't because we can't be reverent, and so we won't."

The big fellow said, "What do you mean, we can't be reverent? We can be more reverent than those little ninth graders that you love so much."

"Yeah," chimed in two or three others. "We can be reverent. You just let us have a devotional tomorrow, and we'll show you reverent."

And so they did. I didn't set out to be a master teacher at that moment. But I loved them, and when I told them about the need for reverence they sensed that I was sincere (not as sounding brass), and they felt that what I was saying was true. At that moment, we rejoiced together.

That wasn't the end of the battle, but we all were now going the same direction. The confrontations were no longer with the entire class, just with some individuals.

One fellow who sat on the front row was the greatest troublemaker of them all. He disrupted almost continually with his light-minded remarks. But to my delight, I learned that if I would move to the other side of the room and speak in a low volume, he would soon drift off to sleep. With him asleep, the class could move forward in a more effective manner.

When the bell would ring, signaling that class was over, I'd wake that student up and the two of us would walk together to the front door of the seminary building. One day as we walked, he told me that he worked at a job every night until two in the morning. I told him how hard it would be for me to stay awake if I went to bed as late as he did. I thanked him for coming to class so faithfully. He could see that I understood, and as time passed, he and I became good friends.

Each day at the end of class I would wake him up as gently and respectfully as I could and then walk to the door with him. He could tell that I liked him, because it's hard to hide something like that. Each day, as we walked to the door together, I had a few moments when I was a master teacher.

As my students and I talked in that fifth hour class, we

often got off the subject. The students liked to talk about sports and polygamy and who is sealed to whom when there is a divorce and the army and college life.

If someone had come in and seen the casual manner of things, I'm sure they would have said, "Poor Brother Durrant. He can't handle those big guys. They know how to make him suffer. He's a good guy, but he's a C teacher at best."

They would have been right. But I knew then of the private moments and the feelings that I shared with those "rowdy ones." They sort of reminded me of when I was younger. Perhaps because of that I had a genuine love for them, and that made it so I could see beyond their foreground. I could see their sky.

## The Message That Stopped In The Heart

I recall fifteen-year-old Jimmy. He was a troublemaker and wasn't shy by any standards. His boisterousness was downright disruptive not only to his own class but to our other seven classes. Jimmy would never listen to a lesson.

About midyear I decided that I as a teacher was saying too much and the students were saying too little in our lessons. The only answers they ever gave were "yes" or "no." I decided that I would change that. I'd get them to talk. So on a special day I said, "I brought some popcorn today. Let's all sit around and eat it, and as we eat we'll talk about what Heavenly Father is like."

I set the stage as well as I could and then softly said, "Now, you each tell me what you feel about our Heavenly Father." For a few minutes all was silent except for the crunching of popcorn.

I gently said, "Robert, do you believe in Heavenly Father?"

The only response I got was some crunching.

"Albert, what about you?"

More seconds of silence, except for crunching.

I gently asked, "Albert, do you believe in a Heavenly Father?"

More silence followed. But then Albert said softly, "Yes."

I asked, "Why?"

After a pause he spoke again. "Because I was in a car and it went off the road, and just before we crashed I prayed nobody would get hurt, and nobody did."

Soon Roy added that he believed in God because his mother had been sick and he prayed and she got better.

The momentum caused nearly all to join in. Even Jimmy was caught up in the sweet comments being made.

Soon we talked of Jesus. Sadie said, "Jesus is bread and water."

I asked, "Why is that?"

She replied, "Because that is what we have in the sacrament."

I explained about the sacrament, and when I finished she said, "Oh," with understanding.

For several weeks we taught in this way of letting these young people make soul-to-soul comments. Then we had a testimony meeting with all the classes together. There the students took turns expressing their feelings.

At this meeting one would get up and slowly walk up to the front. Incidentally, those students could really walk slowly. All would watch as one made his or her journey to the pulpit. That person would say a few sentences of testimony, and all would watch until he or she had returned to sit down. We spent much of our meeting engaged in travel time.

Finally, toward the end of our time together, on the back row Jimmy stood. Those seeing him stand softly snickered.

Jimmy was a clown, and they all laughed a good amount at just about everything he did.

Everyone watched as this strikingly handsome young man in his Levi jacket swaggered his way to the front.

As he held the pulpit with both hands, leaned back, and looked out, a complete silence filled the chapel. All seemed to wonder at once, "What funny thing will Jimmy say?" I, along with the others, held my breath in anticipation.

After a few seconds our wonder ended as Jimmy's voice rang out. He said, "Something strange is going on up here at LDS seminary. I've been coming up here for three years. In all that time, everything the teacher says goes in this ear (he pointed at his left ear) and comes out here (pointing to his right ear)." Jimmy paused for several seconds.

Finally he spoke again. "But lately a strange thing has been going on. What my teacher says goes in here (again he pointed at his ear), but," he said as he put his hand on his heart, "it has been stopping right here."

There was no laughing. Jimmy the clown was now Jimmy the teacher. As he expressed his feelings about heavenly things, the Spirit of the Lord testified to all of us that what Jimmy said was true.

## Teaching The Cool Ones

I recall such a class at my ward. I was president of the Young Men. My biggest problem was that no one was willing to teach the teenage boys each Tuesday evening. I finally told the bishop that if he would release me, he could easily get a new president. Then I could go to where the wild things were and teach them.

I was glad when he agreed, because there was something about this group of guys that really fascinated me. They were unlike any group I'd ever known. At that time there was a tremendous drive among the young folks to be "cool," and this group really considered themselves to be cool. Somehow I got a kick out of that because I thought that as far as I understood the word *cool*, these guys really were. And the more they thought it, the more it seemed to be so.

I was anxious to teach them. I didn't have some notion I'd shape them all up and take away their cool. I think mostly I just wanted to see if I could understand what made them the way they were.

The first night I had a good lesson prepared. It wasn't a highfalutin lesson way above their world. It was down to earth, with just an occasional look toward heaven. But when I presented the lesson, I found that even that was too religious for my young friends. Our discussion soon devolved into almost exclusively worldly subjects.

So I decided to be the discussion moderator. I'd insist that only one speak at a time and that we all stay on the same subject until it was exhausted and then move on.

They were fascinating teachers—or, I should say, students. I recall that one night we talked about the police officer who worked in the halls of their school. I found that fascinating, because when I went to school we didn't have a police officer. We talked of the qualities a good police officer should have. At the end of our hour, just before we went to play basketball, I asked them if I could take a minute and say something. They agreed, and I said, "You know, I've loved being here with you tonight, and I'm so glad that you guys don't have any problems that would involve a bad relationship with any police officers. I'm proud of you. And I love you." They were all silent. I shouted, "Now, let's go play basketball!"

The next week when we were in our classroom, my cool young friends told me all about drugs. It was quite an education for me as they told me what they had observed in the way of drug users. Again they let me conclude the discussion. This time I said, "Thank you for teaching me about the effects and dangers of drugs. I am so glad that you men are wise and strong and that you steer clear of drugs. I love you guys, and you each can be a great leader. Now, let's go play ball."

I liked these guys. I mean, I really liked them.

In the next class, one of them got us going by telling us a communist kid had a locker next to his. They all told me what they thought of communism and capitalism. It was interesting to me because when I was in high school, there wasn't a single communist in my class. None of us in those days even knew what a communist was.

The next week there wasn't room for all of the guys who came in the classroom, because several young men were coming from another ward. I told them they ought to go to their own ward. One replied, "We don't like going there. The teacher there is always prepared, and you never are. That's why we like coming here." I wondered if that was a compliment.

As I write this, I can see those guys in my mind. Oh, how I loved them! To me they were great. We talked of many problems faced by young people, such as pornography, alcohol, speeding cars, and cops. At the end of each discussion, I'd ask for my moment.

One time, after a discussion on driving, I asked one, "Do you speed?"

"No, my old man would kill me if I did," he replied.

"I know your dad," I said. "He's my friend. He's a great man, and he is so blessed to have a son like you."

As I described his father, my big "cool" friend struggled to hold back his tears.

Another who wore big black boots and rode a motorcycle asked, "Brother Durrant, what's wrong with drinking coffee?"

I looked at him as he sat back on his chair with its back tilted against the wall. He continued, "Each day I sluff my third-hour class and go to a cafe to drink coffee, and it don't hurt me."

I asked, "How old are you?"

"Sixteen."

"What priesthood office do you hold?"

"Deacon."

"You're sixteen years old and you're a deacon, and you want to know what's wrong with drinking coffee?"

I kicked his boot with my foot, and it knocked his foot off from where it rested on his other knee. This caused his chair to slam down onto all four of its legs.

Startled, he said, "You don't have to get mad."

I replied, "I am mad. I'm mad at what you're doing with your life. Get on the ball. Be what you can be."

I softened and said, "I love you. It hurts me when you don't do all you can do. I love all you guys. I'm glad we're friends—that's why I want you to shape up and look at the sky and be somebody." I paused and looked at each one. Then I clapped my hands and said, "Now, let's go play softball."

As we journeyed a block or so to the softball field, I walked close to the troubled one.

"I want to say the closing prayer at your missionary farewell," I said.

"What?" he said laughingly. "I ain't goin' on no mission."

"I didn't say anything about your going. I just want to give the closing prayer at your farewell when you go."

"How can you if I ain't goin'?"

In the weeks that followed, each time I'd see him he'd say, "Are you still going to give the closing prayer at my farewell?"

I'd say, "I sure am."

"How can you? I ain't goin'."

Three years later I was serving as mission president in

Kentucky. That student called one night and said, "Can you come home?" I asked him why. He said, "'Cause it's my missionary farewell, and you said you'd give the closing prayer."

Many years have passed since those sacred times when I met with the "cool" ones. As I think back, I realize what a glorious time that was.

## A Teacher Who Understood

Mr. Sorensen had grown up in Sanpete County, Utah, and he had a country-type wit and the kind of wisdom that is peculiar to those who grow up around horses, cows, barns, and irrigation ditches.

I recalled my first day in his class. He called me by name, and because of the way he looked at me, I sensed that perhaps I had a shot at being his favorite. I'd not had much luck through the years at becoming a teacher's favorite, even though I'd longed to be that as much as I'd ever longed to be anything.

The second day of class Mr. Sorensen told a story that made me laugh so hard I thought I'd fall out of my chair. He said in his slow sort of drawl, "Down in Sanpete County there were these two guys who went hunting for birds. One of the two stuttered and the other shook. Well, they saw a bird and argued over who would shoot it. The one who shook was carrying the gun, and so they finally decided that he'd shoot. As he aimed, the gun's barrel shook back and forth. Shaking even more, he aimed . . . and then he aimed a bit longer. Finally he fired and the bird fell. He shouted, 'I got it! I got it!' His friend said, 'Well, you-you-you should have. You-you-you aimed at the whole tree!'"

That night at dinnertime I told my family the story. They laughed some, but not nearly as much as I did.

As the days went by I'd tell Mom nearly every night what Mr. Sorensen had said that day. I remember her saying, "George, you sure do seem to like that Mr. Sorensen." I could tell that Mom liked him too, because parents really like teachers whom their children like.

Remembering those pleasant experiences filled my heart with joy. But then I remembered a most troubling experience I had with Mr. Sorensen.

Two weeks into that same school year a major crisis came into my life. The principal sent a note saying that there were too many students in Mr. Sorensen's history class and that another teacher didn't have enough students. Thus, two students were going to have to transfer from the large class to the small one.

Mr. Sorensen looked sad as he told us the news. I could tell he didn't want to lose any of us. He said, "To make this fair I'll choose two numbers between one and thirty-five. Then you can each write a number on a piece of paper and give it to me. The two of you who choose numbers closest to the ones I have chosen will have to move."

I had a feeling I'd be one of those who would choose an unlucky number. Just the thought of that caused me deep pain.

I watched Mr. Sorensen write down the two numbers, and it seemed to me that he wrote two digits for each number. Therefore, I felt that each of the two numbers had to be ten or higher. If I wrote "1" on my paper, I'd be far away from the dreaded numbers and I wouldn't have to move.

Finally, having gathered and studied the numbers, Mr. Sorensen announced that the numbers he had written were twenty-five and one. He continued, "Betty, you chose twenty-four, so you are to go." Then he paused as his eyes focused on me. "And George, you chose the number one, so you'll go too."

I hadn't cried in many years, and I didn't want to cry then. But I couldn't hold back such a flood of emotions. I didn't cry out loud, but every person in the class could tell what I was doing.

Mr. Sorensen was almost always jovial, but at that moment I could tell he wasn't too far from tears himself.

My classmates became sober on seeing my distress. Silence filled the classroom. After several seconds I heard a girl's voice say, "Mr. Sorensen, Betty and I are friends. I'll go with her and George can stay here."

Mr. Sorensen smiled and said, "Did you hear that, George? Are you willing to stay here with an old codger like me and let Anna go to that other wonderful class?"

I had been looking down so my classmates wouldn't see my tears. But what Mr. Sorensen said caused me to look up. I said in a whisper, "Yeah, I'll stay here." I sniffed, and added, a little more loudly, "I'm willing to stay with you, Mr. Sorensen." He smiled and nodded his approval.

That sort of sealed it, I guess. Mr. Sorensen and I had been close before, but now we were fast friends. I'd never had a teacher before who was my friend. Oh, he wasn't a friend like my friends Bob and Don L. and Delmar, because he was a teacher. But he treated me like a true friend.

I'd come to class as early as I could so that he and I could talk about sports and World War II. He'd tell me stuff just as though I were another teacher. He seemed to respect me, even though I'm sure he knew that that year was a troubled time for me—a time when I didn't have much respect for myself. A time when I did a lot of looking down because of my insecurities. A time when I needed someone to tell me often to look up at the sky.

## Mr. Brimhall Recognized Common Sense

Mr. Brimhall was my fifth-grade teacher at the old Harrington Elementary School in American Fork.

Mr. Brimhall acted as if he was so mean. That memory caused a broad smile to cross my face. I too thought he was mean back then. I recalled that some said, "Mr. Brimhall is mean. But he's fair, because he's mean to *everybody.*"

*But, you know,* I said to myself, *he wasn't mean at all.* How could a mean teacher have been so kindly aware of an insecure little guy like me? How could a mean teacher have said to me almost every day, "George, it's a little noisy out in the hall. You are our official door-closer. Would you get up and go close the door?"

At this request I would go to the door, close it, and return to my seat.

Mr. Brimhall would say, "Thank you, George. You are a good door-closer."

I'd feel as though I were the most important person in the class and maybe even in the whole world, and that Mr. Brimhall was the world's kindest man.

I knew that being asked to close the door didn't have anything to do with arithmetic. I seldom could have been praised for my prowess in that area. But I knew Mr. Brimhall was right—I was a good door-closer. And somehow that made up for a lot of things I wasn't so good at.

One day we were studying fractions. Mr. Brimhall said, "If you had four quarters of a pie, they would all be equal in size." He added, "The four quarters of anything are all equal in size."

I raised my hand and, mustering all my courage, said, "Mr. Brimhall, that's not right."

"Oh?" he said in sort of a mean way. "When is it not right?"

I timidly replied, “Well, my dad shot a deer, and I was helping him cut it up. The hindquarters were a lot bigger than the front ones.”

The twenty-nine other students all laughed at my remark. I suddenly found myself wishing I'd kept quiet as I usually did.

Mr. Brimhall didn't laugh. He stood up from his chair and walked over to where I sat. He stood above me, put his hand on my shoulder, and softly said, “I've never thought of it like that. You are absolutely right. George, you've got what I call common sense, and that is the best kind of sense.”

# MISSIONARY SCONES

## You Can't Score Until You Have Served

I was raised in American Fork. I was not a tall, athletic fellow known for my sports prowess. But I did have one memorable sports victory. In the springtime all the schools in the Alpine School District—Pleasant Grove, Orem, Lehi, and American Fork—would get together for Alpine Day. On that day we had track and field where the gifted athletes ran and jumped and threw heavy objects. Because I wasn't too fast and couldn't throw anything very far, I was a good spectator. I was standing there during my senior year watching what was going on when the coach called out my name said, "We need a bunch of you guys inside the gymnasium. They've decided to have volleyball as one of the events for Alpine Days."

I went inside and I suddenly became a member of the volleyball team. None of us had ever played that sport before as it was new to our area. We started to play against the teams from the other schools who didn't know how to play it, either.

I had been keeping track of the score in my head and finally the referee said we had two points.

I protested, "We made four points. I've counted them."

He said, "There's something you don't understand. You can't score until you've served."

I said, "That's dumb."

He said, "It might be dumb, but that's the rules."

Soon I understood the rule, "You can't score until you serve."

Now I know that is not only a rule in volleyball, but also in life.

## The Right Time To Go Down The Hall With Your Arm Around A Girl

As a sophomore I once saw an older student going down the hall with his arm around a girl, and I thought to myself, "That's what I'm going to do when I get to be a junior in high school." When I became a junior, I saw a senior walking down the hall with his arm around a girl, and I thought, "When I get to be a senior I'm going to walk down the hall with my arm around a girl and be a big wheel." But when I was a senior I was still timid. So I decided that I would wait until I got in college before I would walk down the hall with my arm around a girl. Then in college I decided I'd wait until after my mission.

There were two reasons why in high school I didn't walk down the hall with my arm around a girl. One was the characteristic I've already related, namely, my timidity. The other reason was that there wasn't any big rush on the part of any girl to walk down the hall with my arm around her. But now I look upon these formerly painful circumstances as a blessing to me, because that made it easy for me to graduate from high school free from any commitment to any girl.

## I Thought That I'd Never Catch Up, But I Did

I recall a classmate of mine who was the opposite of me when it came to his relationship with the girls. He boldly walked down the hall of the school with his arm around a girl. All I could do was to dream of doing such a bold thing. He had many dates during high school and was among the most popular boys. He had dark hair and dark eyes, a perfect profile, much charm, and was extremely bold. After high school he went to work as a truck driver and I enrolled in college. I commuted from home to college each day with an older fellow who had a car. One day, right after I had begun college, as we were driving home we passed by my bold classmate's residence. There in his driveway was a new red Chevrolet convertible car. I thought it was the most beautiful car I had ever seen.

Later that day I saw him riding around in that red convertible with a beautiful blonde girl. She looked good in that car. I thought that the only thing that could have made that picture more beautiful was for me to have been the owner of that car and the boyfriend of that girl.

A few weeks later there came an invitation to the wedding reception of my handsome friend and the beautiful girl. The wedding ceremony took place in a garden and was performed by a bishop. Three of my friends and I attended the reception together. We had purchased a gift—it was a lamp that was so big that it couldn't be wrapped. We entered carrying the lamp. We gave it to the youngsters at the door and they carried it over to the gift table. I felt glad that we were able to give such a gift.

I made my way through the reception line. I was not accustomed to such social situations and I hardly knew what to say to the bride or groom. But after awkwardly offering congratulations I took my seat at a table and began to eat my nuts and drink my punch. As I ate I looked across the room to where this handsome couple were being congratulated by well-wishers. I remember thinking: "Why don't I do what they are doing? Why don't I grow up? Why don't I quit school and get myself a car and a girl and get myself married? They're moving forward in life and I'm just going to school. I'll never catch up to them?"

Time went by and I continued to go to college. Then came that glorious day when my bishop asked me if I would like to go on a mission. I replied, "Bishop, I'd give my right arm to go on a mission." So I went. Two years later I came home. By this time my friend had been married for some time and he and his wife were blessed with three children.

Not long after my arrival home from my mission, I was finally bold enough to walk down the hall with my arm around a girl, and I was bold enough, even without the help of a red convertible car, to win the love of a most beautiful girl. Gradually I was able to catch up.

## They Did Not Know That I Was A Dud

In high school I was a "dud." I didn't want to be but I was. I wanted to be student body president, but I didn't get elected because I wasn't nominated. I wasn't nominated because no one thought I'd be a good president. I was the only one who knew that I'd make a fine leader, and I didn't mention it because I thought everyone would laugh.

I wasn't all-state because it's hard to make all-state while sitting on the bench. If a sports writer would look over at me, I'd sit up straight, but they still didn't name me all-state.

So when I arrived in England on my mission, I wasn't exactly Mr. World.

But the great thing about it was that the people in England didn't know that I was a dud. They saw me in my nice navy blue suit and they thought things such as, "I'll bet he was student body president," or "I'll bet he was all-state and popular."

As I said, none of what I thought they thought was true, but I never corrected them. And for two years I wore that navy blue suit and the people kept thinking I was great. (They thought all of us were.)

## Responsible For Your Companion

When I was a missionary, my companion and I were crossing a small footbridge which spanned a river which ran through the city where we labored. Because the bridge was bordered on each side by a high wooden fence and because it turned at an angle just before it ended, it was not possible to see the other side until one turned the corner. Signs were posted, "Do not ride bicycles on the bridge." My companion would put his foot on the pedal, push off with his other foot, and coast. I repeatedly asked him not to do that.

One day, as usual, he did it again. He was about twenty yards ahead of me. He went around the corner and came face to face with an English Bobby (policeman). I arrived on the scene and said, "Officer, if I've told him once, I've told him a hundred times not to do that."

My companion looked at me and seemed to be saying, "Thanks a lot, friend."

The officer, sensing the humor, smiled and said to him, "Now listen carefully, young man. I'm releasing you in the custody of your friend." He then turned to me and said, "From now on you're responsible for him."

I've never forgotten that experience. And, by the way, neither has my companion. I still remind him that he is in my custody. He still reminds me that he really appreciated my thoughtful assistance.

## The Youngest Missionaries Ever

Eleven-year-olds Mike and Trevor noticed their dear friend and Webelos leader Brother Hal Grant had for the last few weeks left the church building at the end of Sacrament services and did not return for Sunday School nor Priesthood meeting. They sat restlessly in Primary longing for it to conclude so that they could carry out their plan. They had determined that if Brother Grant skipped his meetings this week, they would do something about it.

As soon as the closing prayer was said they dashed home. With a pair of scissors they cut some thin cardboard into two small rectangle shapes. Then with a felt tip pen they each wrote their names on one of the small cards. Though they were some eight years away from being missionary age they boldly wrote the word Elder in front of each of their names. Then with straight pins they fixed their name tags onto the left side of their suit coats. Two minutes later, wearing their homemade missionary identification, they knocked boldly on their Scout leader's door.

When Brother Grant saw his two Webelos standing on the porch he was surprised to see their new identification. Before he could ask them what they were up to young Trevor spoke up and said, "I'm Elder Gatenby and this is Elder Poulsen. We are two missionaries from the Church of Jesus Christ of Latter-day Saints."

Brother Grant was speechless as Michael, now Elder Poulsen, announced, "We have been sent here by the Lord give you a special message." Then one of the two youngest Elders in the history of the Church boldly asked, "Could we please come in and talk to you?"

Surprised, Brother Grant decided to go along with the charade. Soon the two young missionaries were seated in the front room where they were also joined by Sister Grant. With their scriptures sitting in their laps, Elder Gatenby asked Sister Grant if she would say a prayer before they presented the discussion. She agreed and did so.

Elder Poulsen then said, "Brother Grant we would like to read a scripture with you. Could you get your scriptures please?"

Soon Brother Grant had his scriptures and said, "I'm ready, what do you want to me to read?"

Elder Poulsen hadn't thought ahead and so he replied, "Just open up your book anywhere and read a verse."

Brother Grant did as he was asked and read a verse aloud. As soon as he finished the young Elder asked, "Now Brother Grant, what does that scripture mean to you?'

When Brother Grant had finished explaining what he felt the scripture meant, Elder Gatenby spoke up and said, "You are the best Webelos leader in he whole world and we love you a lot. But we are concerned that you are not doing the things you should in the church. We have noticed that you come to Sacrament Meeting and then you go home without staying for Sunday School and Priesthood."

Elder Poulsen then added, "We don't think that what you are doing is right."

As Brother Grant moved a bit nervously in his chair Elder Poulsen added with great sincerity, "We are here to challenge you to stay for all three meetings. Will you, Brother Grant, promise us that from now on you will stay to all the meetings?"

Brother Grant loved these boys. They were not only in his Webelos troop but they were also his dear young friends. He could not disappoint them.

He replied that he would try to do as they had challenged him to do.

The two young missionaries then asked if they could say a prayer before leaving. Brother Grant agreed.

Elder Poulsen prayed and part of what he said was, "Please help our dear friend Brother Grant to stay to all three meetings each Sunday."

Sister Grant who had been quiet up to this time asked, "Would you two missionaries like a piece of cake and a cold drink before you go on to your other missionary duties?" The two agreed to this proposal. After eating they said they had to be going. As they left the house Brother Grant told them that he was glad they had come. They had been in his home each week for two years but never before was it like this. The Scout leader could not believe that these two young boys could be so bold as to do what these two had just done. There was a feeling in his heart that had not been there before the young missionaries had knocked on his door—a feeling that would be hard for him to ignore.

## Keeping the Brakes On Going Uphill

Two missionaries were riding their tandem bike up a steep hill. At the top, the one on the front seat said, "Wow! I'm out of breath. That hill was really steep."

The missionary on the back said, "Yeah, that hill was so steep that I had to keep the brake on all the way up to keep us from rolling backwards."

## We'd Be Great Companions

Oh, how often I have wished I could be your companion! We'd really get them—you and I. We'd be the two best average missionaries here. We'd goof off, but only when the time was right. We'd bear testimony to each other. We'd study (but you'd have to help me because I'm not as smart as some). We'd go looking for people each morning. Sometimes we'd feel a little discouraged, but we'd go out anyway. We'd love the members and they'd know it. We'd act in such a way that they'd say, "Don't let the president ever move you two."

We'd teach some great discussions and a few that weren't so great. Sometimes we'd really teach by the Spirit. We'd be good friends with the bishop or branch president. He'd like us a lot. We'd write to each other's parents and encourage them. I'd write to your girlfriend.

We'd eat pretty well, especially pancakes. We'd be sort of self-starters. We'd both want to become successful. We'd get a little discouraged if that didn't happen, but we'd keep working hard anyway.

Then one day you'd get transferred. I'd help you pack. You'd tell people good-bye and they'd cry. I'd wonder if people loved me as much as they did you. We'd go the bus. We'd shake hands and I'd feel like crying.

"I'll see you," I'd say. "Remember, we're going to room together at college. And remember at my wedding you'll be my best man." Then you'd go.

I'd go home and wait in the apartment. At 3:45 another bus would come into town. This time another one of you would come into town and we'd start all over. Just you and me—companions.

I love you, my companions. Together we'll be what we ought to be.

## True Missionary Success

I recall a missionary with whom I talked on a cold winter's day in Kentucky—just he and I alone in a little office. His eyes moistened as he said, "I get the feeling that Mom and Dad wonder why we aren't baptizing anyone." Tears fell as he tried to continue. "They had such high hopes for me, and I'm letting them down. I try, President, I really try; but I just can't seem to do it." I sat silently as he softly cried. Oh, how I loved him! How I hoped that I'd have a son who'd care as much as he cared! You see, I knew him. I knew that when he said he had tried, he really had.

I found myself wishing I could look into his father's eyes and as,: "How did you raise such a son? How did you infuse in him such honor and integrity? How did you teach him to love so completely? How did he come to be so totally responsible?" I could learn many things from the father of such a noble son.

The Spirit of the Lord filled my soul as I sat with him. I knew I was in the presence of a man of God. I told him of my love and respect for him. I told him many things. Then he spoke again, "President, my companion and I will work even harder. I know there's a family waiting for us. We're going to find them and bring them into the Church. You just watch." Days came and went and his full-time mission ended, and he hadn't found the family. But, oh, how he had searched and prayed and worked!

Some time has passed since I last saw him, and I long to see him again. He was one of my most successful missionaries, for he was a real man. As the years roll on, we will meet someday and talk. He will say, "President, I wanted to find a family so much. It broke my heart then and it still does." And then after a thoughtful pause he'll say, "But I sure did try."

I'll look at him with pride and say, "You surely did, you tried with all your heart." And then I'll think, "I hope my own sons will try that hard and be that successful."

## Afraid To Invite For Fear Of Being Rejected

It was the summer between my sophomore and junior years of high school. I don't know what it is about summertime, but back in those days I always seemed to do my best thinking during those warm and carefree months. Perhaps because there wasn't much structure in the summer and my mind was left free to do some wonderful wandering.

Being away from the high school crowd for two months had dimmed my mind somewhat as to how difficult it was for me to fit in socially with girls the way I desired. I suppose my lack of social prowess and having so much time to dream is what prompted me to wait on the front porch for Ronnie Clements to come by to deliver our *Deseret News*. After a several-minute wait, I saw him pumping his old balloon-tire bike up the Alpine Road. As he cocked his arm to heave the paper onto our porch, I shouted, "Hey, Ronnie! Hold up a minute. I need to talk to you." Being a little weary from his ride, Ronnie leaned his bike against our fence, walked up the front walk, and sat down beside me. After a little small talk I said, "Ronnie, don't you deliver papers to the houses on Center Street?"

"I sure do," he replied.

I then asked him if in his work he ever saw a certain really pretty girl who lived in a brick house on the corner. He answered, "Oh, sure. I see her almost every day. As a matter of fact, I'll be down there in about ten minutes. I'm sure I'll see her then." When he said that I got so excited that I could hardly contain myself.

"Would you mind asking her something?" He agreed and wanted to know what I wanted him to ask her.

"Ask her if she would go to the movie with me at seven o'clock this Friday night." He agreed, and after he had got a drink of cold water from our hose, my magnificent messenger was on his way.

The next day I was out on the porch at least half an hour before Ronnie's scheduled arrival. Finally he appeared. I was so fearful that the news would not be what I desired that I did not dare approach the subject. But before I could say anything, Ronnie shouted, "She said yes. She'd love to go with you."

As soon as I heard those words I knew that I had made a

serious error. Up until that time my summer had been stress free. But now, I suddenly had the makings of an ulcer.

Friday night came all too soon. At about 6:30 I set out on foot for her house. As I walked past the old Star Flour Mill, I seriously considered returning home. Conscience alone drove me on. I walked down the mill lane; walking there usually brought me toward a quiet peace. But this time I felt only disquieting turmoil.

Finally I was at her door. I knocked. She answered, and a few minutes later we were walking the last three blocks to the Cameo Theatre. We weren't holding hands as we walked. We weren't even talking. As we entered the theatre, I purchased a bag of fresh buttered popcorn. We went down the left aisle. I don't know why I did that, because always before I'd sat on the right side. I didn't seem to be able to think straight. The movie was entitled *Sentimental Journey*. I didn't know what it was about, because my mind longed not for a sentimental journey but just for a plain old journey home.

I was so nervous that I didn't dare offer her any popcorn for fear she would say no. If she had rejected my offer, I don't know what I would have done. The safest procedure seemed to be to not risk rejection and to just eat the popcorn myself. So that is what I did.

The movie seemed to last longer than *Gone with the Wind*. I've never seen such a welcome sight as when "The End" flashed on the screen. We walked to her house in considerable silence. I came about as close to kissing her good night as the Wright brothers came to flying to the sun. I bade her a quick good-bye and headed home. As I walked the other direction through the old mill lane, this time my journey brought me peace.

## Do Missions Make You More Handsome?

As we were driving home from our recent mission to Canada I asked Marilyn, "Remember how I've said that going on a mission makes a man more handsome?"

"Yes," she replied. "I've heard you say that after each of your four missions."

"Well," I continued, "I was looking in the mirror this morning, and I think it has worked again for me. What do you think?"

Her reply delighted me. "Oh, I agree. To me you do look much better now than you've ever looked before." Then to my dismay, she added, "But of course, with each mission I serve my eyesight gets dimmer and dimmer."

That reminded me of the time when the optometrist asked me which eye I could see better with. "This one? Or this one?" I guess I didn't give the correct answers, because at the end of the exam he told me that my youthful "20/20" vision was now a thing of the past. I hated the thought of glasses. I feared they would mar my otherwise good looks.

Later I got the glasses and went into the bathroom, where in private I could assess just how I looked. My worst fears were verified. I was shocked at what I saw. I just didn't look as good as I had without the glasses.

I complained to Marilyn that I didn't want to wear the glasses because I didn't look good with them on. She told me I looked very good in the glasses. I asked her, "Then why do I feel I don't look good?"

She replied, "Because by wearing them you can finally see yourself."

## Looking Good

I recall a time when I was Mission President in Kentucky. I went to a Zone Conference at Murray, Kentucky. While we were there, I had a wonderful day with the missionaries. I really felt the spirit more so than I'd felt in a long time. Following that long day meeting with those wonderful missionaries, I went to a motel with Sister Durrant. When we walked in the motel, this lady working in the motel looked at me and said, "Who are you?"

I said, "I'm George Durrant."

She said, "I don't care what your name is, who are you?"

I said, "I am a missionary for The Church of Jesus Christ of Latter-day Saints."

And she said, "Oh! I knew it was something special. I could tell by the way you look."

I jokingly answered, "You mean because I am handsome?"

She said, "Oh no, you are not handsome. As a matter of fact, you are not even good looking. But the thing that I noticed about you when you walked in was that you look good."

I really thought that was something wonderful, that you could look good without even being good looking. That's what I mean about having the look of a missionary, having the image of Christ in your countenance. You can do that if His name is written in your heart.

That is what is more important about the way we look than our clothes, even though that is important. But to be able to have the look of Christ in our eyes! That really makes us look good and that is more important than being good looking.

## The Changes That Can Come While You Serve Your Mission

I recall my time in the mission home in Salt Lake City. I had immediate love for my first companion, Elder Mahlon Edwards from Boulder City, Nevada. We seemed to be on the same frequency and could talk to one another about our deepest concerns. We walked some blocks to a place called Heinze Apothecary to purchase some sea sick pills for our upcoming ocean voyage to England.

I recall we had a most meaningful conversation which had been filled with much humor. We were nearly back to the mission home when Elder Edwards said something I've never forgotten. He said, "Elder Durrant, I'm glad we've met and become friends." He then added, "Promise me you won't change while you are on your mission." I'm not sure what I said in response.

But as I look back, I feel that I really didn't change. I didn't change the feelings for my family, my love of sports, my desire to succeed, my sense of humor, or, I guess I should say, I didn't change my personality.

When I came home, I was the same old George Durrant, but in a way, I was really the same new George Durrant. I feel I became more dependable, more considerate, more determined, more committed to the gospel, and boldness became my boldness became more victorious over my timidity. But, I was still the same old George Durrant that I had been when I began my mission and I was glad of that.

## Tracting In The Rain

I remember one instance when a missionary came to me in an interview in Chattanooga, Tennessee. He started to cry.

He said, "My companion is crazy! President, he's crazy!"

Very concerned, I asked, "What did he do?"

The missionary replied, "The other day it was raining. It was *really* raining! And he said to me, 'Let's go tracting.' He's the senior companion so I said, 'We can't go tracting in a rainstorm.'

"He answered me, 'We've got to go tracting.'

"We went out. There we stood on people's doorsteps with the rain coming down out of our hair, dripping off of our noses. There we stood, President Durrant. He's crazy."

I said, "Oh, boy, he *is* crazy."

I knew the next missionary in for an interview was the crazy Elder. I could hardly wait to see him. There he stood in the door, the crazy one, the one who tracted even when it was raining. It seemed to me that, even though he was not a large man, he filled the whole doorway. A lump came into my throat as I greeted him.

## When You Are Bold And Open Your Mouth, The Message Will Come

As a missionary I longed to speak with power and authority and to be bold. Elder Covey was the assistant to the president and he was without a doubt the boldest man I have ever known. He and his companion traveled throughout the mission encouraging all of us to be bold.

Just saying the word "bold" makes me feel a bit bold. Bold is the most bold sounding word I know. Let's say the word bold together. Here we go—"Bold!" Let's do it again, only this time let's say it with more boldness. Here we go, "**BOLD**!"

Elder Covey and his companion came to Hull. They told the ten missionaries in our district some of the bold things other missionaries in the mission were doing. They told of personal experiences they had on buses and at street meetings where they had spoken with boldness.

I recall I got quite excited about being more bold.

That meeting was held in the afternoon. That evening, these two dynamic missionaries and us local ones went out to do some bold missionary work.

Because it was Saturday night, I told Elder Covey that we likely wouldn't find many people at home because they would all be at the movies. Almost all the Hull citizens spent Saturday night at the movies.

Elder Covey suggested we go to a movie house and speak to the people on the streets as they came and went. When we arrived, some 200 people were lined up to enter the theater some thirty minutes later.

"Let's go talk to those people," Elder Covey said as he smiled and rubbed his hands together.

"We can't do that," I replied timidly.

"Why?" he asked.

"Because those people would have to listen. They can't leave or they would lose their place in line."

"That is the idea," he said as he walked toward them.

As we drew closer, he turned to me and said, "Elder Durrant, it was your idea to come down here. I've never done this before, so you speak first and show me how and then I'll speak."

His words left me limp. I knew I couldn't just walk up there and start to speak, but I also knew that I had to just walk up there and start to speak.

The people were lined up against the brick wall of the theater on the edge of the sidewalk. I stood on the opposite edge of the walk with my heels up against the curb and gutter. I was as far away from them as I could get, which was about five feet.

In a panic I removed my hat and held it in my left hand.

A few people noticed me and wondered what I was up to.

With a shaky voice I spoke, "My friends of Hull, I am Elder Durrant and I am a Mormon."

Now some thirty of the closest people ceased their private conversations and all their attention focused on me.

After uttering that first sentence, my panic lessened. I continued, "Many of you might think us Mormons have many wives."

I paused and then added with a smile, "I'm a Mormon and I don't have a wife at all."

They didn't smile but I could tell they were thinking, "We can understand that."

Now I felt more relaxed and excited. I felt a surge of boldness going up and down my spine.

I continued, "Mormons don't practice polygamy in these times. I'd like to tell you what Mormons do believe. In the year 1820 . . ."

I went on to tell them the Joseph Smith story.

As I spoke there was one large man who fixed his eyes on me. He was as tall as I am and even huskier than me, if you can imagine that. His large size and his intent expression caused me to feel uneasy.

I'd sweep my eyes from one person to another. They all looked at least slightly pleasant except for this man who looked deeply disturbed by my words.

As I neared the conclusion of my message, I felt that when I stopped speaking this man would actually attack me. So I spoke a bit longer than usual.

When I stopped speaking, just as I had supposed, he came out of the line straight at me. I couldn't back up because of the gutter behind me. I braced myself for his assault but just as I expected the worst, he stopped, smiled and extended his hand.

I reached out my trembling hand and gripped his in a

firm handshake.

Then he said, "I have never seen anyone with the courage you have." He continued, "You spoke with such conviction. I wish I had your courage and could be so sure of anything." He then thanked me for my words and example.

To me this man for just a few minutes became a spokesman for the Lord to me. This was the Lord's way of saying, "Now, Elder Durrant, don't you ever be afraid to speak up and when you do, I'll be there to back you up."

I spoke at other movie lines, but never did anyone else respond as this man did. But never did I feel that I was so in need of courage as I had been at that time.

True boldness is not a one time act of public display, but it is a continual attitude of speaking the words of the Lord in thousands of almost private circumstances.

## Don't Be Wishy-Washy

I recall a talk I gave a month or so after Marilyn and I were married. As I entered the foyer of the chapel, an old friend of mine pulled me aside and said, "I've got some visitors here with me from England. They are of a high social standing. Inspire them, but be careful what you say so that they will not be offended."

That made me nervous and I said things such as, "It is our feeling that Joseph Smith was a prophet. We know others feel differently, but it looks like from all he did that he was a prophet, or, at any rate, I'm sure that we all agree that he was a great man."

As the talk wore on I found myself diluting all my points. After the meeting, as Marilyn and I rode home, she didn't comment on my talk. I finally asked, "What did you think of my message?"

She softly said, "You were really wishy-washy."

Her words cut me to the very core because I knew they were true. We rode the rest of the way home in silence. It was in that silence that I determined that although I would have other faults I would never again be wishy-washy.

Since then I have constantly tried to present the gospel principles with faith and as facts.

## It Is Easier To Be Bold When You Know You Are The Lord's Agent

As I've mentioned, in high school I felt like a dud. But the classiest, most charming girl in my school was my girlfriend. She did not know that she was my girlfriend. I did not dare tell her for fear that she'd say, "No way!" And I didn't tell my friends for fear that they would laugh. I was the authority on who my girlfriend was, and she was it.

I liked her so much that I did not dare to talk to her.

One day a friend of mine named Don—a big, handsome and fearless fellow who was a favorite of all of the girls—sent me a note. It read:

> "Dear George,
> Ask Louise (That was the name of this lovely girl) if she will go to the movie with me Friday night."

Now, with this note in hand, I was no longer afraid to talk to Louise. She was sitting in the seat just in front of me. I tapped her on the shoulder and with no fear at all, I boldly asked, "Hey, Louise, what are you doing Friday night?"

"Nothing," she smilingly replied.

"Would you like to go to the movie?"

"Why, yes, I would," she answered.

"Good. Old Don over there wants to take you."

In the light of my fears, what made me fearless on this occasion? What gave me the courage to be so bold when I was so timid? It was the note from Don. On that occasion I wasn't speaking for me. I was speaking for him. Thus any rejection (my greatest fear) would not be a rejection of me but of my friend. So it is when we are commissioned to speak for the Lord and ask them for Him, Will you read the Book of Mormon?" "Will you pray?" "Will you come to church?" "Will you obey the Word of Wisdom?" "Will you pay tithing?" "Will you be baptized next Friday at 2 p.m.?"

## That Is Exactly What We Are Saying

I love the book we all know as *The Missionary Guide*. My favorite story in that profoundly important book is the story of Sister Franks.

In this story a sophisticated man, after hearing Sister Franks tell of the origin of the Book of Mormon, said in a skeptical one, "So, you claim this man Joseph Smith saw an angel that told him about this set of golden plates. And he went to the hill and dug up the plates and translated them from an ancient language into English. Is that what you are saying?"

Sister Franks leaned forward, looked into his eyes and replied, "That is exactly what we are saying."

I loved that reply. "That is exactly what we are saying."

Are we saying, "Jesus Christ is the Son of God?"

"That is exactly what we are saying."

Are we saying, "Joseph Smith was a prophet of God?'

"That is exactly what we are saying."

Are we saying, "The Book of Mormon is the word of God?"

"That is exactly what we are saying."

## The Most Surprising Thing We Will See In Heaven Will Be the Surprised Looks On Other People's Faces

While mission president, I once spoke to three sociology classes at the University of Tennessee. At their request, most of my remarks centered on family matters. But, in a question-and-answer session the matter of one true church came up.

The professor respectfully asked, "Mr. Durrant, when this life is all over, are you Mormons going to be the only ones up in Heaven?"

I was perhaps untrue to a former commitment to be bold. I answered in a somewhat wishy-washy manner saying something such as, "Well, we know that there are many good people. So, we'll just have to wait and see who is there and who is not." I smiled and added, "I suppose the most surprising thing we will see when we get to Heaven is the surprised look we see on other people's faces when they see us there."

I would have given him a better answer if he had asked the question in a better way. He should have not used Mormon but instead he should have said, "Are you members of the Church of Jesus Christ going to be the only ones up in Heaven?"

Then with boldness, I could have replied, "That is exactly what I'm saying. Unless a person has become a member of Christ's Church and received the necessary ordinances and has lived a good life he or she will not return to the presence of our Heavenly Father."

## My Senior Companion

Many years ago, before my mission, I came as a freshman to BYU. That is when I first came to know Murray McInnis. BYU was small in those days and so we all sort of knew each other. At least, us "little wheels" knew all the "big wheels" even though they didn't always know us.

Murray was really part of the "in" crowd. The girls swarmed around him and I could tell that he knew how to talk with them and dance with them and laugh with them. He had a manner with the young ladies that I longed to have but was never able to have. Oh, I could have had, but something inside of me held me back. Socially I was more of a retreater than an attacker.

Murray worked at the front desk of the old Grant Library. When I'd go there I'd see him. He was always smiling and he had a most pleasing and seemingly fearless personality. That is, it was pleasing to everyone except me. I was irritated by his charm and his wit. He was the way I wanted to be and because I wasn't the way I wanted to be, I resented him.

As I look back, it seems strange that I had such feelings about him because as I said, I had really never met him. But, of all of my fellow classmates, he was the one I liked the least. But, that was not his problem. It was mine.

After two days of training in London, my mission president, President Reiser said to me, "Elder Durrant, you go to Hull." I was shocked and asked, "Where?" He replied, "Hull." He then spelled it for me, "H U L L." An hour later I was on a northbound train headed for Hull. I didn't know then that it was in Hull that the tall, handsome fellow I'd envied at BYU was now beginning the second month of his mission.

Two days later, I attended my first district missionary meeting. The two elders from north Hull were a few minutes late. Hearing someone come in the back of the chapel, I turned and was shocked to see a most familiar face. It was none other than my BYU classmate, Elder Murray McInnis. As we all greeted each other Elder McInnis and I officially met for the first time.

As he approached me, he smiled broadly and with much warmth in this voice said, "Hello, Elder Durrant. I'm glad you are in the district." He then startled my by saying, "I remember seeing you a lot at the Y."

I stammered and had scarcely said anything to him when his companion—our district leader—took my attention from Elder McInnis to himself. We all sat down to begin the meeting. I couldn't fully focus on what was going on because of the feeling I had in seeing Elder McInnis. His warm greeting had, in an instant, changed all of my past and unjustified ill feelings toward him to feelings of love.

As our three hours together wore on, I was impressed by the way that Elder McInnis smiled; the way he talked; the way he taught; the way he loved. Now, instead of being envious of his attributes, I was admiring him and I was longing to be like him.

A few weeks later, I was elated when I was told that I was to be the junior companion to Elder Murray McInnis. I sensed then, as I know now, that my three months with this natural, spontaneous, unique man from Eager, Arizona was to change me forever.

I wished you could have seen us together as we did our missionary work. I know there have been other missionary companionships that have been dynamic—Alma and Amulek, Paul and Barnabus—but never, according to my memory, have there been two missionaries as dynamic as Elder McInnis and Elder Durrant.

We rode a bicycle built for two. We called it a tandem. It was a classic bit of machinery.

Elder McInnis sat up on the front and I brought up the rear. He steered and I followed. I didn't mind. I loved following him. His constant good mood, his genuine love for me and for everyone, his confidence and friendliness made him so easy to follow.

We wore hats in those days. We chose Homberg hats. They were sort of round on top and had a narrow brim. As the English would say, we were a smart-looking pair of blokes as we cycled down the cobblestone streets of Hull.

Even when we got off and walked along a street we were still like a tandem. Elder McInnis led the way and I was right behind.

"Good morning!" he would say cheerfully. His wide grin would cause even the most disturbed to have a difficult time to keep from smiling back. His natural, spontaneous, genuine love would get us in nearly every heart and in almost every door.

I wanted to be like him and as I tried to do so, I was unlocking part of myself that had long been imprisoned. I was coming out of myself and being more bold and warm. As I tried to be like Elder McInnis, I too, could get people to smile and invite us to come in.

And in we'd go. Before I could warm up as to what to say Elder McInnis would be complimenting them on their children, the pictures on their walls and their kindness. His manners were meticulous. He had the bearing of a king and the graciousness of a secretary of state. Yet, he was as common as a guy from Eager, Arizona could be.

As we taught, he was fearless in asking them to live a Christ-like life. His boldness in inviting them to come to church, to give up drinking tea, to pay tithing, to be baptized, would often shock me and made me nervous. "Don't push them so hard!" I'd say to myself, but then in response to his loving invitation they'd say, "Yes." And I'd want to shout, "Way to go, Elder McInnis! Way to go."

The people loved him and because when I was with him, I was a bit like him, they loved me too.

Those were golden days for me. I was becoming what I had always longed to be. One day—a very sad day—a letter came from the mission office to Elder McInnis. He was to be transferred the next day to go to Newcastle. Our time together was nearly over. I was now to be senior companion to Elder Kenneth Blair.

In the morning, Elder McInnis and I rode the tandem together for the last time. I felt my heart would break. I had become so reliant on his charm, faith and all that he was. Fear filled my heart. Could I possibly stand without him at my side?

At the train station I said, "Elder McInnis, I love you. I don't know what I'll do without you."

Tears filled our eyes.

"You'll do great," he said as he placed both his hands on my shoulders.

"You'll be the best man at my wedding," I said in an effort to let him know how deeply I respected him.

He nodded. We said goodbye. He boarded the train and we watched as he leaned from the window for a last goodbye.

Emptiness is the only word that comes close to describing how I felt. As Elder Blair and I walked out of the station, neither of us spoke. We pulled the tandem bicycle from the brick wall against which it leaned.

I swung my leg over the unfamiliar front seat and Elder Blair climbed on behind. As we headed up the road, everything looked frighteningly different from the front—now there was so much to watch out for—I felt so desperate for direction.

And somehow I found it.

## Arm's Length

Sister Leavitt had her arm around her husband at the couple's conference. I had to kiddingly caution her to remember, "Arm's length!" We asked the husbands of each couple why he loved his wife. Finally we'd all spoken except Elder Johnson, a native Kentuckian. His eyes sparkled as he said, "I love my wife because I just cain't hep it!"

## Call Me Elder

One missionary didn't want to be called Elder when he first came out. He wanted to be called by his first name. In letters home he would always sign his first name and he didn't want his parents to address his letters "Elder." He, having just received a transfer, was saying good-bye to the people in his first area. A little boy started sobbing and begged as he held onto the missionary's coat, "Elder, don't leave, please don't leave, Elder. I love you Elder. Please don't leave Elder." He had never had anything like that happen to him before. When that young boy who loved him so much used the word "Elder" and cried, it really affected this missionary. After that he said, "I didn't want to be called Brad anymore. I wanted to be called Elder."

## The Wild Chicken

One of the missionaries told me that he and his companion were pretty hungry one evening and they didn't have anything to eat. Then they saw a wild chicken, which they caught and roasted over a bonfire. I said, "A wild chicken? I didn't know there were wild chickens around here."

He replied, "It was just a normal chicken, but when we chased it, it was so wild that we had a hard time catching it."

## Love For Those We Teach

Many missionaries have the gift of pure love, or charity. One elder who worked in the office had taught a lady and her family and they had joined the Church. This lady had quite a few problems and she called me, the mission president, several times. I was talking to him about her one day and telling him that she'd called again.

He said, "She's really a problem, isn't she?"

I didn't answer right off and he said, "I'm sorry she calls you so often." Then he started to cry. I leaned how much that family meant to him and I cried with him.

## Guided By The Spirit

Some missionaries at times are deeply in tune with the spirit. One such elder was described to me by his companion. He told me they'd been night tracting. Because it was getting late and he was tired, he said to his companion, "Let's go home."

But his companion just stood there in the street. There was a gentle breeze blowing, and it was a beautiful night. After some silence his companion said, "Elder, there's one more house that we need to go to. Which door do you feel inspired that we should go knock at?"

The elder telling me the story said, "I told him none. It was time to go home."

And then his companion stood silently for a moment and said, "There's the one, right over there."

I reluctantly followed him and we went there and were able to teach a discussion. In two months that family had joined the Church.

## I Knew That I Would Never See My Mother Alive Again

I last saw you when I said good-bye as I departed to serve as mission president in Kentucky and Tennessee. You remember the day of that good-bye. You were in failing health when I was asked to serve. The circumstances surrounding our lives at the time this call came were very different from those some twenty years before, when as a young man I had been called to serve in England.

The earlier call had prompted some questions as to whether or not our family circumstances and finances would enable me to leave. The bishop came to our home and asked if I could go. As our family and Bishop Grant sat somberly in the parlor, Dad said, “George can’t go. I’m ill; I can’t care for the chickens; we will have no money. He can’t go.” I remember the hurt look that came to your face, Mom, as you sat up straight in your chair and through your tears said, “Bishop Grant, Bert is ill. I know he can’t take care of the chickens. But I’m still strong. I can feed them and gather the eggs. I can do the work. We can make it and my son George can go.” And so I did.

Remember how proud you were of me as, dressed in a new navy blue suit that you had purchased for me at Devey’s men’s store, I stood and gave my farewell address. You wanted me to go, but I sensed that both you and Dad realized how much you would miss me. I was your youngest; when I departed all the children would be gone.

Until that time, the times I had ever been away from you were very few. I had been away three days at the Mutual Dell Camp, three days in Salt Lake City at the Newhouse Hotel for the State Class B Basketball Tournament, and five days at a time at National Guard training at Camp Williams. I didn’t know if I could bear being away from you for two years—two years seemed that day to be the same as forever.

We drove to Salt Lake City and arrived at the Union Pacific Railroad station. We didn't say much, you and I. Dad didn't either. Finally the last minutes were gone. There was only time for one more thing—one thing that rose in importance beyond any other word or deed that had ever been spoken or performed. I put my hands on your shoulders, leaned forward, and kissed you on the cheek. A surge of comfort in my soul told me that it would not be for the last time.

We wrote often, didn't we, Mom?

You did gather the eggs and feed the chickens. My older brother John helped you and cleaned out the coops. As you entered the chicken coops three or more times a day, the chickens caught the vision. They wondered at first where I was. When they realized I was on a mission and you, Mom, were working to support me, they decided to do their part. They laid more eggs than any chickens we'd ever had before. You worked harder than a mom should ever work. The Lord blessed us. The money came and I had what I needed.

I wasn't the best Elder in the Church. But I was always doing my best all the while I was in England because I knew what you were doing to keep me there.

Those were wonderful days, weren't they, Mom? I was telling the missionaries and Saints in England about my mom, and you were at Relief Society showing the sisters my picture and saying, "See, here is George; doesn't he look handsome? He is a missionary in England, you know."

But now it was twenty years later. This second mission call was different. You were ill. Dad was gone and you were lonely. You looked forward each week to having Marilyn and me and our eight children come down from Salt Lake City to visit you. With this mission call you knew that those visits would end.

Finally, the time for our departure was just days away. We came to the old family home for our last visit. Our talk together was not as lighthearted as our talks usually were. The dark cloud of separation loomed heavily over our hearts. We ate and did our best to forget what was soon to be. Finally it was time for the good-byes. One by one Matt, Kathryn, Devin, Marinda, Dwight, Warren, Sarah, and Mark hugged and kissed you, their grandmother. One by one they went out the front door and ran toward the waiting car. Finally you stood up and Marilyn embraced you and tearfully said good-bye.

Then it was just you, Mom, and me. We were alone in the spacious kitchen as we had been so many times before. The kitchen where you'd made me peanut-butter sandwiches, homemade noodles, hot biscuits, and one special pork chop. The room where I had kissed you on the cheek at least seven thousand times. You were standing near the old rocking chair by the window where I would sit so many years before on the few occasions when you'd be away. I'd watch the headlights of each car coming up the Alpine road, hoping that they would be the lights of the car that would bring you home to me.

You were weeping openly and I inwardly. I walked closer to you. I felt as if my heart would break and I knew that yours already had. I reached out to put my hands on your shoulders as I had done so many times before. You put your arms around me and held me tighter than I could ever remember.

You begged me not to go.

I didn't want to leave you, and yet we both knew that it was in my going that we would some time be together forever. I pulled away, and as I did, you became calm. I looked deep into your tear-filled eyes. I expressed my everlasting love. I bent forward and for the last time I kissed you on the cheek.

Five months later while in Kentucky I received a phone call from Duane that your tender but tired heart had been stilled. I went to my room and knelt in prayer. My heart rejoiced. Now I knew you would grieve no more. It was then that I felt your presence. You came to me. You were there. You saw our beautiful mission home.

A few days later you got in the car with me and we headed down the winding roads of Kentucky and Tennessee. You saw the green fields, the white fences, the southern mansions. You met all the missionaries. I could tell that you were proud when each of them called me President. I could tell that, even though the missionaries couldn't see or hear you, you wanted to shout out, "This man that you call President—this man in the navy blue suit—he's my son." Then you turned away and went to your new home.

# TESTIMONY SCONES

## My Boss Told Me, "Don't Say The Church Is True." But I Couldn't Help Saying So

Prior to my mission I received a call to come to the office of my bishop. He said, "George, how would you like to go on a mission?" I could scarcely speak as I answered, "I'd give my right arm to go on a mission." I hadn't always felt that way. But now I did.

I went to the service station where I worked and announced to the boss that I was going. He replied, "That's great, George. You'll be a good missionary. You've been a good employee. When you get home you probably won't want to work here. But if you do, I'll hire you back because a mission will really help you. A mission is the greatest thing that can happen to a young man."

He then continued, "I've only got one complaint. When I go to church, people stand up and say that they know the Church is true. Now, there's no way to know that, George. These people can't be telling the truth. No one can know the Church is true. All I want from you is the promise that when you get home you'll not stand up and say that you know the Church is true. George, you're too honest to say that."

All I could tell him was that I thought it to be true at that moment and that I wouldn't promise anything.

That's the way I felt when I set sail for England. As the boat lay in Southhampton harbor on the night of my arrival I saw reflected in the waters the lights of England. At that time I didn't have a lot of confidence. I felt as if I would never be able to knock on doors and teach the gospel in such a way that those I taught would want to join the Church. I stood on the ship wondering if it would be possible to swim home. But then I prayed to the Lord and said, "All I ask for now is the courage to get off this ship." He gave me that courage. He gave me courage to meet my mission one day at a time.

Shortly after my arrival in Hull, England, I was blessed to teach a family the fact that God has a body of flesh and bones, that Jesus Christ does also, and that the Holy Ghost is a personage of spirit. As I concluded that scriptural discussion I knew that what I had taught was true. As we left that house I boarded the back seat of a tandem bicycle. We pedaled to our apartment, and as we did my head and heart were swimming with the glories of knowing the true nature of God. A few minutes later I knelt by my bed and prayed to my personal Father. I was so glad I was on a mission.

The next week we taught the family that the true church should have twelve apostles and should be guided by revelation through a prophet. A few days later we read in the scriptures that the true church was taken from the earth and was replaced by a church that was not true. After reading these scriptures, the family identified the church that replaced the true church as their church.

They said, "If our church isn't true and the true church is gone, and if the true church should have twelve apostles and a prophet, where is that church?"

We replied, "We are here to tell you about that true church and we will do that the next time we meet."

It was that very week that our district leader asked me to give a special talk in our missionary meeting about Joseph Smith and his First Vision. In my every spare moment I prepared for that talk. I read and reread the account of the First Vision and of the life of Joseph Smith.

Finally the time came and I stood before seven other elders to tell the Joseph Smith story. As I began to speak, I said, "Joseph Smith went to the Sacred Grove, and while he was there, in response to his prayer, God and Jesus Christ appeared to him." Having said that, I could speak no more. The Spirit of the Lord settled in upon me and forced tears from my eyes.

I began to cry, a thing I had not done for years; and never had I cried in this way. I looked down at the floor, not knowing where else to look. After a time I gathered myself together enough to look into the eyes of my seven companions. Each of them was also in tears. The Spirit of the Lord was there. As I spoke, I came to know with all my heart and soul that Joseph Smith was indeed a mighty prophet of God.

I talked about the prophet's persecution and finally his martyrdom. When I finished speaking I was a new man. I knew exactly what I needed to know to really live. I knew then as I do now that God lives and that Jesus Christ is his Son. I knew that Jesus Christ was resurrected and that he appeared to Joseph Smith. I knew that it was right to pay tithing; that the Word of Wisdom was the way to live; that the temple was the place to get married; that the prophet then leading the Church was the voice to follow; and that the scriptures were the guide. I knew everything that I needed to know to truly live.

I believe that that day in England I became a man. After that I became the greatest average missionary England ever had.

During my mission the Lord stood by my side and gave me answers to my prayers. And I loved being a missionary. It was still hard at times to knock on doors, but I did it. And the more I did it, the more I found that I could do it.

# THE SCONES OF REPENTANCE

## The Easy Way Is Not Always The Right Way

Two beginning but lucky deer hunters had shot a big buck. They were dragging it to camp when an experienced hunter coming up the trail observed that they were pulling it by its hind legs. He helpfully suggested, "If you fellers will pull that deer by its horns, you will be dragging it with the grain of the hair and it will go more easily."

Taking this advice, the hunters took hold of the horns and dragged the deer for another hour. Finally one said to the other, "He was right; it does drag easier this way."

"Yes," replied the other, "but we are getting farther and farther away from camp."

## When He Came Back, I Swung Him Around Again

I used to swing my children around by holding their arms and spinning around on the front lawn so that they would fly out parallel to the ground. It's great fun. Children love it. (It's getting harder for me to do. The older I get, the dizzier I get when I spin around.) I recall that once when I was doing this one of my little sons came running up and said, "It's my turn." At the same time my little girl who was nearby said it was her turn. I really felt it was my daughter's turn, so I said to my son, "You wait, and I'll swing her first." While I was swinging her, he ran to the house in a rage. He lay down on his bed and continued his tantrum. He kicked his feet and looked up at the ceiling.

Time went by and he calmed down. He started to think. He had a decision to make. He could either stay there kicking like that and causing all kinds of trouble in his room, or he could just simply get off his bed and come back. I was still outside swinging kids around. After some time he decided to come back to the front lawn. He came running up to me and said, "It's my turn." And it was his turn. And I spun him around and he had fun.

Now, my son could have continued to stay in his room while I was still out there spinning people around. He could have lost out on that situation if he had wanted to. But he decided, as the prodigal son did, to come back. And when he came back I was ready with open arms to grab him and spin him around.

## I Lied When I Said I Felt Good About Doing Wrong

My firsthand knowledge about being a poor sport started when I was a pre-teenager out on my home court in the barn. It was there that I first felt the real pain of personal defeat. My brother, four years older than me, came out to the barn. Foolishly he challenged me to a game on my home court. As we got under way, I was playing better than I'd ever played. I was hitting long shot after long shot. I wasn't keeping score, but I knew that I had him down by ten or more. I was therefore shocked when he announced that the score was tied and that whoever made the next basket was the winner. The trouble was that just as he said that, he had the ball and was right under the basket. I lunged to get to him to block his shot but I was too late. The ball came down through the basket, and he declared himself the national champ.

I was beside myself with anger and frustration. I shouted, "You didn't win. I made more points than you." He laughed as he headed out of the barn door. I looked around to get some other witnesses, and there was the cow with her head reaching through the stall trying to get some more hay. I made my appeal to her. She just kind of shrugged her shoulders as if to say, "Don't ask me, I can't count." I was in such anguish that I broke out in tears.

As my brother headed toward the house, I shouted, "I won and you know it."

He shouted back, "No way. I'm the champ."

I didn't know what to do. I thought surely the world had come to an end.

I guess I was really a sore loser in those days, because of what I did next. You see, he had a new baseball mitt that he had just bought with his own money. I saw it laying on the hay. He had forgotten to take it back into the house. In despair I picked it up, looked at it real close, and then flipped it over my shoulder into the pig pen. Then I walked slowly and dejectedly back into the house.

When I got there his first words were, "Hey, everybody, I beat George. I beat George." Then he said, "Oh, I forgot my mitt," and with that he headed out of the back door for the barn. While he was gone I sat staring silently out of our front window. After what seemed like an extra long time, he came in the back door and asked, "What did you do with my mitt?"

I said without hesitation, "I threw it out of the barn into the pig pen."

"You did what?" he shouted as he took off like a shot out of a cannon. Pretty soon he came back, holding the mitt kind of delicately with his thumb and one finger. The pigs hadn't eaten it, but they'd made it so nobody else would ever want to eat it either. I remember him as he held that mitt in front of me. With tears gathering in his eyes, he asked, "See what you've done. Now are you happy?"

I thought for a little while, and then I said, "Yeah, I am." But that was a lie. I wasn't happy. You never are happy when you do wrong.

## A "No Smoking" Sign Hanging In The Heart

A missionary at the Missionary Training Center was caught smoking outside one of the buildings. That was reported to the mission president, who called him in to discuss the matter. The president and his first counselor talked to the missionary. He was fearful that he would be sent home and he really hoped he would be. But the president could tell he had the makings of a wonderful missionary. So he said to the young missionary, "Where were you when you were smoking?"

The missionary described where it was. The president then turned to the first counselor and asked, "Do we have a 'No Smoking' sign on the outside wall of that building?"

The counselor replied, "No, president, I don't think we do."

The president then looked at the missionary and asked, "If we put a 'No Smoking' sign there, will you ever smoke there again?"

"No," came the reply.

The president then asked, "You mean that you will never smoke there again?"

The missionary said that he would not. The president then asked, "What if we hang a 'No Smoking' sign in your heart? Will you ever smoke again?"

The missionary gulped and said that he would not. The president asked him if he himself would hang the sign in his heart, because he was the only one who could do so. He said he would do that.

The president told the missionary that if he would hang that sign there and obey it forever, he could go on his mission; otherwise he could not go. The president then said, "You have done a dumb thing by smoking. But if you keep doing that you'll do a very stupid thing, because you will miss out on all the joys of your mission." Many years later that "No Smoking" sign still hangs in the young man's heart and he treasures the memories of his mission.

## The Wrong Idea Of What Is Phony And What Is Real

A young woman came to see me. She was really upset at me because, years before, I had been instrumental in her decision to cross the line from the world and come into the Church. Now her life was not at all what she had hoped it would be, and she felt that the Church was the cause of her unhappiness. She had come to my office to blame me for her misery.

She told me of her many frustrations, the chief one being that she had found out the night before that the fellow she had been dating was married. She really liked him and had hoped that something permanent would come of their romance. But now her dreams were dashed. She felt that if she had not been a member of the Church she could have continued to see him in the hopes that he would leave his wife for her.

She added that he was not a member of the Church and that was one reason why she liked him. When I asked her why that was so, she told me she didn't like Mormon men. She said they all seemed to be too soft-spoken and unmanly. She said none of them seemed to be real men. She added that before she became a member of the Church she had been free. If she wanted to date a married man or a single man and be intimate with him, she could. If she wanted to drink, she could. If she wanted to be part of the world, she could. But now the Church had taken all her freedom.

As I listened, she bristled all the more. She said she was sick of hearing of a house and a spouse and wall-to-wall children and fireplaces and apple pie and all that sort of phony baloney.

Finally I had heard all I could take, so with slightly raised blood pressure I said, "You call a fireplace and apple pie and children and marriage phony baloney. But I'll tell you something, I have been there. I have felt love at home. I have come home to a wife and children. I have sat with them by a fireplace eating apple pie. And I want to tell you that those things are not phony baloney. Those things are real. The things that are a bunch of phony baloney are the things that you say you wish you could do out in the world. And if that is the phony baloney that you want, why don't you leave the Church and go get those things?"

Her frustrations and my words caused her to cry. After many tears she said, "I know what you say is true. It's just that I long for so many things that I can't seem to get and so I get discouraged." Then she added, "I can't leave the Church because I have felt more joy and peace since I joined this church than I ever felt before. And besides, I know the Church is true."

## Elder Cowley Made Me Want To Be Religious

In high school I was not certain that I wanted to be religious. Whether it was real or just imagined on my part, I felt that many who were religious had a "goody-goody" attitude that didn't fit the pattern of what I wanted to be. In college I began to wonder what my direction should be.

While in this state of mind, I walked alone to the Smith Fieldhouse and took my seat near the back. Some eight thousand BYU students were there for our weekly devotional assembly. President Ernest L. Wilkinson introduced a man I did not know, nor had ever heard of before. The man then began to speak.

Somehow the words he spoke reached way back to where I was seated, and the spirit he conveyed caused the words to sink deep into my heart. He spoke of miracles, healings, the Maoris of New Zealand, and the power of the priesthood. His words were impressive, but more than words impressed me that day. I sensed that this conveyed real religion.

His words were sometimes sobering and made me wonder. But at other times, his words were humorous and caused me to chuckle and smile. From his first sentence to his final amen, I felt feelings that I had never felt before.

After the closing prayer, I wanted to go down and speak to him, but instead I slipped quickly out of the side door and hurried up the hill toward the CougarEat.

As I walked, many thoughts filled my mind and joy filled my heart. Nearing the Joseph Smith Building, I said to myself, "I want to be like that man. I want to be religious, and at the same time I want to be real."

I know that Jesus Christ is the pattern, and our goal ought to be and is to be like Him. But, oh, how glad I am when someone who, like me—a struggling ordinary man—shows me a close-up pattern of how to live.

Matthew Cowley, an Apostle of the Lord, did that for me on that day so long ago, and I have never forgotten the goal that I set that day.

## Staying A Long Way From Sin

A returned missionary desired to reform some of his pre-mission friends who had wandered away from the Church and into the world. To do this he went with them to bars. He did not go there to drink, but only so that he could be with them and influence them to return to Church activity.

You can guess the outcome.

This situation is a bit like the man who fell into the lake. Someone asked him, "How did you come to fall in?"

He replied, "I did not come to fall in; I came to fish and I fell in."

When we go into the world, we may say, "I did not come here to fall into sin. I came here because I wanted to see the world, and I fell in."

## If It Is To Be, It Is Up To Me

I can't say I recall being called to Kentucky and Tennessee as a mission president. My son Matt was at the time a ninth-grader in a Salt Lake City school. There he had made many friends and had enjoyed an excellent social life. His keen sense of humor and other characteristics had helped him find satisfaction at school. It was my lot to advise him that this pleasant life with its comfortable environment was to change.

I chose as the place for this news conference with my son a local restaurant—a place where you could go through the line and get all the food you wanted. After we had gone through the line and were sitting at the table, the only way I could see him was to look around the masses of food that balanced precariously on his plate.

After our prayer, and just as he started to eat, I broke the news. He was of course shocked, but as he swallowed the food he was eating, he said, "I'm ready to go, Dad. I'm proud of you, and I'll do my best." I don't think he realized then, and nor did I, how difficult the years ahead would be for him.

We arrived in Kentucky just in time for him to start his sophomore year in the largest school in the state. His only acquaintances were three or four other Mormon young people whom he had met a week or so earlier in church. As the first few weeks passed by he got right into his studies, and his grades appeared to be excellent. But his social life suffered. He didn't feel that he belonged there. He had no real friends. Although he didn't discuss this with me, he spent many, many anxious days wishing he was back with his old friends.

He became depressed. But he had hope, because it would soon be time for the basketball team to be chosen. He was certain that this would be the doorway to happiness. He made the junior varsity team but often found himself seated on the bench. Although he was good, he was not yet as good as he had dreamed he might be. So basketball, his last hope, was not giving him the satisfaction he needed. His sophomore year was not a happy one.

Then came the beginning of his junior year. He had grown considerably and had practiced basketball all summer. Many at the school had gained respect for him because of his straight "A" grades, an unusual thing on that particular basketball team. He had some satisfaction in that, but he wanted satisfaction along different lines. He wanted social satisfaction and athletic satisfaction. He felt that he had to prove himself. To him, the place to do that was on the basketball court.

The time came for the varsity team to be chosen. He had played well and was hoping to be on the main five. He enthusiastically entered the gymnasium to look at that all important list posted by the coach. He stood with others looking at the names. He read from top to bottom. His name was not on the list at all. He had been cut from the team. In his mind that meant he had been cut from everything.

He returned home that day before school was out, went to his room and stayed there. I knew of the deep grief he was suffering but didn't know how to help. On the second day of his sorrows, late at night I went downstairs to his room. His light was still on and he was looking up at the ceiling from his position lying on the bed. We talked. We talked for a long time. He told me of his deep sorrow and wondered if he could ever return to school. He told me that he had prayed and asked the Lord to help him make the team. And now he said, "I've prayed for strength." But there seemed to be no help and there seemed to be no hope. I thought my heart would break as I saw my son suffer. I listened, I loved, and I silently prayed.

After a while he said to me, "Dad, I'm just going to have to start over. I'm going to have to build on something else. I know no one else can do it for me. I've got to do it for myself." With tear-filled eyes he said to me, "Dad, I want to be like Elder Jibson and I think I can be." He had named one of the elders who was serving in the mission. He continued, "I'm going to be like him. I'm going to learn to smile like him, and to love and care like him. Dad, I'm going to make it. I'm going back to school and I'm going to start over." We knelt in prayer together, and then I told him of my love for him and of the great pride I had in him.

The next day he went to school. During that season he played basketball for the church team, where he was a star. He started to make many friends at school. He seemed to be relaxed, and he returned to and further developed his keen sense of humor. As time went by I heard him saying such things as, "Dad, these guys are great! I love this school. I love this town and I love Kentucky. I even wonder if after our mission we could live here."

The beginning of his senior year arrived. Because of some difficulties in the school system they had not yet elected the student body president for the year. He decided to run for president. By now he had many friends. He carried on a great campaign based on positive, fun-loving things about how he could help the school to be a better place. He was elected by a landslide. Of course, he was thrilled.

But there was one last dream at his school and that was something he hadn't been able to get out of his system. He wanted to be on the basketball team. The coach had announced that he wouldn't carry any seniors who hadn't played as juniors. Instead he wanted juniors on the team who could help him in the future. Thus there seemed to be no hope for Matt, who was a senior. Nevertheless he practiced long and hard, and the guys who were the stars on the team came to love and respect him.

When the list was posted, once again his name did not appear. As much as he had tried to build himself in other directions, he was again heartbroken. He came home and told me of his problems. At the time I was just departing on a journey and I wouldn't return for five days. All that I could do while I was gone was pray.

When I got back I found that Matt was not home. He was at basketball practice. I inquired if he was practicing with the church and I was told that he was practicing with the school. About that time he arrived home. "How come you practice with the team?" I asked. "You told me you were cut."

"Well, Dad," he replied, "the guys on the team all went to the coach and told him they wanted me on the team. The coach did something he'd never done before. He put me on the team because the guys said, 'We need Matt.' They convinced the coach, so I'm on the team."

He continued his friendly ways. School was composed of both blacks and whites. He befriended them all. He became a great influence in the school—to help unify it, to help all to have more pride in it. On one occasion in a senior class meeting there arose a division among the black students and the white students over who should play the music at the last dance. The blacks wanted a black group and the whites wanted a certain white group. Some of the more vocal groups of both factions began to shout, and a potential little riot seemed to be shaping up. Matt got the microphone.

"Quiet, quiet," he said. And then when there was silence he continued. "I have a solution. There's a group up in Cincinnati we can get. It's five Chinese guys."

His announcement was first met with silence, but then came a unanimous burst of laughter. Tempers cooled and a sensible discussion followed.

Matt and the other Mormon kids, as a group, set a great example at that school. A Mormon girl became vice president and she was also named Miss Seneca, the highest honor the school could bestow upon a young lady.

Matt still felt bad about basketball because he was usually on the bench. One night at a team meeting the projector broke down and game films could not be shown as planned. The team and the coach just sat around and talked. Matt sort of entertained the group. For the first time the coach really found out who Matt was. In the next game he played for over half the game. From then on he was a major factor in many games and gained recognition as a superior athlete.

Finally it was graduation time. He was chosen to give one of the talks. The humor in the talk caused a good deal of laughter. But it was also a serious talk. Toward the conclusion of his remarks, he spoke of the joy he had known there—the warmth of the people, the love he had for the other students. He closed by saying, "My dear friends, in a few days my parents and I will be returning to Utah. As you know, I am a Mormon. I conclude my remarks by using the unforgettable words of a great Mormon prophet Brigham Young. His words describe my feelings. I love all of you because of the way you've treated me and the happiness and joy I've had here. And so I say to you, as he once said, 'This is the place.'" The students and the public rose to their feet and gave him a standing ovation.

Matt had made many steps toward his destiny, a journey which started in a quiet room where, after a trial of his faith, he made a decision to start over, a decision which could be paraphrased by the words, "If it is to be, it is up to me." He had decided to build first upon the idea of reaching his destiny as a special person. As he did that, other things fell into place.

## Church Is Better Than Cleaning Out The Chicken Coops

That is the way it was with my father. In many ways my father, "Bert," was not true to the faith, but he surely did want me to be.

As I have said, when I was young I had a desire to become less involved in the Church. I decided I needed to sleep in on Sunday morning more than I needed to get up and go to church. This greatly bothered my mother, who never missed church and who thought I should get up and go. But my father did not go to church, and I felt that because he did not go it ought to be all right for me to not go.

After I had missed two weeks in a row my mother was greatly distressed, but there was no way that she could make me go. I recall that the next Sunday morning my father came to where I was sleeping and said, "George, if you don't want to go to church you can get up and go out and help me clean out one of our chicken coops."

I had no excuse, so I spent a miserable Sunday morning

deeply involved in chicken manure. After that I was always up and off to church before my dad could enlist me in his chicken coop crew.

## Dad, I Don't Want To Go Play. I Want To Stay Here With You

It was a summer and our sacrament meeting ended early, so we decided that we'd hold our home evening after the services. The children were told before we departed for church that right after we got home we'd go to the back lawn for family home evening.

As we arrived home, some of the neighborhood children were playing nearby. They had a huge cardboard barrel that one of them would sit in and ride head over heels while the others rolled the barrel. It looked like great fun, even to an old father like me, and I'm sure the enticement for small children was unusually strong. But nonetheless we had little difficulty getting the children to gather with us on the back lawn. After the opening portion of our family gathering, and just as I was beginning to tell a story, our five-year-old son, Devin, announced that he had to go in the house. His reason was one with which I could not argue, so he was excused to go.

We awaited his return, but he didn't come back. We carried on for a while but then closed the activity a bit early. I went past the front of the house and out near the street. I pulled him out of the cardboard barrel. I was a patient, kind, wonderful father as I calmly said, "Come in the house with me."

He had a hostile tone in his voice as he announced, "I want to stay here. You never let me play."

I was no longer quite so calm. I raised my voice and stated, "That's about all you do is play." He replied and I replied and we headed toward the house. He came willingly because he had to; I was holding his hand. I walked faster than he could walk but he kept up because I was dragging him.

We went down the hall toward the room where he slept. I opened the door, pulled him ahead of me into the room, hit him hard enough on the rear to hurt his feelings, and as I closed the door I raised my voice above his screams and said, "If you can't stay at family home evening, maybe you can stay in your room." As I slammed the door I said, "Now you stay in there and don't you come out."

There we were: I was sitting in a chair on one side of a door and he was kicking and screaming on his bed on the other side of the door. As I sat there I began to calm down. I wondered why I couldn't handle such a matter without getting so upset. As I looked at the closed door that separated my son and me, I started to pray. "Why does it have to be this way? Why do doors that ought to be open sometimes get closed? Why can't my son and I understand each other?"

As I sat in my chair looking at the closed door I wanted so much for it to open. And I began to hope that this little boy that I loved so dearly would forget my words and come through the door to me.

Soon my wish was granted. The door flew open and out he came. In a rebellious tone, he announced, "I'm coming out!"

I quickly jumped up, pulled him back into his room, and said, "I told you to stay in there."

The door had been opened, but not the right way. And now it seemed closed tighter than ever. Again we were separated by the door. Again I searched within. Time passed, and my heart was filled with an overwhelming love for this boy, my son. Again, I prayed for the door to open. I considered opening it. But I knew I must open it right or else it could teach what I didn't want to teach.

By now the little son had ceased his cries and his room

was silent. After a time, the door opened just a crack, and then a little wider. Finally it was opened just wide enough that I could see him. He was crying again. Only this time he was crying in a different way. This time his tears were not those of rebellion but rather they were the tears of the heartbroken. As I looked into his eyes and he into mine, he spoke with softness, "Daddy, I'm sorry."

My reply was quick and sincere. "My son, I am, too." I then beckoned him with my hand and said, "Come here." He came over and stood by my side as I sat in the chair. I put my arm around his shoulder and pulled him close. How good it felt to have him with me again! I told him, "Devin, did you know that when you left us tonight we didn't have a family home evening? When you left, we didn't have a family because you were gone."

I talked to my son. The Spirit of the Lord was there. What a joy it is to talk to your son when the Spirit of the Lord is there! I told him of my love for him, of my pride in him. I told him that because he was so easy to like, everyone admired him. I told him of the great good he could do if he'd just be where he ought to be and do what he ought to do. I talked to him about his future and even about the time when he would serve a mission. Because of the Spirit that was there he seemed to understand all that I said.

Then I realized that he was just a little boy and that I'd talked to him a long time. I decided I should let him go. I hugged him one last time, whirled him around, and hit him again on the rear (the blow was as hard as before, only this time it didn't hurt), and said, "Now you go and play."

He crossed the room to leave. But just as he was about to disappear down the hall, he stopped. He turned around and looked back at me and said, "Dad, I don't want to go and play. I want to stay here with you."

I called him back. This time I took him on my lap and held him as close as I could. We sat in silence and rocked back and forth. The Lord's quiet warm influence bound us together as a father and son and we were as one.

## Mom, You'll Never Go To Church Alone Again

While I was growing up, my father raised white chickens. They laid white eggs. I bought some brown eggs and put them under a white setting hen. They hatched out as little brown chickens, and when they got big they laid brown eggs. We put my brown chickens in the coops with the white ones. I helped gather the eggs and take care of the chickens. The pay for my labors was brown eggs—all the brown eggs laid were mine. There were a couple of dozen a week, and I raised a little money by selling them.

This money gave me some popularity with my older brother and his friends because they had a 1931 model A Ford car, but they were seldom fortunate enough to have money to buy gas. They advised me that I could go with them any time I wanted to if I would provide the money for the gasoline. I felt kind of big as I rode around with these guys. They were all older than I was and were athletes as well. I thought it helped my prestige to ride around town with them in the Model A.

I remember waving to my friends as we passed them, and I suppose my friends were saying, "There goes old George—he's kind of a big wheel riding with those guys." So I thought my money was being well spent.

Week after week we'd go out in the Model A. During that period of time, I regularly attended church with my mother. There weren't too many young men in our ward, so my friend Herbie Pawloski and I blessed the sacrament every Sunday. I enjoyed blessing the sacrament. I'd kneel down at the table and try to read each word just right. As I did this, a good feeling would come into my heart. I also liked breaking the bread while the people sang the sacrament song. I'd softly sing along, and as I stood there helping the Lord I'd really feel special.

Each Sunday afternoon, I knew that my mother was expecting me to go to church and the bishop was expecting me to bless the sacrament. But one Sunday, a little while before the time for church, my brother and his friends came and told me that if I had some money they wanted me to go with them in the Model A. I did have some money. And I thought, "Because I've attended church so regularly in the past, perhaps today would be the time when I could miss."

As I was about to get into the Model A, my mother asked me where I was going and I said I was going with the fellows. "Will you be back for church?" she asked, and I replied, "I don't think so." She looked hurt, but I got in the Model A and away we went. We rode around and had a good time. I thought from time to time about the fact that I ought to be in church. That sort of dampened the fun, but it sure was good to be with those big guys.

It so happened that we were driving past the church shortly after the meeting had ended, and the people were coming out. My mother was coming down the stairs all by herself. I wondered who would walk home with her and I wondered who had helped Herbie bless the sacrament. I wondered if the bishop had missed me.

Suddenly I found myself feeling very miserable. Tomorrow would be Monday and I would have to go back to school. The thought of going back to school on Monday always used to be something of a hard thought for me to face on Sunday night. I didn't dislike school, but it seemed as if Monday wasn't a very happy day and consequently I usually didn't feel happy anticipating it during the last hours of the weekend. But on this Sunday night, after the Model A ride was over and I was home again, I had a deep case of misery. I finally asked Mother who the bishop had asked to help Herbie bless the sacrament. She told me one of the men had. I sat silently for a time and then I said, "Mom, next week I'll be there." She smiled. Just saying that made me feel better, and I started getting over my misery. The next week I was there.

## I Finally Spoke Up, And It Made A Real Difference

My sociology teacher had said something controversial—I believe he did so just to get a reaction out of the students. But when he asked if anyone wanted to comment on what he had said, the class was silent.

I wanted to say something because I didn't agree with him, but I never made comments in my classes except when I wanted to be goofy and make people laugh.

Now, this class was filled with more than eighty students, and for that reason I had never said a word during the semester. So naturally I didn't comment. The teacher asked again, "Any comments?" I felt a great urge to speak up, but my lack of courage would not allow me to do so.

The teacher paused.

And suddenly, almost against my will, I was speaking. My words were coming from my heart, and my whole body seemed to vibrate with nervous energy.

Everyone listened while I tried to make my point. When I finished, the teacher asked, "What is your name?"

I replied, "George."

"George who?"

"George Durrant."

"Students, did you all hear what George Durrant said?"

Soon the class discussion moved on, but I kept thinking over and over about the teacher's words: "Students, did you all hear what George Durrant said?"

That was the highlight of my college career.

## The Lord Said, You Go Home And Bless Her

When I think of seeking and obtaining forgiveness, I think of an experience my wife and I had some years ago when we were living in Brigham City, Utah. Our children had had a restless night. It had almost seemed as if they had conspired together, as if the oldest had said, "Now listen, fellows, here's how we'll do it. I'll cry from twelve to one, you wake up at one and cry from one to two, and then he'll wake up and cry from two to three. That way we kids can all get some rest, but we'll be able to keep Dad and Mom up all night."

So my wife had been up with the children most of the night. (The reason she was up and not me is that when my children cry at night I smile and I think, "That's one of my precious children." Then I nudge Marilyn and she gets up and I try to go back to sleep.) Neither of us got much rest that night, but she got less than I did.

The next morning I had to go to Salt Lake City early. I decided I'd quietly get out of bed and not even wake Marilyn up. I'd just prepare my own breakfast and do everything that needed to be done. (I'd say that's being rather a fine fellow, when I think about it.)

Starting to get dressed, I went to get a white shirt. There wasn't one ironed. As I asked myself, "Why hasn't she ironed my shirt?" I wasn't feeling quite as wonderful as I had felt ten minutes before. (Incidentally, every morning of my married life except that one she has had a shirt ready for me.)

A little disgruntled, I got a clean shirt and ironed it in the places where you have to iron a shirt if you're going to wear a jacket. At this point I was still feeling pretty good about myself. I then decided I would get myself some breakfast.

I set my mind upon some nice toast with honey. (I don't want to boast, but I make really good toast on our toaster.) But when I went to get out the bread—no bread! I looked in other possible places with the same result. It's difficult for even a talented person to make toast without bread, so by now I was upset. "Why isn't there any bread?" I thought to myself, "What does she do all day?" (Incidentally, there has been bread at home every morning except that one.)

As visions of toast and honey slipped away, I decided to make hotcakes. I began by following the recipe, but that was too slow. Because of the time factor, and because I decided I knew what things went into hotcakes, I discarded the recipe. Hurriedly throwing in my ingredients, I mixed them all together.

Finally the hotcakes were done and I sat there in a lonely kitchen and started to eat. The first mouthful was terrible and all the others more than matched it. With each bite I took I became more and more upset until I was almost beside myself with disgust, frustration, and self-pity.

Now, perhaps you've noticed that it's no good being upset if you're all alone. It's just a waste of energy. So, if you're going to be upset, you've got to be able to show somebody you're upset. I knew that the best way to show people that I'm upset is just to be quiet, not say anything. Then when they say, "What's wrong with you?" I can say, "Nothing's wrong! Why do you think anything's wrong?" Pretty soon then I'm getting even more mileage out of my "upset" condition.

But that method doesn't work if you're alone, because

there's nobody there to see that you're being quiet and not speaking. So, realizing on this occasion that the silent treatment wouldn't work, I decided to use "Plan B." This plan is just the opposite of silence; it consists of "banging around." So I banged around.

You can really bang around in great style in the morning when others are asleep. I banged around and banged around until I knew I'd awakened Marilyn, then I went into the bedroom for the final part of my act. There was a sliding door on the closet which contained my suit coat, and I knew that if I slid it with great vigor it would hit against the other side and make the last big bang. In case any doubt remained, that would definitely let Marilyn know that I was upset. So I vigorously slid the door across and it banged on the other side. Out of the corner of my eye I saw that Marilyn jumped at the noise. Now I knew she was awake.

I then made a cold and calculated decision that I would really let her know how upset I was. I would just put on my coat and leave without saying good-bye. And that's what I did. And that's how I left the house that morning, I who was supposed to be a "priesthood man," a man who everybody at church thought was a fine fellow and all that sort of thing.

At the time I was a branch president and had an office in the nearby chapel. I now went down to that office to get some papers to take to Salt Lake City to my meeting. As I picked up the papers it occurred to me that I should pray, because that's what I did every morning in the office. So I knelt down to pray. As I was praying there was only one thing that I could think about, and that was to ask Heavenly Father to bless my wife Marilyn that she would have a happy day. I asked the Lord for that blessing for her, and after that request I couldn't think of anything else to say. As I knelt there speechless, Heavenly Father spoke to me. At least, he put an idea into my mind. He suggested, "Why don't you go home and bless her? You're closer to her than I am."

As I arose from my knees, I knew that in order to bless her I had to do one of the hardest things in the world. I had to give the most difficult speech there is to give. Short as it is, it's terribly hard to deliver. I rehearsed it in my mind and I prayed for the courage to be able to say the words. I went home, and for some reason Marilyn was up and around. (Apparently something had awakened her earlier.) As I approached her I looked into her eyes and I could see the hurt that was there. I took a deep breath and gave the speech. I said, "Marilyn, I'm sorry." Then came the speech that regularly follows the words "I'm sorry," spoken between family members, and it goes, "And I love you." And there's something that follows those words, when spoken to one's wife or husband, and it's not a speech at all. I hurried out of the house again. This time I was a real priesthood man and I was ready to do the Lord's work. And, by the way, Marilyn told me that she did have a happy day.

## Being Prepared Leads To A Lot Of Work And To A Lot Of Joy

Every Friday in this particular class it was the practice of the teacher to allow those who desired to do so to give a report on current events. As she called the roll at the beginning of class she expected one of two responses from each of us. When she called out our names we could either answer "Prepared" (which meant that we were ready and willing to give a talk) or "Unprepared" (which meant that we were not prepared to talk). Because I was a bright young man I quickly figured out this system. I found that I could avoid these talks by using the word "unprepared." My friends in the class also used this word. We supported each other as supposed friends do.

Those who said "prepared" had to give a talk, while we who said "unprepared" didn't ever have to move. But we weren't just idle, because we caused a little trouble in the back of the room by sometimes laughing just a little. This made the person giving the talk aware that we were making fun of him or her. Perhaps this is why I was fearful of speaking. I could not bear to have anyone laugh at me.

Week after week went by, and each Friday when the teacher would call my name, "George," I would answer "Unprepared." I knew that my long list of "unprepareds" would be the raw material for an "F" on my report card. I didn't want to take such a grade home to my parents, but to me that was easier than risking my pride in front of the class. So I kept saying "Unprepared." I even imagined that I got so that I could say it with quite a bit of dignity. But now I know that the word unprepared can never be said with dignity.

In the class was a girl I liked. I liked her as much as a ninth-grader can like a girl; and, as I recall, that's quite a bit. I liked her to the point where I didn't even dare talk to her, let alone really express myself to her about my feelings. She was one of those who had both a pretty face and "scones in her heart." She was one of those who seemed to care about everyone. But she seemed to care about me in a special way. Sometimes in my dreams I imagined that she was in love with me. What she said meant a great deal to me.

One Friday as the teacher was calling the roll, she called the name "George." In my usual way, I said "Unprepared." At that time, to my surprise this girl turned around and stared at me. I quickly looked away from her, but I knew she was looking at me, because you can tell when people are looking at you. I looked first to one side and then to the other. But she waited me out until, not knowing where else to look, I looked fully into her eyes. As I did so, she spoke with firmness, "Why don't you get prepared?" Then she turned away.

Her words seemed to explode into my heart. For a time I couldn't even think. As I began to calm down I found myself wondering, "What does she care, unless she cares." All day long I thought about what she had said. You know how our minds work; yours is always working, and so is mine—thinking thoughts, ever thinking thoughts, all sorts of thoughts.

That night I clipped an article from the newspaper and began to memorize it. Finally I had done just that. Every word was in my mind. The great accomplishment of memorizing that much material was not made easier by my rather average ability to memorize. But intelligence always has been tempered greatly by desire and motivation, and I was now motivated by the very force that makes the world go around. Finally, when I knew I had every word memorized, I folded the paper neatly and put it in my wallet and carried it with me all the week.

When the next Friday arrived I was sitting up a little straighter because this was a different kind of a day. The teacher was at the front with her roll book. (I had seen this roll earlier, when I had visited with her. As you know, some students get to visit with the teacher more than others do.) It was her habit to put a negative sign by the names of each who answered "Unprepared," and a positive sign by the names of the prepared. When I had seen the roll book a week or so earlier I noticed that on the line headed by the name George Durrant there was a long row of negative signs. These negative signs seemed an accurate appraisal of the way things were going for me. But this day was different.

The teacher was calling the roll. She didn't look up, because if a teacher does that she gets the marks on the wrong line. Finally she got down to the D's. I heard the word "George." There was a brief second or so of silence, and then I softly responded, "Prepared." The teacher stopped calling the roll and looked down to where I sat. I nodded my head up and down. She looked amazed. My friends all looked over at me as if to say, "You traitor!" The girl turned around and looked into my eyes and smiled.

But now the glory was over, and I wondered, "What in the world have I done? What have I said?" For I knew that by saying "Prepared" I had committed myself to get up and perform. Only those whose insecurities equaled mine can imagine how I felt.

I found myself wishing that I hadn't said it. Time raced right at me as one by one the other prepared students gave their talks. Now it was my turn. The teacher looked down to where I sat, and I knew that it was an invitation to come forward. I somehow made my way to the front. I took a deep breath, lifted my head, and looked out at my fellow students. To my relief I found that they weren't laughing. They were all looking up at me in complete amazement as if they could not believe what they were seeing.

I started to speak. I remembered the first word, the first sentence, the first paragraph. I remembered every word of the entire article. Desiring to be truthful at the risk of being boastful, I feel compelled to say that that was the finest talk ever given at American Fork Junior High.

When I had finished speaking, and as I was still momentarily standing there in front of the class, there surged through my body and my soul a thought that hadn't been there for quite a while. That day in the roll book the teacher, out of habit, first put a minus or a negative sign by my name. But when I said "Prepared" she added a vertical line that made a plus or positive sign by my name. The memory of that thrills me. Why, that's the highest of all marks! To have a plus by your name is an honor of the greatest magnitude.

## Look At The Sky

I recall the first art class I took, way back in my early college days. It took all the confidence I could muster just to enroll. I knew that everyone else in the class would be as talented as Leonardo da Vinci and I'd suffer much self-inflicted humiliation as I compared my meager abilities with theirs.

I did my first painting for the class in watercolors. It turned out a little better than I thought it might when I first put the paint on the paper. Even so, I was shocked and filled with fear when the teacher announced, "I see that most of you have completed your first painting. So let's all put them up here along the wall. When they are all in place we will criticize one another's work."

I thought to myself, *I didn't know I'd have to put my picture up to be criticized. If I had known that, I would have never taken this class.*

But having no choice, I reluctantly put my picture on the far right of the display. I hoped that the criticism would begin with the pictures on the left side and maybe the class time would end before it was my turn. Or I hoped at least they'd use up all their criticisms on the other paintings before they got to mine.

As the discussions of the first few paintings were taking place, I didn't say anything about anybody else's efforts. I hoped my silence would indicate that I had no desire to criticize their work, and then, if they were Christians, they wouldn't say anything about mine.

But the clock moved so slowly and the discussion so rapidly that with five minutes remaining, all eyes except mine focused on my work. My insecurities made it so that I could not muster the courage to look up. As everyone looked at my painting, there were several seconds of silence.

Then I heard a girl's voice. In a quiet, kindly tone she said, "I like the sky." Those four words gave me a small feeling of confidence. I lifted my eyes and looked up at the painting. To myself I said, *By George, that is a nice sky.*

From the other side of the room, a fellow spoke up. "But he has got the foreground all fouled up."

In my mind I responded, *Why don't you look at the sky?* And then I thought, *Next time he won't be able to say such a thing, because next time my foreground will be as good as my sky.*

## Keep Things Level And Square

When I was a beginning seminary teacher in Brigham City we had a little house with a very small back yard. By going out our side door, turning right and going down three steps there was an area that was a perfect place to build a small patio.

Because, at that time I was teaching Navajo youth at the government school, I envisioned in my mind the patio having the look of a Navajo rug. I decided that by making the patio from red and green cement block that I could, lay them is such a manner that they would form the pattern of such a rug.

I drew on paper the way that I wanted the patio to appear. I went to the lumber yard and bought the necessary number of blocks. Then I brought in some sand. That was on Friday. Saturday I would get up early and construct my patio.

I wanted the work to be perfect and so I knew my two most important tools would be level and a square. With these in hand I began the work. I made certain that the small board that would form the outside frame of the patio was perfectly square. That took me some time. Then I shoveled the sand in and smoothed it so it was about two inches deep. I laid the level on the sand to make sure that it was perfectly level. That took longer than I thought that it would.

Finally I was ready to lay the flat cement blocks into the sand. I looked at my drawing and laid the first block in the corner. I used the square to be certain it was right. Then I used the level to make sure it was perfect. Then I stood back and looked. It looked very good. I repeated that process with the next several blocks.

About that time Marilyn came out the side door and looked down on the patio. She watched as I took time to lay the next block. Then she said, "That is taking a long time."

"Yes it is," I replied. "I want it to be square and level."

She answered, "I wanted to go shopping this afternoon but it looks as though you will be working there all day."

When she went back in to the house. I looked at my work and decided, "I've got the hang of this now. I won't need to be slowed down by using the level and square. I can just sight things in with my eye. That way I can move along faster and I will be able to go shopping with Marilyn." I started to hurry and as I did the work was moving faster. I worked harder and faster.

Marilyn came out again at mid-afternoon and looked down at that patio which was now nearly finished. I was just putting the last blocks in, but they did not fit with the square frame. I solved that by hitting the last few blocks with hammer until they fit.

As Marilyn looked at my work she did not say anything. I went up and stood at her side and looked down. The patio looked terrible. Finally she said, "We can have some good dinners on that patio." I knew my work had disappointed her. And what was worse, my work had disappointed me.

When friends came that Sunday (the next day) I made

sure that they did not go out the side door where they could see the patio. I did not want them to see the patio because I was ashamed of the way that it looked. I did not want them to see what I had done.

That was a busy week and I could do nothing around our place.

Friday night I spent a very restless night. The next morning I had planned to sleep in. But I woke up very early. I soon had my level and square in hand and was headed outside. Marilyn asked, "What are you doing?"

"I'm going to work on the patio."

"It is already finished," she replied.

"I'm going to do it over and this time I'm going to do it right."

Without even eating breakfast I was at work. Soon I had all the blocks out and stacked up. I smoothed out the sand. I lifted the first block and used the level and square to get it right. Marilyn came out and asked, "How long will it take?"

I answered, "It will take all day."

Finally in the late afternoon it was nearly finished. Marilyn came out, looked down and said, "George! It is beautiful."

I went up and stood at her side. I put my arm around her and I could scarce contain my joy. It looked just like a Navajo rug.

The next day company came. I took them out the side door where they could see the patio. They said, "Wow! Look at that. It is so beautiful. Who did it?"

I shrugged as Marilyn said, "George did it."

I wanted them to see what I had done.

## Just Deciding That Made Me Feel Better

I love those wonderful days of waiting for Christmas. One particular year it seemed to be coming slower than usual. Each day was filled with a little of the pain that always comes with waiting and a lot of the joy that comes from knowing that pretty soon something really good is going to happen.

How can you look forward to Christmas when you know exactly what you are going to see under the tree when you get up on that cold December morning? At the same time, I'll have to admit I did like magicians and I'd always wanted to be one. I was eager to open that box and to start doing magic tricks.

I tried making the coin disappear but I couldn't do it quite right. Mom told me to read the directions again. I did, but I couldn't really understand what they were telling me to do. I hated to admit it, because I was a year older, but I missed my Tinker Toys. They worked just fine without any magic words.

There were a lot of feelings I had on that Christmas day that I didn't tell anyone about because I couldn't really explain them.

Dad was out feeding the chickens, Mom was in the kitchen cleaning eggs, and Kent had gone to play basketball with his friends. I was all alone, sitting in the parlor by the Christmas tree. Kent had given Dad a little silver metal toy gun for a present as a joke. It shot BBs, but wasn't any threat to the neighborhood birds because it had about as much power as a girl slugging you in the arm. And even with a dead aim you could barely hit the ground.

While I was sitting there feeling bad about feeling bad, I picked up Dad's gun and looked at it.

I shot it a couple of times at the cardboard lid of my magic set box, which was leaning against a chair. Then I looked over at the Christmas tree. I drew dead aim on a blue ornament hanging way out on the end of a branch about halfway up. Of course, I didn't shoot because nobody in all the history of mankind had ever shot a Christmas tree ornament. It just isn't right. It's almost worse than shooting a robin in the springtime.

I lowered the gun and was about to set it aside. The trouble was, I was so sad that I just felt like shooting at something. I raised the gun again, aimed right at the ornament, and slowly squeezed the trigger. It was almost impossible to even hit the tree with that gun, much less the blue ornament, but, incredibly, the ball exploded into hundreds of silver and blue fragments. I was shocked at what I'd done. Then, as luck would have it, Mom entered the room. I've never seen her look more startled. She turned from the mess on the floor and looked at me. I was still holding the gun. There was no use telling her I hadn't done it. Kent wasn't home, so I couldn't blame him.

She didn't get angry. She just looked at me for what seemed like a long time. I didn't want to look back but I knew that I had to. I could tell she couldn't believe that her son George could have done such a thing. I was wishing she'd get mad because I knew you couldn't be both disappointed and mad at the same time. The most painful thing that could ever happen to me was to have my mom disappointed.

I told her I'd pick up the pieces. She didn't say anything, just turned and walked out of the room, her eyes moist. In a few minutes I went in to where she was sitting in her rocking chair. I didn't say I was sorry again because she could always tell how I felt and she knew I was about as sorry as anybody had ever been. She reached out and held my hand. As I stood close to her, I felt that toys didn't matter much. The only thing that counted was not hurting people and doing good things instead of bad things.

Later that day I tried to pick up the pieces of the broken ornament and put them together with glue. I soon knew I couldn't do it, any more than I could put a broken egg back together. I finally gave up and just sat there. I hadn't cried in two years. And I didn't cry then. I wanted to, but I couldn't.

I decided then and there that that would be the last ornament I'd ever break. Just deciding that made me feel better.

I lay down on the floor on my back with my feet close to the base of the Christmas tree. I put my hands under my head for a pillow and looked at all the colorful decorations. I looked up at the star. It seemed more beautiful than it ever had before. As I was lying there, I wished I could go back to the way Christmas used to be. I felt that way because I remembered the happiness of the past, but at that time I didn't know anything about the joy of the future.

## The Christmas That I Remember Best

My senior year in high school was the year when I'd grow tall, girls would discover me, I'd be student-body president, and I'd be a bona fide basketball star. But that year had come and none of that was happening.

One night after a poor basketball practice I dejectedly walked home. Mom greeted me at the door and said, "George, you are just in time for dinner."

I sadly saw that she was cooking potato soup and said in disgust, "Ma, why do you cook that stuff?"

"Because, your dad likes it."

"Why don't we ever have what I like?"

As if she had not heard me, Mom smiled and said excitedly, "Your dad went downtown and bought a Christmas tree. He didn't say it, but I can tell that he wants you to decorate it."

"Why me? Let him do it," I replied.

"He thinks you'll do it. You can do it tonight."

"I'm not doin' it tonight."

"Why?"

"Cause I'm going someplace."

"Oh, George, why can't you stay home more?"

"Cause there's nothing to stay home for. It's Christmas time and I'm about as happy as the hunchback of Notre Dame."

Dad came in from doing his chores and we all sat down to the potato soup. I could tell he was pleased to have such a good meal. I reluctantly took a big spoonful and couldn't help thinking, "I hate this stuff but when Mom makes it, it is pretty good." I had two full bowls.

After dinner I heard a car honk three times. It was Lum Nelson in his dad's 1941 Chevrolet. I almost slipped on the ice-covered walk as I hurried to the car. I heard Mom shout, "George come back and get your coat."

A few seconds later I was back inside. Mom was surprised and said, "I thought you was leaving."

I smiled and replied, "I changed my mind." Dad was sitting in his rocking chair reading the front page of the evening newspaper. I walked over and sat close to him and said, "Dad, I was thinking I'd like to decorate the tree."

He lowered the paper and looked at me. He didn't say anything, he didn't ever talk much. As he lifted the paper up again I thought I saw him smile a little. I got the decorations from above the closet in the back bedroom. The tree was in the parlor just waiting to be decorated. I said, "Don't you two come in here until she's all finished."

Decorating a tree with an artistic flare takes a lot of time, especially if you are hanging each ornament just right. I wasn't in any hurry because I was happier than I'd been in a long time. As I worked, I was singing real good, "Silent night, holy night."

Nearly finished, I moved a red ornament to where a blue one had been and vice versa. I was thinking so hard about what to do next that I was startled to hear my mom say, "George, your dad and I wondered why it's taking you so long." Then she saw the tree. "Oh, it's beautiful!"

Excitedly I said, "I'll plug in the lights and it'll look even better." As I walked over to be near Mom and Dad, I could see the red and blue reflections in Dad's dark brown eyes. He didn't say anything, but I could tell that he liked what he saw. We all three stood there for a few seconds with the kind of feelings that you have when you are with your family and you're happy. Then Dad in his low and slow voice said something that I will never forget. He said, "George, don't forget the star." I looked up at the top of the tree and sure enough I had forgotten the star. I went quickly to the piano bench, picked up the star, stood on a wooden chair, and gently placed it on top of the tree. Dad didn't speak, but he nodded his approval.

I don't remember what presents I bought for Mom and Dad that year. They couldn't have been much. But I'll never forget that night when I and gave myself to mom and dad by staying home, decorating the tree, and making them happier than I could have done in no other way.

I don't remember in much detail other teenage Christmases, but I remember that one. It was that Christmas that I stopped dreaming of what I could get, and started dreaming of what I could give.

## The Prayer That Brings Immediate Results

One young man told the following story in our sacrament meeting:

"One morning I arose from my bed and came into the kitchen where some of the other family members were. They asked me, 'Did you leave the water running outside last night?' Whoever had done so had left the hose close to the basement window, and the water had flooded the basement.

"I said I hadn't left it running, but somebody else said he knew I had. Father said, 'I think it was you; you were out there last.' There were some sharp exchanges of words, and the family had an argument. There was a negative feeling in the home. I felt that I'd like to tell everybody off, and even that I'd like to punch a few of them.

"Then Dad looked at the clock and said, 'Well, I've got to go to work. It's time we had family prayer.'

"I felt like saying, 'What do you mean, family prayer? We don't have the right to have family prayer, the way we act and shout at each other. Besides that, everybody has accused me falsely for something I didn't do.' But I didn't know what else to do, so I knelt down.

"Then to top it all off my father looked at me and said, 'It's your turn.' He said it rather sharply. I looked at him and he looked back at me.

"He finally outlooked me, so I closed my eyes and said, 'Heavenly Father.' And then I didn't know what else to say.

"After a while, I said, 'We haven't got any right to pray. We've got a lot of contention and dissension in our home.' My spirit changed a bit when I said that. I continued to pray by saying, 'Heavenly Father, we don't want to act in this way. Help us that we can talk to one another in a normal way and love one another and not accuse one another. For everything we've done wrong we're sorry. Please help us to have love in our home.' Then I said amen.

"I stood up and my prayer was answered immediately. The whole spirit in our home was changed by that prayer. I looked at my dad and my dad looked back at me, and we embraced; and I kissed my mother. My brothers and sisters gave me a warm look. We just all felt like standing there and singing a chorus of 'There is beauty all around when there's love at home.'"

# SELF ESTEEM SCONES

## The Great Race Is To Keep Up With Yourself

Three of my children were swinging in a park. Two of them had learned to pump themselves in swings. Our little daughter had not yet mastered this skill. The two who could pump themselves were on the two outside swings and the little girl, who was only moving because of a breeze, was in the middle one.

Devin, on one outside swing, was going as high as the swing would allow. He noticed that Kathryn, on the other outside swing, was doing the same. He shouted, "I'm keeping up with Kathryn." Swinging in unison with him, Kathryn shouted back, "I'm keeping up with Devin." Little Marinda, who was scarcely moving, looked first at one and then the other and then humbly said, "I'm just keeping up with myself."

That is the race you are to run, a race in which your eternal goal is to keep up with that spark of divinity which is best described as yourself.

## The Great Discovery Is To Find Yourself

One day my four-year-old son was hiding from me. I knew where he was, because I could see his feet sticking out from behind a chair. But wishing to contribute to his fun, I shouted, "Where is he?" Then I added, "I think he is in the bookcase." I removed several books and announced, "He isn't there." Then I said, "I think he is in the lamp." I turned it off and on and exclaimed, “He isn’t there.” Then I went near his hiding-place and stated in a loud voice, “I can’t find him. I guess I’ll have to go and buy an ice cream cone all by myself.” At that point he jumped from behind the chair and announced, “Daddy, I’ve found myself.”

## You Are Still In There

A man was wrestling on the floor with his two little sons. He grew tired before they did, which is often the case when fathers and sons wrestle. To get some rest, he decided to act as though he had fallen asleep. As he lay there the boys wondered if he had died. The older of the two, not knowing what else to do, reached down and with his thumb pulled open one of his father’s eyelids. Then he looked at the smaller boy and reassuringly announced, “He’s still in there!”

## You Are The Best Size Of All

A girl came to my office and wanted to talk to me. After talking about some rather unimportant matters, she became very serious. She said, “I have something else I want to talk about.”

“What’s that?” I inquired.

“I don’t want to be this tall,” she said. “I’m taller than many of the boys. I haven’t been getting any dates. I think one reason is that there are only a few boys taller than me and that limits me so much.” She went on to say, “I wish I hadn’t grown so tall.”

“That’s interesting,” I said, “because ever since I first saw you in my class I’ve admired your tallness. That is what makes you look like a model.”

“Yes, but how do you get to be a model?”

I replied, "I don't know, I've never been a model. But to me you sure look like one. I like the way you stand up straight to the full extent of your height."

She seemed to feel a little better, but she added longingly, "I just wish I could get more dates."

"If you keep close to the Lord and as you stand up straight as you do," I said, "you'll get more dates. At least you'll get the important dates with the right guy. Until you do you'll just have to keep doing good—and I know you are good because I see in your countenance something very special."

This beautiful girl is one of the multitude of people who wonder about their physical stature.

## Son, Having You Help Me Is Like Having A Man

When we moved from one town to another, my young son and I were taking a table from the home to the moving van. The table appeared too big to go through the door. I was puzzled about how to get it through and I asked my son what he thought. He considered the matter and said, "If we turn it on its end and take these legs through first, then I think it will go."

I said, "Let's try it." We did as he had suggested and it worked. As we went toward the truck I looked at him and said, "You know, having you help is just like having a man."

He's always remembered that, and he says to me, "Remember when you told me that having me help was like having a man?"

## Giving Yourself A Big Hand

There was no more beautiful spot in all the world than Saratoga Swimming Resort on an August night with a full moon. I was there one night long ago. Just a little more than two years had passed since high school graduation. A large group of my former classmates and some others were there for a swim in the naturally hot water of the two big pools. Then we all gathered for a picnic.

I moved away from the group and stood alone under the giant cottonwood trees. The moon gave a special illumination to the lush green leaves that danced in cadence due to the slight warm summer breeze.

A young lady who had gone to a car to get her sweater saw me standing alone. She came over. For a few seconds, we stood together in silence. Then she spoke, "Quite a party, isn't it?"

I replied, "Yeah, it sure is."

After another long pause, she spoke again, "You don't drink beer, do you, George?"

"No," I replied in an almost inaudible voice. Then as she looked at me in silence, I sort of felt the need to repeat a little louder, "No, I don't."

I looked away from her and gazed out across the dark calm waters of Utah Lake. On a far shore, I could see the reflection of the burning flame of the distant steel mill. She spoke again with a tone of deep sincerity, "George, I sure do respect you."

With that she quickly departed and I stood alone. Over and over again in my mind I heard her words, "George, I sure do respect you."

To myself, I gently whispered, "I respect me too." And as I stood there on that moonlit night, I had an inward feeling of self-applause. It was not haughty applause; it was not proud applause. It just seemed to be respectful applause-applause which only I could hear; applause which caused me to take a little inward bow; applause which satisfied my soul.

## The Greatest Lesson That You Taught Me Was That You Remembered My Name

I recall a student I once taught. Like many of us, he always seemed to wonder if he really was the "right stuff." Two years after he had been in my class, I returned to the school as a substitute teacher for a friend who had to be absent from his teaching chores for a day.

The students were all seniors and I asked each one to take a turn and tell the class what they planned to do during the next year after graduation. I remembered the name of a girl on the far side of the room in the front seat. So I said, "Barbara, let's start with you."

While she spoke, I remembered the boy's name behind her. Because I had known the students quiet well, I was able to call each by name.

About in the middle of the room and at the back sat my rather "unsure of himself" friend. While the girl in front of him gave her brief report, I noticed he seemed pale and apparently very frightened.

With considerable gentleness I said, "Dennis, what are you going to do?"

Suddenly the fright seemed to vanish only to be replaced by overcoming emotions. Dennis was choked to the point where he could scarcely speak. It wasn't until four months later that I learned just what had occurred.

What do you think it was?

Dennis had had an attack of the greatest fear known to mankind–the fear that he and he alone would go unrecognized. When I said his name "Dennis," it released the vent up fear and had totally softened his heart.

In his own words, Dennis told me with the same emotion that he had felt that day, "Mr. Durrant, the most important thing that you ever taught me was that you remembered my name." He told of how he felt as one by one I had remembered all the others. Hearing each of their names, he became more and more certain that I would not remember his. Recalling his name that day was one occasion when I rose to the rank of a master teacher.

## I Still Lie A Little

I recall a time when I had an appointment to see a very important leader of the church. As I entered his office I was a bit nervous. His first question was, "How are you?"

I replied, "Nearly perfect!"

He seemed pleasantly startled and asked, "Oh, is that right? Just what is it that is keeping you from being completely perfect?" I quickly replied, "I lie a little." I thought for a minute he might fall out of his chair with laughter. The atmosphere in the office was no longer stressful for me, because he and I had had a laugh together.

# FAMILY HOME EVENING SCONES

## Popcorn Popping In The Front Room

Sometimes we get out our electric popcorn popper and put a sheet down in the front room and take the lid off the popper and dive for the kernels as they fly from the popper. Sometimes one of us hides and another finds him and hides with him and another finds her and hides with all the rest, and then another, and then another, until the entire family is hiding under a bed. Sometimes we play marching music and turn it up real loud, and we march single file as a family all over the house. You can see why we pull the drapes. We don't want anyone seeing us. They might think we are strange.

## From Now On, Could Mom Teach The Lesson?

Early that evening I prepared a long lesson on a subject which I felt would help the children correct some of their misbehavior.

The children's attention lasted only two or three minutes into my lesson before they began to fidget. I was slightly irritated and raised my voice a bit. They began to poke one another and to whisper little insults at each other. This upset me and I became very stern and told them to sit still. I changed from teaching to preaching. They were quieter now because they sensed that I, their usually calm dad, was getting more and more upset. I felt as though they were not supporting what we were trying to do. I decided it was time to really lay down the law. I told them that our prophet had asked us to have family home evening and all they wanted to do was goof off and hit each other. I was really wound up now. I told them that there were a lot of things they were and weren't doing around the house and that things were going to change. I reminded them of undone dishes, unmade beds, too much TV and too little study, too much bickering and not enough cooperation. I went on and on.

By now they were completely subdued. They were each sitting straight in their chairs and I was definitely in charge.

Having won the battle, I did not feel the thrill of victory because in my heart, I knew I had been a little harsh. So I asked, "Do you like to have family home evening?" They didn't respond but I could tell they were thinking, "Oh yes! We love to have you get all upset and shout at us and tell us all what to do and make us feel like we are not worth two cents. That is really fun. We love it."

Then I asked, "What can we do to make family home evening better?"

Our oldest son, eight years old, meekly asked, "Next week, could we have Mom teach the lesson?"

His request said it all.

## To Say All The Good About Mom Would Take All Night

We sat in our front room using the family home evening manual. The lesson we were discussing centered on saying good things about each other. One by one, each child was the target, and all the rest of us took turns saying good things about that child.

A beautiful spirit came into the room.

Finally, it was Marilyn's turn to be the one. Each child quickly stated something good about her. Finally it was our ten-year-old son Matt's turn to speak.

He softly said, "Dad, if I said all the good things that I know about Mom, we'd be here all night."

Having heard these words, a feeling of love and gratitude came forcefully into my heart.

After pausing long enough to take a deep breath, I said, "Oh, my dear son, I feel the same way about her. I love her with all my heart."

# HOLIDAY SCONES

## I Hope You Don't Get All the Things That You Want For Christmas

Without bragging too much, I'd say that I was better at making windmills out of Tinker Toys than any other kid in American Fork.

Of course, that might have been because I had so much practice. You see, nearly every Christmas from the time I can first remember such things I'd get a long, round box full of Tinker Toys. I recall one Christmas I wanted a scooter that had pretty good-sized wheels on both ends. You could hold on to a handle that came up on the front. Then you could put one foot on the scooter and put the other one on the ground and push off and away you would go. My friend had gotten one the year before and the two times he had let me ride it I had gone as fast as the wind. I couldn't wait to go lickety-split on that beauty out on the Alpine Road.

You can imagine my disappointment that particular Christmas morning when Santa Claus got confused and, instead of what I'd ordered, he left me another box of Tinker Toys. It was hard to see how he could get scooters and Tinker Toys mixed up, but I guess he has a lot of orders and in those days there weren't any computers to keep things straight.

In an effort to make the best of things, I sat down and pulled the lid off the box and dumped those Tinker Toys out in front of me. In a few minutes I felt a whole lot better, because it's impossible to be unhappy when you are pushing a foot-long little wooden rod into a round hole in a little round wooden wheel. I must have made fifty different Tinker Toy contraptions before Mom told me that my oatmeal was ready. So, in spite of Santa's error, that still turned out to be a fine Christmas.

By the time December was about to roll around again, I'd lost interest in scooters. Remembering the mistake Santa had made the Christmas before, I didn't want to take any chances, so I ordered a little earlier. I did that by telling everybody, including my friends and my brothers and mainly my mom and dad, that I sure did want a Red Ryder BB gun. I mentioned it so often that my brother Kent said that he was sick of hearing about it and told me to shut up. My mother usually got after him for saying "shut up," but for some reason she didn't make a peep that time.

I still can't figure out what went wrong that Christmas. The only good thing was that the box of Tinker Toys was bigger that year and I could make a much fancier windmill out of those rods and little wheels. Besides that, this year those little flat pieces that you put on the ends to make the windmill blades were out of plastic instead of cardboard.

I had a lot of fun that Christmas day. Oh, sure, I'd be lying if I said I didn't feel bad. I still longed for the BB gun. Still, I had no resentment because it's hard to feel that kind of feeling toward somebody as good as Santa Claus. Besides, I knew that I'd get the BB gun the next Christmas.

Eleven months later, just two days before Thanksgiving, I was sitting in my classroom at the Harrington School, which was located just a block north of the downtown stores. We were drawing turkeys and pilgrims and Indians, but my mind was on the BB gun that I knew I'd soon be firing at just about everything in sight. With that thought filling up my mind from one side to the other, I was startled when I heard the 3:30 bell ring. Mom told me that I always had to be home by 4:00. But I couldn't wait to go down to Gamble's store and see if they had the Christmas stuff in yet. With that in mind, I headed south instead of north. About two minutes later I was walking along Main Street. I knew that if I walked faster than usual I could make up the lost time and still arrive home in time to meet Mom's deadline. Besides I wanted to be there in time to hear Terry and the Pirates and Jack Armstrong on the radio.

I hurried east along Main Street. Before I knew it, I was right in front of Gamble's store. I got so close to the window I touched it with my nose. As I was gazing in to try to see the BB gun, I saw something that made me decide I could live forever without Red Ryder's favorite firearm. There in Gamble's window was the fanciest bicycle I'd ever seen. I wish I could describe it. The word Hiawatha was printed in gold letters on that fat piece just in front of the seat. It was painted with a color somewhere between purple and red, with white on the tips of each fender. I had never seen anything so beautiful.

From the second I saw it, I started thinking about owning it. I doubt if anyone anytime anywhere ever wanted anything as much as I wanted that bike.

I stood there gazing in that window for a long time. Then I knew I had to head for home. I hardly knew where I was as I walked through the old mill lane. All I could think about was that Santa Claus had to be informed about my desires in such a way that he couldn't possibly get confused. We American Forkers didn't write any official letters to the North Pole, as far as I can recall. We just figured that if we talked about what we wanted to our friends and to our brothers and sisters and to our fathers and mothers that somehow Santa Claus would get the message.

It was hard to concentrate on Terry and the Pirates that night because I was thinking about that beautiful Hiawatha. It was two days to Thanksgiving. Then I'd have about thirty days to tell everybody I met that I was getting a Hiawatha for

Christmas. If I talked about it like that for that many days I just knew that jolly old St. Nicholas would surely get the word. To myself I said, "This year there will be no mix-up." Then I added, "At least there'd better not be." Having said that, I hit my right fist down on the table to show that I wasn't just kidding around.

I never fell asleep for the next month without having that bike appear in the front part of my mind. I could see myself riding it up the Star Flour Mill hill without even having to get off and push. No kid in the history of American Fork had been able to pedal up that steep hill—I mean clear to the top. In my mind I could see Lelee and Dickie Hampton standing there watching me pedal by. They'd be as jealous of me as I'd been of them when they'd gotten to go to California the summer before. I could see myself riding up north to the canal and then coming back down so fast I'd be nothing more than a purple-red flash.

Finally the long waiting period was nearly over and it was Christmas Eve. It had always been hard for me to sleep on the night before Christmas, but that night falling asleep was as hard as trying to make a snowman in July. Somehow, after what seemed like a couple of hours, I drifted off into the Land of Nod.

It seemed like I'd only been asleep one or two seconds when I woke up. I could hear Dad taking the round metal lids off the stove so that he could put the newspaper and the kindling and the coal in. Hearing that, I knew it must be morning. I jumped out of bed and in the same sweeping motion I pulled on my overall trousers. As I hurried out of my room like a cowboy coming out of chute number one at the Lehi roundup rodeo, I could see the bike in my mind and I knew that Santa had come through. This time he'd kept the record straight. This time the bike would be mine. Without going to the bathroom or even hardly breathing, I hurried through the big kitchen that separated my back bedroom from our parlor.

I was so excited my heart was pounding faster than the motor of a Model A going up American Fork Canyon. I hurried past Dad, who had just struck a match to light the fire, and I entered the door to the room where I knew I'd see my bike near the Christmas tree.

In my haste to cross the room to find the bike, I nearly tripped over the biggest Tinker Toy windmill ever built. I looked straight ahead. There was no bike there. I turned and looked to the right, no bike; to the left, no bike; behind me, no bike.

I stood silently in the shock that comes when disappointed is just too weak a word. Then from behind me I heard the voice of my mother. "Look at this," she said excitedly. "Who could have built this?" I looked and she was pointing at the windmill.

My father, who had followed me into the room, spoke up and said, "I got up this morning and came in here and there was old Santa a-workin' on that. I talked to him and he said that he thought George was such a good boy that he wanted to not only give him a bigger-than-ever box of Tinker Toys, but also wanted to personally build him a windmill."

That was quite an honor, and a little bit of a desire to go on living came back into my heart. I walked over closer to the windmill. I'd had a few questions about Santa Claus lately because of what Bobby Jackson had said the week before during recess, but the windmill Santa had built proved that Bobby Jackson was wrong. I couldn't wait to tell the kids at school.

I'd be kidding you if I said I wasn't unhappy about not getting the bike. Yet at the same time I couldn't blame Santa. After all, he had built me a windmill. If he'd done that for every kid, he'd never have even made it out of Utah County that

Christmas. I knew I must have been one of his favorites. I couldn't hold any ill will in my heart for him. Besides, I was already looking forward to the next Christmas.

I didn't want to take the windmill apart because of who had built it but I felt he'd be the first to understand if I did. There were a lot more pieces this year, and I built some amazing things.

Two days later I was sitting in my Sunday School class. The teacher was telling us about eternity being a really long time. I kept thinking, "Eternity might be a long time but it can't be as long as the time it takes to get from one Christmas to the next."

My New Year's resolution that year was to get the Hiawatha bike the next Christmas. When I went back to school after the time off for the holidays, Floyd Vest came riding to school on the Hiawatha bike. As I saw that, I started wondering a little about how fair old Santa really was. But then I remembered he'd built me a windmill. I talked to the other kids and he hadn't done that for any of them, so I felt sort of good, at least for a minute or two. But then I'd start thinking that I wished he'd built a windmill for Floyd Vest and then he could have been the lucky one who was Santa's favorite and I could have been riding the Hiawatha. Of course, it didn't matter much because I'd get the bike the next year. But I wondered if Santa knew how hard it was to wait from one Christmas to the next.

## Christmas Alone With The Savior

In mid-November of that year, I had left the New York harbor aboard the great ship Maritania, bound for a two-year mission in the British Isles. After a seasick week I arrived in Southhampton, England. I spent a few busy and eventful days in London, and then received my specific assignment. Now, as

Christmas approached, I was in a city called Kingston Upon Hull. The excitement of travel had worn off and had gradually and completely been replaced by discouragement. I'd been in Hull, as it was called, just one month and I had been homesick since I'd arrived. As day by day and hour by hour Christmas came closer, that most painful malady of the heart grew ever worse.

To add to my woes, the cold damp foggy air filled my lungs as, with my companion, I pedaled my bicycle for miles to call upon those who would listen to messages of the restored gospel. Under such conditions my nose began to run on December the twenty-second. I began to cough on the twenty-third, and on Christmas Eve I had an almost perfect cold.

As soon as I had arrived at my assigned area, I had written home:

> *Dear Mother,*
> *My address is Elder George Durrant, 4 The Paddock, Anlaby Park, Hull, England. Please let all the family and all of my friends know that if they and you desire to send me Christmas cards and gifts they can send them to that address. Please call as many people and advise them of this as quickly as you can.*

I hopefully supposed that this letter would get home in time for the returning mails to bring me some measure of Christmas joy.

Each day I'd wait almost breathlessly for the postman. He'd be laden with so many cards and gifts that instead of trying to slide them through the mail slot in our front door he would bang the brass door knocker. I'd throw the door wide and reach out and grab the entire pile. Surely at least one-half of these would be mine. With trembling hand I'd pull one from the pile and read. The first one was addressed, "Elder Tagg." The next one, "Elder Tagg." The third, "Elder Tagg." One after another the same name appeared. I was soon willing to settle for just one. But there wasn't one. In all, during the week before Christmas Elder Tagg received thirty cards and several gifts. As he'd open each card, I'd have to look away.

Finally, it was the last mail delivery day before Christmas. I had prayed fervently that I'd receive some Christmas greeting from home. The mailman came up the walk. The door knocker clanged. He reached out and so did I. To my joy there were seven cards and a small brown package. One by one I read the addresses and handed the first, the second, and finally all of the cards to Elder Tagg and then I tossed him the present. I could tell that he was deeply sorry and I knew that if he could have he would have given me any one or even all of the cards and the gift.

I turned away and ran up the stairs to our bedroom. I felt that I needed time to think. As I sat there on the side of my bed, I placed my coupled hands against my bowed head. I wanted desperately to somehow turn the clock and the calendar ahead and just skip Christmas. I knew I could make it through the other 729 days in England but I didn't feel that I had the power to weather this first Christmas.

As I sat in deep silence, the landlady, Nellie Deyes, and Elder Tagg came to the open door. She said, "Elder Durrant, I've come to say good-bye for a few days."

I looked up and she was looking away from me and I could sense that her heart was also heavy. "What do you mean, good-bye?" I asked in surprise.

Without answering she turned and was gone. Elder Tagg spoke softly, "They fear that she has cancer. She wanted to wait until after Christmas to go to the hospital but she just learned this afternoon that a bed has opened up at the hospital and so she must go now."

I was shocked. She reminded me so much of my mother and I'd grown to love her in the month we'd lived in her home.

I went downstairs to where she and her loving husband were just ready to leave for the hospital. I'll forever remember the look in her eyes as she said, "Elder Durrant, I love you. Now you be sure and have a good and happy Christmas." Then she asked if Elder Tagg and I would give her a blessing. Elder Tagg anointed her head with oil. As we both laid our hands upon her head, I poured my heart out to the Lord in prayer that she would soon be well. Later that night she went into surgery. Christmas Eve she died.

When I learned the news, I wanted to pray but I could not. I had had so much love, so much hope, so much faith—and yet she had died. I wondered about many things that foggy Christmas Eve.

Sister Guest, the Relief Society president, had two weeks earlier invited all four of us who served as missionaries in Hull to come at noon on Christmas day for a goose dinner. On Christmas morning at about 11:00 the two other elders came from their home some four miles away to the place where my companion and I lived. The plan was that Elder Tagg and I would proceed on with them to the dinner. We were all greatly saddened by the passing of Sister Deyes but we knew that she would want us to go.

My cold had indeed worsened and the two elders who hadn't seen me for a few days commented on my apparent ill health. After discussing the matter with Elder Tagg we decided that I shouldn't go out into the damp air. Pop Deyes was at home and I said I'd stay with him. The others agreed and soon the three of them were gone.

Pop Deyes was in his quarters and wished to be allowed to remain in solitude, so I was left to myself in the front room. It was Christmas day and I was more alone than I'd ever been and more alone than I thought anyone else had ever been.

There were no gifts. There were no cards. There was no Christmas tree. There were no carols. There was nothing. The silence of the room was broken only by the mechanical working of the cuckoo clock. It was now just past eleven o'clock in the morning of the saddest day of my life and it was Christmas.

I moved closer to the fireplace, which was the only source of heat. The glowing embers seemed to be trying to act as my private Christmas lights. Resenting their attempt to brighten my soul, I picked up the nearby metal poker and pushed at each one to crush out its glow.

I lowered my head and cradled it in my left hand. I sat that way until a "cuckoo" brought me back from where I had been. It was noon.

The room was growing colder now. I arose and poured some coal onto the few embers that remained. Now the fire gave off no heat because the new coals had covered the hot ones. I pulled my chair closer to the fireplace. Almost accidentally I looked on the mantel and there I saw my Bible. I stood and reached out and grasped it and sat back down. I really didn't want to read. I was far too sad to read. Yet at the same time, as a new missionary, I needed to know so much. The others knew so much and I seemed to know so little.

It wouldn't hurt to read a little—just a page or two. I opened the book beyond the middle and found my eyes focused on the words, "The gospel according to St. Matthew."

I didn't want to read. I wanted to be home. With clenched fist I hit the open book and then shook my head almost as if I could by saying "no" cancel every painful feeling that filled my sorrowed soul.

Because the pages were right in the line of my sight, I found myself staring at all the words at once. Without a conscious effort I focused on the first verse. I read, "The book of the generation of Jesus Christ, the son of David, the son of Abraham."

Like obedient servants my eyes continued reading the genealogy of Jesus, but my mind was not willing to let the words become thoughts. A few seconds later it was almost as if the words on the page forced my eyes to call my mind to attention. With full concentration I read, "Now the birth of Jesus Christ was on this wise: When as his mother Mary was espoused to Joseph, before they came together, she was found with child of the Holy Ghost."

Placing the fingers of my left hand at the bottom of this sacred verse I looked up at the mantel above the fireplace but I really wasn't looking at all. I wondered, "What does this mean? How did it say it?" I looked back at the page and read again, "She was found with child of the Holy Ghost."

I felt an incredible sense of wonder. Somehow, through a process beyond my intellect, I sensed that what I had just read was among the most important truths ever known. My eyes lifted slightly and I read the entire verse again, this time in an audible whisper, "Now the birth of Jesus Christ was on this wise: When as his mother Mary was espoused to Joseph ..." I paused and wondered, What does espoused mean? I read on, "... before they came together, she was found with child of the Holy Ghost."

Without looking at the verse I read again from the memory of my mind the words, "... of the Holy Ghost."

I knew I had heard all this before. But somehow I'd never really heard it with my heart.

To my mind my heart whispered, "So Mary is his mother, but Joseph isn't his father."

I noticed a small letter "i" near the words "of the Holy Ghost." I looked at the footnote and read "Luke 1:35." I rapidly turned the pages ahead and eagerly read, "And the angel answered and said unto her, The Holy Ghost shall come upon thee, and the power of the Highest shall overshadow thee: therefore also that holy thing which shall be born of thee shall be called the Son of God."

Letting the book rest in my lap, I touched my chin with my left hand and stared at the coals, which were just now beginning to turn from black to orange. Gently I whispered, "The Son of God." A surge of energy went up and down my spine as I felt my soul fill with light. In a louder voice and with pure knowledge I softly said, "Jesus Christ is the Son of God." That thought caused me to sit more erect.

With half a smile, I turned back the pages to Matthew.

I read on until I came to the words, "... the angel of the Lord appeared unto him in a dream." I wondered, Are there really angels? And within my soul I heard the glorious message, "Yes, there are angels."

A few seconds later I was in the midst of my own Christmas pageant. "Now when Jesus was born in Bethlehem of Judea in the days of Herod the king, behold, there came wise men from the east to Jerusalem,

"Saying, Where is he that is born King of the Jews? for we have seen his star in the east, and are come to worship him."

Again I let the book rest in my lap as my mind flooded with memories. I remembered when I had proudly taken the part of a wise man in the Christmas pageant. Because of that memory and the feelings of my heart, my face was now fully covered by a broad smile.

I read on, "...the star, which they saw in the east, went before them, till it came and stood over where the young child was.

"When they saw the star, they rejoiced with exceeding great joy."

As I pictured in my mind that holy star, I could see my

mom and dad in the doorway looking in at the newly decorated tree. I could hear Dad's words, "George, don't forget the star." That thought caused me to sit and just stare at the glowing embers. Oh, how I loved my dad and mom—and for a few minutes I was at home with them.

I continued to read, "And when they were come into the house, they saw the young child with Mary his mother, and fell down, and worshiped him: and when they had opened their treasures, they presented unto him gifts; gold, and frankincense, and myrrh."

The fire was now giving off a great warmth but it seemed that the greater fire burned within me. For, in my soul I knew that Jesus Christ was the Son of God, that he had been born in Bethlehem, that a star had shone over where he lay. As I continued to read, I knew that he was baptized in the waters of the Jordan, I knew that he was tempted of the devil but that he overcame all temptation. I knew that he was speaking and challenging me when he said, "Blessed are the pure in heart: for they shall see God." Oh, how I longed to be pure in heart! Of all the goals of life, I could think of none that would be so desirable as to be pure in heart.

As I read every page, paragraph, line, and word of the book of Matthew, I could see and I could feel. As I read of his crucifixion, I remembered the words of the song, "Were you there when they crucified our Lord?" And I was, for as I read I was there and in my heart I trembled. As I read of his resurrection, I rejoiced. My soul was filled with hope as I finally read the last two verses of Matthew. I could almost hear his voice as he spoke directly to me:

"Go ye therefore, and teach all nations, baptizing them in the name of the Father, and of the Son, and of the Holy Ghost:

"Teaching them to observe all things whatsoever I have commanded you: and, lo, I am with you always, even unto the end of the world. Amen."

Slowly I closed the book and with both hands I held it close to me. To myself I said, "Jesus Christ is the Son of God. There are angels. He did live and teach and love and perform miracles and was cruelly crucified and then he rose again. He is my Savior and this is his Church. I'm one of those he has sent forth. He is with me forever."

As I sat there holding my Bible, it was late on Christmas afternoon. Never had I been so happy in such an inward way. On that glorious day I had found the one who is the heart of Christmas.

I had found him when I felt forgotten by my family and friends. I had found him when I felt the pain of being away from home. I had found him when the death of someone I loved had torn at my heart. I had found him when I felt hopeless. I had found him because I'd followed the star. I had learned what so many have learned, that following the star, and never forgetting, is not always easy. Sometimes the nearer the star takes us to the stable and the garden and the cross, the more difficult the journey becomes.

That Christmas in England I learned that Christmas can be Christmas without a multitude of things. Mistletoe, colored lights, green-boughed trees, yule logs, greeting cards, and Santa Claus each have their own special way of gladdening our senses and delighting our hearts. But Christmas cannot be Christmas without Christ. On that holy day uncontrollable circumstances had pushed all else aside and left me free to follow the star. On that day I learned that Christ does not fit into Christmas. He is not part of Christmas. Jesus Christ is Christmas. In the years since, I've learned that the pressures and selfish desires of life can push themselves between me and him. If I want to "not forget" the star, I must take the time to be alone with him. I must read of him, think of him, and pray to be near him. Then in the east I see the star. I follow it. I find him and when I do I feel free—free to let my soul soar into the realms of the sacred and indescribable joy that I found first in England many Christmases ago.

## Better To Give

Christmas was coming, and each of us first graders in Miss Booth's class had drawn the name of another boy or girl to whom we were to give a Christmas gift. It was to cost no more than fifty cents.

On the day when the gifts were to be brought to school, I arrived early and put my gift for Walt under the Christmas tree. Then I sat in my seat waiting to see who would put a gift for me under the tree.

Bob came in with a big box wrapped in red paper with a large white ribbon. Each of the children hoped that this gift, which was by far the largest one would be for him. Then Bob shouted, "This big present is for George."

I had never been so happy. The biggest present under the tree was for me! All the other children in the class wished that they were as lucky as I was. I could hardly wait for the end of the day, when the gifts would be opened. Many times that day a boy or girl would say to me, "You are so lucky. I wish I was you. I wish that the big present was for me."

Finally the time came. Miss booth said, "All right, boys and girls, it is time to open the gifts. We are all so excited to see what is in that large present bob got for George. So let's start with that one. Bob, would you come up and take your gift to lucky George?"

My heart pounded with excitement. All eyes were upon me. I could tell that everyone else wished they were me.

Bob placed the large red box in front of me. I began to tear the paper away. Then I opened the box. I could see much crumpled-up newspaper. I pulled each of the papers from the box. Then, down at the bottom of the box, I saw a book. I pulled it out and saw it was a coloring book.

Suddenly all of my happiness changed to sadness. I didn't like coloring books.

Then everyone said, "I hope I don't get a coloring book. I hope I get something more exciting than what George got."

Now, instead of feeling like I was the happiest person in the world, I felt that I was the saddest. I didn't even want to watch to see what the other boys and girls received for their gifts. I even felt that I didn't like Bob, because Bob had made me feel unhappy.

Finally the teacher said, "Now for our last gift. It is the gift that George brought for Walt. George, please come up and get your gift and give it to Walt."

As I walked to the front I felt sad. Everyone in the class had received a better gift than I had received. I took the gift to Walt and then I sat down.

A minute later Walt shouted, "Oh, look at this! This is what I wanted! It is a walk-o-meter. You pin it on your belt and it will tell you how far you have walked."

Walt put it on his belt and began to walk around the room. All of the other boys and girls were really excited. One boy said, "I wish I had that. That is the best gift of all the gifts. I wish George had drawn my name."

A girl said, "Next year I hope that George gets my name."

Then Miss Booth said, "George, you sure do know how to give good gifts. Everyone in the class wants to be able to make others as happy as you have made Walt."

Walt turned around and looked at me and said, "Thanks, George, for making me the happiest boy in the class."

Suddenly I didn't feel sad inside. I looked at my coloring book and saw a picture of some pirates. I loved pirates. I wanted to get out my crayons and go to work, but it was time to go home.

As I left to go home Bob shouted, "Merry Christmas, George." I said the same thing back, and I felt that this would be my happiest Christmas so far.

## The Winner Is Father

Radio News:. . . *the Transit Authority announced that, if the okay is given to proceed with the project, it will require four years for completion. That's the news. And now back to the Marve Levy Show.*

Marve: Hello, and welcome back. This is the Marve Levy Show. If you were listening during the last hour you heard our guest Nolan Simmons outline his views on the increased role personal computers will have in the education of our children. Fascinating man—maybe we can get him back again.
This last half-hour will be open line. I'm sure you don't want to hear another of my tirades on the world's ills, so call in and you can go on your own personal gripes... Richard, you're on the air.

Caller: Hello, Marve. Am I on?

Marve: You sure are. What's troubling you?

Caller: Marve, I don't have anything to complain about, but I sure enjoy your show. That last guy was great! Anyway, I work in my little wood shop in the evenings and I'm a regular listener of yours. I've heard you enough to know you hate sentimental stuff. So I'm a little hesitant to call, because I don't have any great thing to say or profound question to ask. But Marve, don't cut me off. I'll only take a minute. I just had to call and announce that two hours ago my wife gave birth to a six-pound, four-ounce baby girl. And that has made me the happiest man in the world. I'll hang up now so you can get on with your other calls.

Marve: Oh, good. Just what the world needs—a "Happiest Man." I'll tell you what the world needs. It needs more guys who know that if we don't get on the ball, nobody will be happy at all. Old Richard needs to quit smelling the roses and start pulling some weeds. I can't believe it. Fifty thousand watts being used to announce the birth of a baby! It's no wonder this country is in such bad shape. We've got a bunch of know-nothing people out there who can't see the big issues because they are too busy bragging about having a baby. We'll see how happy that guy feels as he watches that baby grow up in a world as corrupt as this one... Yeah, go ahead, you're on the air. What's on your mind? Probably how to get your cat to eat the new calorie-free cat food. What is the world coming to? Go ahead.

Caller: Hey, Marve, lighten up. I've never heard you so ornery. You must have sat down on the wrong side of your microphone. Give the guy a break. Maybe what this country needs is more guys who feel they are the world's happiest men. Marve, quit being so cynical. Just relax and listen to what I've got to say and don't get upset. I just wanted to congratulate Richard on his new little girl. But I feel like I'm seven times happier than him because my wife and I have seven beautiful children.

Marve: Seven! Haven't you ever heard of family planning?

Caller: We sure have, and we're still planning—to have two or three more.

Marve: That's disgusting. And just who's doing the planning? You? I'll bet your wife isn't.

Caller: Oh, yeah. We plan together. She always wanted a big family. She loves being a mother, and there's nothing in the world that is as much fun as being a father. You know that, Marve. I've heard you mention your two daughters, so you know what it is. Hey, I've gotta go, but I challenge old Richard who just called in. I'll bet I'm happier than he is.

Marve: Okay. If you say so... I'm glad he hung up before I had to cut him off. I give up. Ignorance is bliss. What's the use? I try to talk sense, but maybe tonight we'll just turn the phone lines over to the village dumbbells who want to talk about "happiness."... Jim, you're on the air. Don't tell me you're happier than our last caller because you have twelve kids. Man, I can't believe it! Two's enough for me. I love 'em, but I just wish... Oh, well, I guess being a family man isn't my thing. But anyway... so you've got twelve.

Caller: No. We don't have twelve. We just have one. But it took us twelve years to get that one. The first year we were married it broke our hearts when we found out we couldn't have a baby. We kept praying and hoping, but it just didn't happen. Then just a year ago we adopted a little boy, and I'm holding him on my lap now. He's grabbing at the phone. I wish you could see him, Marve. Today the final papers were signed. I just didn't know until we got this little guy how I could ever love anyone so much more than I love myself. I'm glad Richard is now a father, but there is no way he could be as happy as I am. Even that guy with seven can't be as happy as me. When it comes to happiness, I'm the champ.

Marve: Ah, well! We're on a roll. Let's just go ahead and waste the entire half-hour. Okay, so this guy thinks he beats out everybody so far. Let's limit our calls to men. You gals leave the calling to the men. Then later, when we need some people who understand big problems, we'll let you ladies take over the show... Hello. You're on the air.

Caller: Marve, I've been listening, and I love what I'm hearing. I've never called in before, but tonight I can't hold back. I don't think these other guys know what real happiness is. I'm the father of three. My former wife has them living with her. I know that doesn't sound like a happy story—as a matter of fact, it has completely broken my heart. When Judy and I married we dreamed we'd be the happiest couple who ever lived. But it just didn't work out. I don't know exactly what happened, but everything fell apart. There was a lot of bitterness. But today, when I took the children back after having them for the weekend, Judy met me at the front door and we stood there and talked. She seemed to have a different spirit about her. She told me that the children like being with me and that they love and respect me. I've never heard anything that meant more to me than hearing that. Just before I turned to go, each of the two smallest ones hugged me and said, "Thank you, Daddy. I love you." Then there's Nick, our fourteen-year-old—he has resented me since the divorce, and that hurts. But as I was about to go, he asked, "Can you come to my game Thursday?" Before I could answer, Judy quickly said, "He told me he always tries harder when his dad is there." I looked into his eyes and choked out the words, "Sure, son, I'll be there. I'll always be there."

He smiled, and something deeply meaningful went between us. My tears were flowing as I turned to go. Then Judy said, "Thanks, Sid, for being such a good dad." Excuse me, Marve. I can hardly talk here... but anyway, that sure did make me happy—maybe even the happiest man in the world.

Marve: Hmm! That one hit me hard. I knew what he meant when he said that somehow everything fell apart. I just hope that I... well, that I can keep being there for my girls. But that's personal, and I'm not gonna uncover my heart. The rest of you can go on expressing your feelings, but I've found you can't trust feelings, so count me out. That's what Sarah has done. Anyway, when it comes to happiness, well, I'm a long ways from being a winner. Maybe our next caller will be our winner.

Caller: Marve, I sense a real human streak coming out of your supposedly hard shell. But as you continue to air applications for the happiest man, I feel I'm your winner. A lot of people would disagree, and at times I would too. But right now, this very moment, I feel I'm indeed the world's happiest man. You see, I'm married to my childhood sweetheart. During my life, I have had a history of having all my dreams come true. Just about everything I've ever wanted, I've got. Even this year's Super Bowl winner was my team.

Marve: Well, no wonder you're so happy! My team didn't even make the play-offs. We'll put you down as a potential winner. Thanks for bringing up sports. Sports, I understand—it's family life that baffles me. Thanks for the call.

Caller: No, no, I'm not finished. I didn't call to discuss sports. Charleen and I have three teenage children. All of them are ideal kids. I'm a supervisor at work and have had several promotions. But two months ago, while I was playing basketball during my lunch hour, I suddenly felt exhausted. The next day I didn't have the energy to get out of bed. Charleen drove me to the doctor. One exam led to another. I hoped for the best, but I got the worst—I've been diagnosed as having bone cancer. They have filled in for me at work, and things are going fine there. My overriding concern has been the family. Charleen has been brave, but at times I hear her crying in the night. The children couldn't seem to bear the news when I told them. They never want to discuss the subject. They try to act cheerful, but there is gloom in their eyes. They've never wanted much in the way of fancy clothes and that, even though we've given them good things. I think all they've really wanted from me was for me to just be a good dad.

But the reason I called isn't to burden you with these things. I wanted to call because just an hour ago the three children came to where Charleen and I were sitting in the front room. They said they wanted to talk. The oldest, Kevin, had been appointed spokesman. As best I recall, he said, "Dad, we, uh... we've been, uh, thinking, and, uh..." His voice broke, and for a second or two he was silent. But then he took a deep breath and continued. "Dad, we need you. We've done some praying, and we feel you won't die."

The others nodded their agreement, and Kevin continued. "But we don't know what will happen. So we, uh, well, we want you to know something. You see, Dad..." Kevin then began to sob, as did the other two and Charleen. Finally, he continued. "You see, well, it's just that you're the best father who ever lived. And whether you stay here with us or die, we promise you that we'll live our lives in a way that will make you the proudest man who ever lived."

None of us could say more. Charleen and I stood up by the three kids. I held Kevin in my arms and never wanted to let go—then Clark, and then thirteen-year-old Laura. Then I held my sweetheart. Finally, all five of us were in one big embrace.

Marve, as we stood there as one family, for just a few minutes there I knew what heaven is like. And knowing that makes me feel that I'm your luckiest, most blessed, and happiest man.

*(Silence fills both phones. Then the caller softly says:)*

That's it, Marve. And Marve, I sense that things aren't so good for you and Sarah. Hold on to her, Marve. Hold on to her. And to all you other guys out there, take real good care of your wife and those wonderful children. See you later, Marve.

Marve: Hmm! I feel like I should sign off and go home. At least I wish I could go home. But... Who's next?... You're on the air.

Caller: Marve, I don't know if I can pull myself together after that. I agree, that guy's the champ. But I had a good few minutes today, myself. My wife had to go out tonight and I was home alone. At least I would have been home alone if it hadn't been for our three-year-old and the seven-month-old twins. I can manage the fast food place where I work, but, man, getting the kids fed and bathed and in bed—that takes more than an MBA! But I did it! Then I cleaned up the kitchen and vacuumed. I mean, things were standing tall when Maggie came home. When she walked in the front room and heard the quiet and saw the order, you should have seen the look on her face. I'm learning my father did most things better than I do, but I'm a better house-husband than he is. And the way Maggie looked at me and hugged me tonight makes me feel that I'm at least the minor league happiest man in the world.

Marve: Well, a happy house-husband. Maybe I should have been a bit more helpful. But too late now... Hello. You're on the air.

Caller: Good show, Marve! I didn't intend to call, but what I've heard those other fathers say has got me all emotional-like and made me start thinking about my own dad. I've shed a lot of tears already today, because we buried him this morning. He was seventy-eight and had been failing for the last few months, so it wasn't a shock; but the tears came, because I'm sure going to miss him.

Marve: Quite a dad, huh?

Caller: Well, yeah. He was quite a dad. His life was kind of tough. He married Mom when they were both young. In ten years they had six children. One day he went to work as usual—and never came home. I guess the pressure was too great. We didn't see or hear from him for forty years. Then nine years ago somebody knocked, and when I opened the front door I saw this man on the porch looking at me and grinning. I knew as quick as I looked into his eyes that he was my dad.

Marve: Wow! Home after forty years. So what next?

Caller: Well, I just acted like he'd been away at work that day, and I asked him to come in. It was quite a shock to

Susan when I called her into the room and said, "Honey, this is my dad." A few minutes later our two married children happened to drop by, because it was Susan's birthday. As the first one came in I said, "Charles, I'd like you to meet your grandfather." I did the same when the second one came in. I've never seen as many shocked expressions as I saw that night. Later I called each of my five brothers and sisters and told them that Dad had come home.

In the days that followed we learned that he was not well and could not care for himself. For the next four years he stayed with Susan and me for a while and then with his other sons and daughters. And like I say, we buried him today.

Marve: No hard feelings about his deserting you?

Caller: Oh, yeah, of course. But all that's painful water under the bridge. We had nothing to gain by having bad feelings. But by forgiving him we could gain a father. And you know, Marve, next to a mother, there just isn't anything in this world that a child of any age can have that is as wonderful as having a father. And now for the past nine years we've had a father. We came to love him with all our hearts.

Marve: Didn't you have a desire to tell him to hit the road?

Caller: Oh, no! No, no! You see, Marve, he's our father. Yeah, I would have liked to have him around in all my growing-up years. He would have come in handy on a number of occasions. Life can be tough without a father. But I'm glad he finally came home, and even though today is a sad day I still feel like having my dad come home has made me the world's happiest man.

Marve: Well, I don't know about all that. That guy has a more forgiving heart than I do. I think if that had been my father I would have told the old guy, "Hit the road, Jack."... Hello. You're on the air.

Caller: Come on, Marve. You think you're tough, but I'll bet you'd have done just what that guy did.

Marve: Well, I'm not sure. Who knows? My dad was always there. But that didn't seem to do me a lot of good. He and I didn't see eye to eye. To him, everything was either black or white. He had his mind made up on every issue. About the only time we talked it was a contest of wills. That's why I joined the navy when I was eighteen. I wanted to get away. I never thought I'd miss the old guy, but I did. Even now as I think of him I find myself feeling more sure of just who I am.

Caller: Is he still alive?

Marve: No, he died two years ago. And you know, they talk about life after death and I don't know much about that, but the funny thing is that each year that goes by I find myself becoming more like him. It's sort of like he still lives through me. But wait a minute! The longer this show goes, the more I feel like I'm letting my heart get in the way of my head. So, I'm gonna say less and let you happy guys do all the talking. I challenge all you guys who feel like you're the happiest man alive!... Go ahead, you're on.

Caller: Hey, Marve! You're confirming what I've suspected for the last year. You're not the hard guy you try to be. At heart, you're a softy.

Marve: Don't be too sure. If I was a softy, then maybe... Well, let's get on with it, here. Do you have a claim to happiness, or are you just calling to psychoanalyze me?

Caller: No. Well, yeah. I do. I'm not married, and I have no children and I'm free. Marve, that's happiness.

Marve: Come on, fella. When you've known marriage like I

have and you've got children like I do—and then suddenly when you know you're losing all that, you can't stake any legitimate claim to happiness. Anyway, I'm not here to judge, but I'm taking you off the list of the candidates for the world's happiest man. . . . Hello.

Caller: Marve, this is Gail.

Marve: Gail, didn't you hear our rules? If you've been listening you know this is an all-male show.

Caller: I know, but don't cut me off. I called to talk about a man, so that ought to qualify me to speak.

Marve: Okay. For you, we will make an exception. Who is this man about whom you desire to speak?

Caller: Oh, Marve, he is the world's greatest man.

Marve: Oh, yeah! Who is it?

Caller: Marve, he is my husband, and he's the handsomest guy in all of Cedar Falls. He is an athlete, and tonight at dinner he was voted the number one "one-on-one" basketball player in our family. Our oldest son didn't vote for his father, but for himself. That one negative vote didn't go over well with my sweetheart, so they are out on the driveway court now settling the issue.

Marve: So you've got a hoop out there?

Caller: Yes, we do. John—he's my husband—he puts a hoop up before he plants a lawn. He loves basketball with a passion. Of course, he loves tennis nearly as much, but he can't beat me at that so he takes pride in his basketball prowess.

Marve: So you're a tennis star?

Caller: Yeah, I'm pretty good. John insists that we all do a lot of playing together, so we are all pretty good at most sports—even hopscotch.

Marve: When you find out who wins the game, let me know and I'll come down and thrash the winner. I'm from

Indiana, so you know I've got the credentials.

Caller: Hey, they're coming in. I'll ask who won. My husband is smiling. He must have won.

Marve: Hey, Gail, put your son on and let me ask him.

Caller: Okay. His name is Jason.

Marve: Hey, Jason, how did you do against the old guy?

Caller: He beat me.

Marve: He beat ya?

Caller: Yeah.

Marve: Why'd you let him do that?

Caller: Well, he was the referee too, and that helped him down the stretch.

Marve: Is he a good player?

Caller: Oh, sort of. But he was mostly just lucky. But tomorrow night I'll get him.

Marve: Tomorrow? Do you play every day?

Caller: No, not usually. Just two or three nights a week.

Marve: Sounds like you and your dad spend a lot of time together. Is he a good father?

Caller: Yeah, he's the best.

Marve: The best? What makes you think so?

Caller: I dunno. He's a good man, and he's fun to be around.

Marve: Put your mom back on... Sounds like your husband spends a lot of time with you and the children. Does he ever work?

Caller: Oh, yes. He was just made a vice-president at General Electric. But he's a clock watcher there. He says he works his head off while he's on the job and then hurries home to do the more important things, such as being a husband and a father.

Marve: You mean things at home are more important to him than things at work?

Caller: Well, in a way. He does well at work. But he says that if he left General Electric they'd keep going just fine without him, but if he ever left me and the children, we'd miss him forever. He has a saying behind his desk at work that says, "No other success can compensate for failure in the home." Marve, I've got to go. He's in teasing the children and they're having so much fun I need to get in there and protect them.

Marve: Hey, before you go... Tell him he has been drafted as a candidate for the title of the world's happiest man. Sounds like quite a guy. I wonder if General Electric knows that one of their VPs is a clock watcher who considers his family more important than their big-screen TVs? How would it be to be the family "one-on-one" champ? How would it be to be any kind of champ in your own home and to have your wife feel like she was married to a... Anyway, we've got time for one last call. Hello. You're on.

Caller: Marve, it's Sarah.

Marve: Sarah... You've never called before.

Caller: Marve, please come home.

Marve: I thought that last week we decided... or, uh, you decided that that was it. It wasn't worth it.

Caller: I've been listening. Marve, please come home. The girls and I... we need you. We love you and we need you.

Marve: I, uh, I'll be there in an hour. No, Sarah, make that forty-five minutes... It's news time. This is Marve Levy. We have a winner. The winner is me and every father everywhere.

## Over The River And Through The Woods

One year a terrible thought crept into the minds of our family. Someone proposed that we all go out to a restaurant to eat Thanksgiving dinner. Grandmother Marilyn even jumped on the bandwagon. They had the momentum of a team of runaway horses. It took all the power and ingenuity that I could muster to first slow the idea down and then to finally stop it and turn it around.

Thanksgiving dinner away from home! I couldn't bear the thought. That would mean that the grandchildren and the children couldn't head over the river and through the woods to Grandma's house. It would mean that we wouldn't have Grandma's hot rolls. I've never had one of those rolls melt in my mouth without believing that I was in heaven. It would mean that the turkey dressing would be made by someone who didn't fully understand the sacred nature and the perfect blending of the fine ingredients of that perfect food. It would mean that the gravy would be stirred by hands other than Grandma's masterful hands.

But more than that it would mean that the grandkids couldn't come and see their cousins and the turkey and the three tables that fill two rooms. They couldn't enjoy the combined emotional frenzy caused by the double excitement of both seeing their cousins and looking forward to the delicious meal that would soon follow—the very smell of which could give the family a desire which could send all of them out of their minds. And besides, Thanksgiving food just doesn't taste right if it isn't flavored by the atmosphere of Grandma's house.

If we went out to eat, after dinner we couldn't all push back our chairs and just sit around in a daze and half sleep and half talk. Sure the family could eat at a restaurant and then come over to Grandma's house. But that is like going to a gymnasium when the basketball game is already over.

There is no place at a restaurant where I could sit on a couch and hold the newest little grandchild on my lap and for a moment or two hug him or her in complete security. In a public place, I couldn't find a quiet corner and a special moment to tell each granddaughter and each grandson of my love for him or her and let them know of their unique place in my heart.

But of course this is all easy for me to say. On Thanksgiving Day, I help out by setting up the tables and chairs. But it is Grandma who gets out of bed before dawn to put the turkey in the oven. It is Grandma who does the masterful work involved in creating the dressing and the rolls. Sure the kids bring some items, but the real responsibility is on Grandma.

It would be impossible for me to be Grandpa at Thanksgiving if it weren't for the selfless service of Grandma. I couldn't be Grandpa on any day if it weren't for the caring of Grandma. It is no wonder that everyone loves her in a slightly different and in a little deeper way than they love me. I always rely on Grandma to be the main event. I'm just a wonderful sideshow.

I don't know how long Grandma can keep making my Thanksgiving dreams come true. All I can do is hope that it will go on for another twenty years. I know that the decision to go to one of our children's houses or to a restaurant for Thanksgiving dinner will come someday. But, even then, I'll keep making my appeal to stay at home. It is so much easier to be Grandpa when everybody is in Grandma's house, and the food is on the table, and the whole house is filled with family love.

## Grandpa, Are You Awake?

"Grandpa. Grandpa! Grandpa! Are you awake?"

If I hadn't been, I was now. It was 5:30 in the morning in Houston, Texas, just two days after Christmas.

As I forced open my eyes, I saw my four-year-old grandson, Kolby, standing at my side and studiously staring at me to see if there were any signs of life. Seeing his face through the dimness of the early morning light was like seeing the sun come up, and suddenly I could answer with great enthusiasm, "Yes sirree, Kolby! Your grandpa is wide awake."

"Get up, Grandpa. It's time to play."

Five minutes later I was sitting on the front room floor pushing Thomas the Tank Engine down his wooden track as Kolby, who sat at my side, drew Thomas on his Etch A Sketch. It was for moments like this that I had made the long journey from my home in Provo, Utah, to Kolby's house in Houston, Texas. It was for moments like this that I thanked the Lord for the joy and privilege of being Grandpa.

As I looked at what my grandson was drawing on the Etch A Sketch, I was intrigued by how that little machine worked and I said, "I get to play with the Etch A Sketch next. Okay?"

"Okay, Grandpa. I'll be through in a minute. Then I'll let you have a turn. Right now you just keep pushing Thomas, okay?"

"Okay," I said with a little feeling of impatience.

As I looked at Kolby's excited expression my heart welled up with love for him, and I reached out and pulled him close to me and said, "Grandpa needs a hug from his friend named Kolby."

"Don't hug me right now, Grandpa. You made me make a line that I didn't want to make."

As he pulled away I asked him, "How come I love you so much, Kolby?"

He laughed and said, "I don't know." He then quickly added, "Maybe it is because I let you play with my toys." I smiled and thought to myself, "That is only part of the reason. There is more to it than that. Much more."

But this serious thought was not for now, so I turned and pushed Thomas the Tank Engine down the track past Sir Topham Hatt, the railroad superintendent.

I found myself being glad that Kolby's parents were still sound asleep. We had all been up late the night before, and so they needed their rest. But the greatest reason I was glad was that I could have Kolby all to myself. And that was a bit like being in heaven without dying. The only thing that marred those golden moments was my longing to get hold of the Etch A Sketch. And maybe soon even that would happen.

## I'd Like To Be That Kind Of Grandfather

While I served as president of the Missionary Training Center in Provo, it was my sad responsibility to tell several missionaries of the death of a father or mother. As you would do, I made a fervent appeal to the Lord for his help, for myself and for the grieving young missionary.

Much more often than informing them of the passing of a parent, I told missionaries of the death of a grandparent. I felt that this would be easier. But in that, I was quite wrong.

I recall the first time that I informed a missionary of this sad news. I sat with a young elder in my office to inform him that his grandfather had died. I, of course, had a great concern and was a gentle and considerate as I could be.

I said, "My dear friend, it is my sad duty to tell you that

your grandfather passed away last night."

His reaction, to a slight degree, surprised me. It shouldn't have, and it did not thereafter. But it did this first time. He started to cry. A seemingly endless flow of tears fell from his eyes. I sat in silence, sensing his deep emotional distress. When his gentle sobbing had almost stopped, I softly said, "Tell me about your grandfather."

Wiping the tears away, his eyes brightened as his mind filled with the memories of his living grandfather. A smile came upon his face as he began to speak. He told me of the experiences he had shared with his grandfather. They had spent time fishing and farming and just being together. He told me of how his grandfather had so often affirmed him when he felt discouraged and unimportant. He told me of the faith of his grandfather and of the love that his grandfather and grandmother had for each other. He told me many more sacred things about the relationship that he had with his grandpa.

I asked, "Was the news of the passing of your grandfather a surprise to you? Did you know that he was sick?"

"It was not a surprise," he replied. "Grandpa had been sick for more than a year. I knew that he wouldn't be there when I returned from my mission. Mom and Dad have cared for him in our home for the past two years. He couldn't talk the last several months, but he could listen, and I used to talk to him each day when I'd come home from school or work. He got so he could remember hardly anybody, but I could tell that somehow he could remember me."

With that he began to gently sob again. But then it appeared that a quiet revelation entered his heart, and the tears of this noble elder ceased. A perceptible glow of hope lighted his countenance. He sat up straighter in his chair and said, "At least now Grandpa and Grandma will be together again."

I asked with deep respect, “Do you really believe that?”

“I know that,” he said. “Grandma and Grandpa taught me that.”

After this young missionary left my office, I knelt among the sweet, sacred memories of what I had just heard and felt. I prayed that the Lord would continue to comfort this young grandson of a most noble grandfather. I prayed that I would leave such a legacy as this grandpa had done and that someday my grandson or granddaughter would speak of me as this missionary had spoken of him.

# TEMPLE SCONES

## Father Has Finally Joined the Church

While I was mission president, a member of a large family wrote to me and asked me to teach the father of his family, who lived in the area, the gospel. The letter told me that many years ago all the members of this family had joined the church except the father and the mother.

The conversion to the Church of the family members began when of the sons served in the army. There he met a Mormon and joined the church. He attended BYU. One by one each member of the family came to BYU and while there each joined the Church. Finally they were all members.

The father, who was a preacher for his own church, did not like the Mormons and was embittered when his children all became members.

So I went to see this man. When he learned who I represented, he became enraged and in our conversation, he turned me every way but loose. I could not get a word in edgewise.

The next day, I sadly wrote to the family telling them that I had failed.

Several years later, I saw on of the family on the street in Salt Lake City. He excitedly told me that his father had, just the month before. joined the Church. I was astonished and asked, "How did it happen?"

He replied, "Well he died and I, with my brothers and sisters, went to the temple and I was baptized for him."

I have no doubt but what this man now rejoices in his baptism, ordination to the priesthood, his endowment and sealing to his wife (deceased) and his children. He was a good and honest man. I was happy with this joyful news.

## Why Was Your Name and Address In Our Son's Pocket When He Died In Vietnam?

Early one morning, some thirty years ago, I boarded an airplane in Calgary, Canada. I was tired and wanted to sleep. A marine officer came and although there were many seats available he sat right next to me. He was a large, handsome and very personable fellow. He told me that he was on a speaking tour to the young people who were part of the Navigator organization, the group whose theme is the picture of a young man steering a ship with Christ standing right behind him.

He was fascinated when I informed him that I was a Mormon. As the plane took off he said, "Tell me what your Church can do for me in addition to what I already believe."

I felt the importance of his question. As the plane made its way toward Billings, Montana, I told him of the temple and of eternal marriage. As I spoke and he listened the Spirit of the Lord was with us. He was deeply touched. In that short time, I felt a great love for him and I could tell that he felt the same toward me.

He had a talk to give in Billings. In the last few minutes we had together, I asked him for his address so that I could write to him and I tell him more. He told me that he was headed to Vietnam the next week and that he would write to me and tell me his new address.

We said good-bye. Tears filled his eyes and mine. The time with him had been a sacred experience for both of us.

Several weeks later I received a letter. I opened it and read, "Our son was killed in Vietnam. When he died, he had your name and address on a paper in his shirt pocket."

They wanted to know how I knew him. I wrote them a long letter telling of our experience together.

A week or two later they told me by letter that they did not favor the LDS Church and that they would not like to hear more of the matter.

I had a friend who lived in their state go see them and inquire if I could take his name to the temple. They adamantly said that I could not.

I long to go to the temple for him but without their permission, I cannot.

## They Are Sacred And Are Part Of His Religion

Prior to serving with the Army, I had been through the temple many times, and there was married to a beautiful wife.

Wearing the temple garment was among my most sacred blessings. While serving in Korea I lived where there were very few private facilities for showering or dressing. Thus on many occasions it was necessary for me to dress and undress in an area where people would see the garment.

I always tried to be as little noticed as possible. I would pull the one piece garment on up to my waist and then quickly put on my trousers. Then I would pull the garment on over my shoulders. Many times I was able to do this so that others would not notice that my underwear was any different than theirs. But there were those times when someone would look perplexed and wonder why my underwear was so different.

For several months it was my duty to play basketball for my division. Often as we dressed before or after the game, my teammates would notice the garment. Many times they would sort of laugh and say, "What are those?" I understood the reasons for their sometimes jocular query, and never became upset, but would merely say, "They are part of my religion and when the time is right I'll tell you why I wear them." As time passed, they became a bit more inquisitive, and also as time went by, we became very dear friends.

An appropriate place for the basketball team to live seemed to be in the gymnasium. Therefore, we acquired some lumber and built a small bedroom into one end, just off the playing floor. It wasn't a very large room and we, the twelve players, all slept there on double bunks. Because of the close quarters it was possible in the night, when it was quiet, for one man to talk and all the rest to hear with ease.

One night we were all retiring early because we had a basketball game the next day. As I was getting into bed, one of my fellow teammates said, "George, you have told us many times that you would explain why you wear those underwear." I felt that the time was right. I got into bed and looking up at the ceiling, I began to talk. The subject was intensely interesting to them, and apart from my voice, there was not a sound in the room.

"Have any of you ever seen a Mormon temple?" I asked. Each replied that he had seen a temple at one place or another, and all agreed that these were among the world's most beautiful buildings. "After the temples are dedicated to the Lord, the only people who can go inside are those who are members of The Church of Jesus Christ of Latter-day Saints and who are living according to the commandments of the Lord." I then added, "I have been inside of one of those temples in Salt Lake City, and that has something to do with why I wear these garments.

"You recall that on many occasions when I receive letters from my wife and pictures of my little boy, I go off by myself to look and to read. Thinking of my family brings me greater joy than any other thought. And when I get a letter, it is indeed a choice experience."

Continuing I said, "My family is the dearest thing in the world to me. Several years ago, when I knew I was deeply in love with my wife-to-be, I asked her if she would marry me and she agreed. We went inside the temple at Salt Lake City to be married. While in the temple we made promises that we would keep the commandments of the Lord, and try with all our hearts to build his kingdom upon the earth. In one of the beautiful rooms within the holy temple, my bride and I knelt down and held hands across an altar. There, with our family and friends looking on, we were married by a man of God who had power to seal on earth and in heaven. We were not only married for this life, but forever.

"In a sense what happened there was this. In the temple we made covenants that we would keep our Heavenly Father's commandments and fulfill all the promises we had made that day. We promised to be honest, to serve our fellow men, to be morally clean. In return, the Lord covenanted with us that if we would keep our promises, when we both had gone beyond this life we would be together as husband and wife forever, and our children would be with us through eternity. That moment of our eternal marriage was the most sacred of my life."

Silence filled the room as I paused and then I continued. "Part of what we did in the temple was to be privileged thereafter to wear these holy garments. Now they remind us, every moment of every waking hour, of the promises we made in the temple and the promises the Lord made to us.

"Men, I just can't explain to you how much this temple garment means to me. I am a long way from any Mormon chapel and I am a long way form my family, yet I am very close to everything that is dear to me because of these sacred garments. So you ask, 'Why do I wear them?' Well, I've told you why—it's because I love my family and because I know that if I wear these garments and live true to what they symbolize, I will never be separated from my family. Being in Korea, thousands of miles away from them is almost more than I can bear, and the thought that someday I might not be with them at all would cause me my greatest sorrow."

As I think back on that experience, I don't remember each word that I said, but I shall forever remember that the spirit of the Lord was there and that for a brief few minutes that little bedroom in the gymnasium in Korea became a most holy and sacred spot. Each man's heart had been touched. In concluding I said, "My dear friends, what I have just told you is true. I know that this Church to which I belong, The Church of Jesus Christ of Latter-day Saints, is the Lord's Church. I know that I am married to my beloved wife forever and that our children will be ours eternally."

Then I said no more. It was dark in the room, not much time had gone by until everyone, except me, had closed his eyes in sleep. As I lay there, I silently called upon the Lord and thanked him for blessing me with the privilege of wearing the temple garment and being privileged to explain why.

As time passed, I had to dress and undress again in the presence of others, and again people would ask, "What are those?" and they would laugh a little. But from then on, I never had to make an explanation. When some stranger would ask the question, "What are those?" one or the other of my teammates, who was nearby, would say, "If you knew why he wore those, you wouldn't laugh. They are sacred and are part of his religion." And when they would say that, I would silently express my deep gratitude to the Lord.

I don't know what happened to all of those men. I lost track of them one by one. But I know this. They, along with me, once had a very sacred experience in a land far, far away.

# GOSPEL LIVING SCONES

## Helping Your Mom Always Pays Off

My father raised chickens and we sold the eggs. That's how we made a living. Because cracked eggs didn't sell, my mother would use them in her cooking.

One day she said in dismay, "Oh, I wish I could make a cake; but there aren't any cracked eggs, so I guess I can't."

My older brother thought for just a moment, picked up two whole eggs, banged them lightly together, and handed her the cracked eggs. "There, Mother," he said, "I've solved your problem. Go ahead now and make the cake."

Mother was speechless for a second or two, but then she smiled; and soon there was a cake. When you do things for your parents, it seems that the result is always a cake of one type or another.

## A Walk Along The River With My Little Dog

I'll sometimes say to Marilyn, "I'm going for a walk." I'll shout at my little dog, Skoshie, "Side!" "Side" is dog talk for "Let's go outside and go for a walk." Skoshie will bark with uncontainable joy and run quickly to the door, wagging her tail behind her.

We will drive to the Provo River, park our car under a big tree, open the door, get out, and head down the river. Skoshie will run all four directions at once. I will stride along the path that follows the riverbank. My thoughts will run back and forth through my mind in the same exciting motion that Skoshie's legs will take her small body.

I will see others running along the path. Some of them will have electronic radios or tape players that plug sound into their ears. I'm sure that they enjoy that. But for me, the only sound that I desire to hear is the sound of my own thoughts. I haven't counted, but it seems to me that I can think of at least seventeen hundred wonderful things in one walk along the river.

My thinking may be a little foggy and sometimes negative as I begin my journey, but by the time I cross the river bridge and arrive at the duck pond, things will begin to clear up. Skoshie used to bark at the ducks. But one day when she did that, I told her in a harsh voice, "Skoshie, if you ever bark at those ducks again, I'll never bring you on another walk." She understands that kind of straight talk, and that was the last time she ever barked at the ducks.

I won't bring enough bread to feed all those dear water fowl. Other people do that. I just bring enough for one special duck. He can't see. Even though he knows the bread is there, his most frantic effort seldom brings him success. I go over by him and drop some right in front of him so that he gets two or three pieces before the others get all the rest. Skoshie cocks her head and seems happy at the blind duck's success.

Then we will walk over to the grove of trees in the primitive part of the park. There is a little stream there which curls its way around the grass and bushes. Skoshie likes this part of our walk the best. She runs all about trying to frighten the gray birds from the bushes to the highest limbs of the tallest trees. I stand close to the tree that seems to be the father of that little forest. There I think and pray and ponder. Thinking seems to go a lot better for me when it is mixed with prayer. I don't kneel down, because other people wandering along the path might think such an act a bit beyond normal. I don't even speak out loud. I just think my prayers. Heavenly Father has good ears and he seems to hear my every word. I silently speak of people I love, the hopes that I have, and my motives that need some adjusting. I feel so much of both heaven and earth as I stand there with my mind wandering in and out of my dreams.

Both Skoshie and I hate to leave our humble little forest to start back to the car, but time finally insists that we move on. Sometimes as we walk along, if no one is there, I sing. The sound of the river currents provides the accompaniment, and I seem to sound real good. At least, Skoshie never complains.

Finally, we are in the car. As I turn the key to start the motor, I say to my dear little friend, "Skoshie, was that fun?" She wags her tail vigorously, comes from her side of the car to mine, and licks my hand, which is her way of saying, "It was our best walk so far."

## A Counter Attack On Bad Language

While in the army barracks, I heard many filthy things. Such talk disgusted me. But I didn't feel I could allow others to make me disgusted all the time. I don't really enjoy being disgusted. I find that being disgusted all of the time is disgusting. I had to live in the barracks, unless I wanted to sleep outside.

So I'd counterattack their filth with my corny humor. I'd say such things as, "I was raised on a farm where we had chickens and we sold eggs for a living. I used to have to work around those chickens, and that is where I first learned to dislike 'foul' language." About the chickens, I added, "I didn't like their yokes at all. It seemed that they were always egging me on." And to get even more corny, I'd say, "I had a pig on that farm. We called him Ball Point. That wasn't his real name but it was his pen name. He got lonely and we couldn't afford another pig, so I drew a big picture of a pig and put it in his pen. It wasn't a real pig, but it was a good paper mate."

I could go on and tell you more of what I told those guys, but I'll spare you the rest. Anyway, such stories seemed to overpower their vulgarity—at least in part. I'd kid them along, and in so doing I could talk them into cleaning things up a little. Gradually things changed. I came to have a deep love for those men and I believe they felt the same toward me. But it was humor and not disgust that provided the oil to make things run more smoothly.

## Unlock Your Heart And Follow Your Feelings

When I was a senior at American Fork High School, I knew a girl. She was a most beautiful girl. But although she had been my classmate for twelve years, I cannot now nor could I then really describe what she looked like. What made her so beautiful was not the way she appeared, but who she was. To me, she was like a vision: whenever I saw her or even considered her in my heart, I was lifted far above my ordinary thoughts and feelings.

In those days my outward behavior was governed by the deflated role that I had cast for myself many years before. But she always caused me to see myself not as I was but, almost mysteriously, as how I knew that I could somehow be.

In my most inward, never-disclosed thoughts and feelings, I found great satisfaction in knowing that this outgoing, achieving, dynamic, respected, beautiful person was my girlfriend. Of course, she didn't know she was my girlfriend, because I never really announced it to her. And I surely didn't want to give my friends the kind of laugh they would have were

I to tell them that she was mine. So it remained my most edifying secret.

But now, during the cold winter months of my senior year, my soul was being stirred by deep-down and very small ideas that I was not to remain a dud. Occasionally, my personality would be nudged to do something slightly delightful. She seemed to notice these rare manifestations of the real me. Perhaps that is what prompted her to use her position as an editor for the mimeographed, two-page school paper to send an almost secret message to me. As I recall, it said, “What girl who works on this paper would like to ride on George’s sleigh at the annual senior sleigh ride?”

The school papers were passed out during Mr. Hap Holmstead’s first-hour American Problems class. Three of my friends, reading this exciting edition, got to the secret passage first. Whispering back and forth, they made such a disturbance that Hap told them to keep it down. But by then, I saw what they’d seen. I was quite pleased. A minute or so later when the girl behind me told me that she knew who the secret girl was, I didn’t have the courage to ask for further details. But even though I didn’t ask, she couldn’t withhold the information and whispered the name.

I couldn’t believe it. All my dreams suddenly came true. My heart pounded and I thought it would explode. Over and over again I thought, “This is my best day so far!”

Later in the day I saw her. It took some real courage to ask her, something that in social matters I had in short supply. But encouraged by some of her friends, who assured me that my request would not be rebuffed, I ventured.

“Oh, yes,” she replied. “I’d love to.”

“Wow!” I thought. “Wow!”

My sleek sleigh was just two years old, and it was quite long. I got it out of the shanty that was attached to our house and polished up the runners.

Finally, the night that promised to be my "night of nights" arrived. We seniors were all to meet at the high school. I'd agreed to meet her there because the school was halfway between her house and mine. I was a little late getting there because I'd had a hard time finding my mittens. As I walked up carrying the sleigh, she broke loose from a bunch of classmates and walked toward me.

When she was just a yard or so away, she melted my heart by saying, "Hi, George."

Soon we were in the big truck that was to transport us up American Fork Canyon. It was crowded because we had a lot of seniors in our class. That, plus the sleighs, made for a full load, so naturally I was sitting quite close to her. I liked that but at the same time it made me nervous. I wasn't good at talking to girls, and especially not to her.

I was glad when we got up past the cave camp and were near the ranger station. As soon as the truck ground to a halt, everybody clamored to get out and start the exciting journey down the ice-covered canyon road.

I carried the sleigh and laid it gently down. I didn't exactly know how to sleigh ride with a girl on the sleigh. As I stood there thinking, she said, "Get on and I'll ride behind." So I did, and she did, and we were off. I hoped maybe the journey would take three or four weeks.

We had only gone about twenty-five yards and were just picking up a little speed when suddenly, for some unknown reason, we were sliding down the ice on our sides, then on our backs, and then head over heels. Finally we slid to a stop. "Oh," I said apologetically, "I'm sure sorry." She was gracious but did admit that she felt a bit of pain in her knee.

I helped her to her feet, and we cautiously recovered the sleigh which had crashed upside down into a snow drift at the edge of the road. I soon discovered that one of the runners had snapped—and with it, my dream was also broken.

Disappointed, we silently carried the sleigh back to the truck. The driver was in the cab. There were two senior girls in the back. They were sitting on the straw and were covered by blankets to stay warm. We joined them.

She and I sort of sat close again to stay warm. As we did so, I felt a bit less sorry that the sleigh had failed. The two girls asked me what I was going to do after high school. I replied, "I think I'll be a movie actor like Gary Cooper." They laughed and so did she. I sort of relaxed, and somehow the conversation turned more serious. I was doing most of the talking, which was highly unusual for me, and they were all listening. It seemed as if they were hanging on my every word—especially the one sitting close to me.

I'd never talked like that before. Even though I'd felt like it, I'd always kept such tender feelings inside. Now I was saying how I felt deep in my heart. I was saying things with sincerity and with no desire to be clever.

I told them about my mother and my family, about how I felt about the Church and how I felt we ought to treat other people. Sometimes, I'd amaze myself with what I was saying. If I paused at all, they'd ask me questions. I watched the way she would listen and the way she'd look at me. I could tell the other two girls were sort of wishing that they had asked to be on my sleigh.

I wish I could tell you all that I said that night, but of course I can't really recall every word. But I'll never forget how I felt. I felt refreshed, as you do when you tell someone whom you love how you feel about the things that you love.

For the first time in my grown-up years I was me—the me that she brought out in me. All too soon the driver started up the truck. A few minutes later we were grinding down the canyon in low gear to pick up the successful sleigh riders. They had had quite a thrill coming down that old canyon at breakneck speed. But I had had the greatest thrill of all. I had unlocked a door to a room in my heart that had been locked too long and that could never be fully closed again.

## I Think That You Are The Nicest Boy In The Class

It was in the early afternoon, just before we were scheduled to rehearse how we'd march in for graduation, that I saw her standing with three of her friends under the giant weeping willow tree that shaded the lawn in front of dear old American Fork High.

She smiled, and that gave me the courage to ask her if she'd write in my book. I was astonished when she replied, "I sure would, if you'd let me take it someplace where I could be alone."

"You can do that," I said.

She took it and held it close to her and walked back into the school. I didn't know whether to sit down or go for a walk or shout or what.

Finally, in about half an hour, she came back and handed me the book. I thanked her and she replied, "I hope you don't mind my taking up a whole page."

"No, it's okay," I replied with syllables of pure sincerity.

As time went on that day, I had plenty of chances to read what she'd written. But each time there were people around. And I just couldn't read something that sacred without being completely alone. Besides, the longer I waited to see what it said, the longer I could dream about what it might say.

But now the time had come. I was alone and could take a moment to read. Again I read, "Dear George." That was the first time she'd ever called me "Dear George." I read on. "I think that you are the nicest boy in the senior class." I'll have to admit I was a little disappointed that the first thing she'd mentioned about me was that she thought that I was nice. I had hoped that other things about me stood out more than my niceness.

I had sort of hoped she would write, "Dear George, You are the most athletic boy in the senior class," or "You are the most popular boy in the senior class," or "You are the most handsome boy in the senior class." Of course, such words would have been stretching the truth a bit. But in a yearbook inscription, that's not the world's greatest sin.

Even calling me the nicest boy in the class didn't do justice to Clifford Laycock and Val Stoors and at least twenty others. But, of course, in her defense she didn't say I was the nicest. Instead, she had just stated that as her opinion.

I guess having her list being nice as my leading quality was only disappointing because being nice had never been even on my top ten list of qualities I wanted to be noticed for. It wasn't even as high as being studious.

If she had really picked out something about me that would have pleased me to perfection she would have written, "I think that you are the toughest boy in the senior class." That would have correlated with what I wanted to be.

All my life I'd wanted to be tough. Oh, I didn't want to be tough enough to get in fights. A guy can get hurt by being that tough. I just wanted to be tough enough that my classmates would say, "There is old George. He sure is tough."

"Of course, she doesn't know what tough is," I reasoned. She specializes more in what nice is. And if she said I was nice, then that was okay.

The message on the rest of her magnificent page went on to tell me what she thought a nice guy like me ought to do in life. She listed some things like college, a mission, and other things I'd not considered doing.

That was all right, but I was looking for a line or two of love. When I came to the last word, I was inspired but disappointed. So I read "Dear George" three more times and then closed the book on the entire matter.

Now, after high school has drifted back into the past, being called nice sounds good. Come to think of it, I believe the greatest thing she could have said to me on that long ago day in May was "Dear George, I think you are the nicest boy in the senior class."

## Don't Blame The Ref

I often think of Christ and what he would do at ball games. As I was thinking about that one day, I imagined in my mind the following: Nazareth was playing Capernaum. Both teams were undefeated in league play. Peter had a son playing for Nazareth and invited Christ to come with him to the game. They sat together. Jesus wanted Nazareth to win because he knew all of those boys better than he knew the boys from Capernaum. The game came down to the last seconds and was tied. Then Capernaum's star was fouled and he went to the line and hit the first of a one-and-one, but missed the second. There were only seconds now to go as he missed the second shot.

Peter's boy had played spectacularly. They worked the ball around and just with a couple of seconds to go it came into his hands. He faked right and went left, and took a jump shot. It appeared to be right on target, but it hit just to the left of center and rattled back and forth and hit against the backboard, came back and hung on the rim and then fell off. By the time the ball fell from the rim, the game was over. Jesus could have goal-tended by putting the ball back on course when the shot was in the air. Nobody would have ever known, but he didn't. He let the ball go where it was shot. After the game as they walked out, Peter said, "The referees did it again. They stole the game from us again."

Jesus replied, "Oh come on Peter, don't blame he referee. You just need to feed your boy more fish."

The next day Jesus would have come to see Peter to talk about Church business. Then he would have said, "Where is your son?"

Peter might have said, "He's in the back studying. He has some final tests coming up."

Jesus said, "Could you ask him to come out and see me a minute?" Peter's son scarcely could look up because of his sorrow at losing the game. Christ would have put his hand on the young man's shoulder and said, "I was sorry about you losing the game last night, but you sure did play well. I was so proud of you and I love you very much. How are you doing in getting ready for your mission?"

Peter's son would have looked up into the Savior's eyes and said, "I'm getting ready."

Christ would have said, "I love you, my son. God bless you."

That's just a story I made up. I often think of the Savior and what he would do.

## I've Never Felt Such A Strong Desire To Go To Church

When I first arrived in Korea after joining the army, I felt alone, even though I had friends in my new barracks. I arrived there on a Tuesday and I felt as though my very life depended upon being able to attend church on the coming Sunday. I inquired of the Protestant chaplain, on Wednesday, as to where the LDS folks met for Sunday services. He said that as far as he knew there was no such church in the area. But he kindly told me that I was most welcome to attend his Sunday services.

On Thursday I visited all the other barracks in our battalion seeking other members. But my search was unsuccessful. I felt desperate.

On Friday I learned that there was a fellow from Utah in a camp just three miles distant. That evening I walked to his camp, and after an hour's search I was able to find him. I was so thrilled to have finally found a fellow member.

The two of us talked of Utah and sports and other matters. Then I asked him where he went to church on Sundays. He looked down as he told me that he did not go to church. I asked him if he would join with me so that the two of us could have a simple Sunday service. He told me he would rather not do that. Try as I would, I could not change his mind. He had, for the time, departed from the faith. I walked back to my barracks with my shoulders slumped in deep disappointment.

When I arrived back at the barracks I was elated to see a note someone had left on my bed that said there was an LDS fellow down at the "I Corps" base, which was just six miles away. The note had his name and a phone number where he could be reached. The next day I called him, and to my joy he said he too wanted to go to church. We decided to meet at a camp that was halfway between us.

It was a beautiful Sunday morning when we each made our way to the small Quonset-hut chapel that served the religious needs of all who desired to come there. When I arrived, the Catholics were holding services. I stood on the sunny side of the chapel and waited. Soon I saw a stocky fellow huffing and puffing his way towards me. Somehow I could tell that this man was my brother in the faith. Soon we stood face to face, and as we met I felt as though I had come home. We were instant friends.

Following the Catholic services we made our way to the

chaplain's office. We told him we wanted to have church each Sunday. He said, "You sure can. The Catholics meet at nine-thirty and the Protestants meet at eleven. You would be welcome at either." We told him we were not of either of those two faiths. He asked what we were, and we told him we were members of The Church of Jesus Christ of Latter-day Saints. He asked how many of us there were, and we said there were two. He looked at us as if we were a little odd, and we looked at each other and knew he was right. He told us we could hold church anytime we desired on Sunday afternoon, as the chapel was free at that time.

We had services every Sunday thereafter. It was a wonderful church. All of our members sat right up front. There was no backbiting in our congregation. Every other week, one or the two of us got to give a talk. Each week each one of us offered either the opening or closing prayer. We also blessed and passed the sacrament. And we each knew that if either of us did not come, none of these things could happen. So we never missed.

## Justice Is Not Always Easy, But It Is Always Right

The American Fork National Guard team I was on had won four straight softball games and now was poised to play for "all the marbles." I'd never played for a championship before, so naturally I was pretty keyed up about it.

The games thus far had been played in the early evening, but the finals were scheduled for Saturday afternoon. Just prior to the time when we were scheduled to take the field, one of our battalion officers advised me I was assigned to pick up the food rations for Sunday. I told him that I'd attend to it right after the game. He replied, "That won't do. It will be too late."

I answered that I'd get the supply clerk to take care of it.

He replied, "No, as the supply sergeant you must be there personally."

I said, "Come on, Captain. You know about the game. We've played hard to get to the finals, and I need to be at first base. The team is counting on me and I want to be there."

"I know that, Sergeant Durrant, but the men have to eat and that is a lot more important than any ball game. So you be there."

Of course, I was beside myself with disappointment. I didn't know what to do. I felt that I had to follow the order, but the game—I just couldn't miss the game. Besides, the supply clerk would be happy to get the rations. And maybe the game would be over in time so that I could get them myself. It just didn't seem necessary for me to miss the big game.

I mentioned the dilemma to some of my teammates, who said, "Hey, he knew about the game. He could have easily worked things out. Let your clerk do it. He can."

The appeal of the game was too great. I was there. I played well and we won. After the game I checked with the clerk, and to my relief I found out that he had obtained the rations. So all was well.

Monday morning I received word that the captain wanted to see me. I walked to his office with no fear because it seemed to me that the matter had concluded with no harm being done.

He greeted me in a most amiable manner and put me at ease. Then, as he looked me in the eye, he said, "Sergeant Durrant, I was very disappointed in you Saturday. You've always come through for me and I've been one of your greatest supporters, but Saturday you disregarded my order."

"Sure," I replied, "but I worked things—"

"Don't interrupt," he said sternly. "I'm not interested in excuses. I know we got the supplies, but that was because the camp supply officer called and said the supply clerk, and not the sergeant, was there. I told him to let the clerk have the rations. He did it, but it made me look foolish."

After a long pause, he said, "What do you think we ought to do about this? We can't just let it go, you know."

I felt that he was making a big issue over a little thing, but I didn't feel that I should tell him what I thought.

As I was thinking, he said, "I've decided to give you a choice. First, you can write and submit to me an official apology, or you can be reduced in rank to private."

I couldn't believe that he would reduce my rank. There wasn't a man at summer camp who had worked harder than me. I felt irritated.

"I'm sure the written apology would be the way to go," he said softly. "Get it done tonight and submit it to me tomorrow morning. Will that be all right?"

I sat in silence. I just didn't feel that I could apologize.

"Well?" he said in a questioning tone.

"Sir," I replied, "you knew about the ball game, and you knew that with your help the clerk could get the rations. Why are you making such a big deal out of this?"

"It's always a big deal when orders are disobeyed."

"I know that, but in this case it just doesn't make sense, and I can't feel good about apologizing. I can't do it, sir. I just can't."

He looked at me and I returned his stare. After a few seconds, he said, "You leave me no choice. I'll start the proceedings for you to be reduced in rank." Then he smiled and added, "I was thinking of reducing you to private. But instead"—he paused and my hopes soared—"because you are a first-class fellow, I'm going to reduce you to private first class."

With that he laughed and stood up. He came around the desk and shook my hand. As he did so he said, "I like you,

Durrant. I like you more than you'll ever know." I could see his eyes moisten as he looked into mine.

"I like you too, Captain."

As I departed I could not remember all that had happened. All I could remember was the look on his face—the hurt look. I sensed that the pain he felt was not because I had disobeyed the order but rather because he had had to punish me.

That night I walked out under the stars that shone down on Camp W. G. Williams. I wondered if it was too late to apologize, but then I thought, "No, I still don't feel like I should do that." Besides, maybe the captain had done the fairest thing after all. I still had a lot to sort out about that experience. Only time would help me to fully understand all that had happened. But somehow I sensed that the captain, with his kind, love-filled justice, had done the right thing.

## I Could Tell That She Had Mercy

I remember once when I was teaching at Brigham Young University and I taught a class in a rather small room. It was a very popular time of day and it was a Book of Mormon class. All the freshmen needed to take it and a lot of them wanted to get it at that hour. Many came to the class and they were sitting in front on the floor and on the isles on window sills and standing in the back. I thought as time went on a percentage of them would be sick each day and we would have enough seats. Therefore, I signed all their add cards, which was a very foolish thing to do.

The problem was that but few of them ever missed the class and they were sitting all over. I tried to get a larger room but at that hour that was not possible.

I remember going over there once after the teaching

hours and kneeling down in the room and praying that somehow it could expand itself and accommodate all the students. But the room didn't change size. But there was a great miracle just around the corner.

As time went by the students did not liking to sit on the floor. They noticed that a sewing room across the hall was not used that hour. So they brought chairs across from there and put them in our classroom. I told them they were not supposed to do that but they did it anyway.

One day I went to my office and there was a note to call the lady teacher who was the proprietor of the sewing room. I have always been afraid of women. I hardly dare go in a hospital for fear a nurse will tell me I'm walking the wrong direction or something. So I became petrified to call this woman. I knelt in my little office and said, "I've got to call her and I know what she's going to say. I don't know how to deal with it. Please help me."

Then with a trembling finger I dialed the number. Soon she answered, "Hello."

The way that she said hello caused me to be less frightened because I could tell from the tone of this one word that she was a merciful woman.

I said, "I'm George Durrant."

She said, "Oh are you?"

And I said, "Yes."

She said, "Your students are taking chairs out of my room."

I replied, "Yes they are."

Then she said, "They're not supposed to do that."

I answered, "I know."

She said warmly, "You know, Brother Durrant, you must be quite a teacher to have so many students. Would you do something for me? I want those students to be in your class.

But would you tell them to try to put the chairs back exactly where they got them from."

I couldn't talk to her anymore. I just kind of clumsily hung up. I saw her in a dinner line not too long after that and I watched her in awe. She could have justifiably pounded me into the earth. And yet she had the great spiritual gift to be merciful and to forgive me. She had every right to make a big deal over this matter, but she was somebody who was willing to overlook my blunder.

## You Don't Have To Be A Starter To Be A Star

During my senior year in high school, my dream of being a starter for the American Fork Cavemen had long since eroded away. It seemed that the coach liked me best. So during the games he had me sit on the bench near him. In my heart I always felt that the time would come when I'd be needed in the game. Finally destiny beckoned and I was ready.

One Friday night American Fork was playing Brigham Young High School. It was a crucial game—perhaps the most important game in all recorded history. Our main center, LeRoy Griffin, was called for three fouls in the first half. His fourth came at the beginning of the second half. I'm sure the coach considered taking Griff out to save him for the final minutes. Then he looked down the bench at me and decided the only hope was to keep old Griff in there. Three minutes later he was whistled for his fifth foul. Now came one of those long time outs designed to allow the coach time to figure out what to do. Again he looked down the bench at me. He looked away, then in apparent anguish he looked back at me again and said, "George, get your sweat suit off." I did. My time had come. The game was tied. American Fork was playing well. Up until this terrible moment it looked as if we at least had a remote possibility of beating this top-rated group of superstars. But now without Griff it appeared that all was lost.

My cousin Boyd Durrant was a policeman, and he could go anywhere in the gym that he wanted. He came down, touched me on the shoulder, and said, "George, don't go out there and embarrass our family. You get out there and you play."

Knowing that I was needed, I played better than I had ever played. I jumped high and I gathered in rebounds. I did all that I needed to do. The game went back and forth, back and forth. In the last quarter the lead must have changed hands five or six times. Finally we were down to the last minute. The game was tied. I hadn't scored any points, but I had defended and rebounded and passed without error. With thirty seconds to go I was fouled. There wasn't any one-and-one rule back then—I just had one shot. With the score tied and thirty seconds to go, I stood up to the line. Usually I had stage fright when I was playing, but I didn't now. I had to make it. The fate of all mankind was in my hands. The referee gave me the ball: I took a deep breath, and shot it. It was in! Now if we could just hold on.

We came down the floor, and Harold Christenson, the best to ever play for B.Y. High, got the ball and scored. We were down by one point with only ten seconds to go. We brought the ball across midcourt. Max Smith passed it to old Spud Stiener. Spud was left-handed and wasn't known for his great accuracy as a long-range shooter, or even a short one for that matter. But time was about to run out so he had to fire it up.

The shot was at an angle out on the side. I was right under the basket, and I watched the ball fly towards its target. It was off course just a little. That caused it to kiss the backboard enough to put it on course. It swished through the net and dropped sweetly into my hands. The game was over. I'll always remember the coach coming out and taking me into his arms. Together we cried tears of joy. I had only made one point that night, but we won the game by that one point. I was needed. I was a sub but I was needed.

## Giving Is Best, But Receiving Is Pretty Good Too

While I was in the army, I was stationed in Texas and then was transferred to Arkansas. As part of this transfer, I was supposed to go home on leave. But I suddenly learned that I didn't get to go home. I arrived in Arkansas very discouraged and went to the army camp. Immediately upon arriving there I threw my duffel bag down inside the barracks. Somebody said, "Durrant, you're supposed to report down to the kitchen to do KP."

I spent the entire afternoon and evening preparing and serving the dinner, and after the dinner I was assigned to clean up the stoves and the pots and pans. It takes a long time to do that. By the time I finished it was after ten p.m. and it was pitch dark. When I returned to the barracks the lights were out and everyone was in bed. I had no place to sleep. I stood in the doorway I was as discouraged as I'd ever been. I entered the barracks and kind of stumbled around a minute. I heard a voice and the voice said, "Durrant." I went in the direction of the voice to a fellow who was lying on the lower bunk. He said, "That bunk up above mine is yours." He said, "I knew you wouldn't have time to get any bedding. So I got it for you. I made your bed and there it is."

I climbed into bed without kneeling down to pray. You don't always have to kneel down to pray. I was lying there in the bed looking up and suddenly I wasn't discouraged anymore.

The whole world had changed from a lonely hard world to a warm and loving place. I was about as happy as I'd ever been. Down below me was the man who had made it so. I don't think he was as happy as I was. He had served me and there is joy in service, but I don't believe his service brought him as many inward blessings as he had brought to me. I could hardly hold back the tears as I was lying there on my bed thanking God for the beautiful world and all the opportunities and joys of being alive.

The man's name who did that was Riggens. I can't remember anybody else's name in the barracks, but I'll never forget Riggens because he helped me when I couldn't help myself. And what joy that brought to me.

## The Girls Couldn't Tell Whether I Was Coming Or Going

When I was a junior in high school, I wanted to be rich. I wanted to have a car. I knew if I had a car I'd be popular. I found out by growing celery you can make a lot of money. I told a farmer that I'd grow the celery if he'd buy everything and I'd do all the labor. At the end of the harvest we'd split the profits. At the beginning of the summer it looked like I would make a enough money to buy a new car. While I hoed the celery, I drove my car in my mind. While I weeded the celery, I drove my car. I never was hot or uncomfortable in that summer sun because I was always dreaming of my car. I remember once as I was hoeing away I could see myself in that car. The car I had decided to buy was a 1949 Studebaker. That car that year was the most beautiful car ever made. It was a car designed so that you could not tell the front from the back.

As I labored in the celery field in the hot sun I could see myself in my dream driving that car and I was going down Center Street in American Fork. Some girls on the sidewalk seeing me drive by were talking. One said, "There goes old George."

One of the others said, "How do you know he's going? He might be coming. You can't tell in a Studebaker."

Just as harvest time came the bottom dropped out of the price of celery and I only made enough to buy a bike. But all summer in my dream I was always coming (or was I going?) in my Studebaker.

## Family Histories Are The Most Important Histories

The great histories have been written. It's now time to write the histories of the heart—the histories of the simple folk. Histories that have occurred not on the battlefront or in Parliament but histories that have taken place within the walls of our own homes. Histories which when written would make kings say, "I wish I could have lived that way." These histories will form a seed bed in which all other histories grow.

A birth certificate proves that you were born. A personal history proves that you lived—you really lived.

A pedigree chart proves your ancestors were born. A family history proves that they lived and because of them you can live.

## Talking To A Beautiful Bush

It was in the fall of the year as I was walking off from the hill of BYU campus. I saw a bush that had been turned from green to red by the fall frost. It's bright, fiery glow made it almost like a bush that was burning and not being consumed. As I walked by, I noticed it and I loved it. After having gone several paces beyond it, I felt impressed to stop and return. I starred at the beauty of this wonderful bush and then seeing that no one else was around to think me strange, I said, "Thank you for being so beautiful." My soul tingled as I felt the deep appreciation of the bush. Then I walked on home knowing again through small experiences that God lives and cares.

## God Answers Prayers In His Own Way

I've often prayed in my desperation for the help in a solving a difficult problem and all the Lord has told me is simply, "Get up and get going." Once as a mission president I was feeling the pains of failure as one missionary had returned home and another was emotionally ill and deeply troubled. It was late at night and I didn't know who to turn to for an answer. I went outside the mission home and knelt under a big tree and poured my heart out to God. I was desperate for answers. And the answer came in a single sentence, "George, go in and go to bed. You are tired." I did so. The next day the solutions came.

## I Would Have Missed So Much If God Had Answered My Prayers In The Way I Desired

I used to sit on the bench during the basketball games because the coach liked me the best and liked to keep me near him. It's all right to be on the bench if you're just full of confidence. You can say to yourself, "Even though I'm sitting on the bench in basketball, I play the trumpet in the band and I'm popular with the girls and all that." But I didn't play the trumpet in the band and I wasn't popular with all the girls. That left a mark on me and it caused me to know a couple of things. It caused me to know how people feel who sit on the sidelines when they want to be in the middle of things. It caused me to know how people feel who don't get elected student body president, who don't get to be cheerleaders, and all those kind of things.

If God had answered my prayers, I'd have been a lot different chap than I am. First of all, I would have been very popular with the girls and I'd have been student body president. I would have made all-state in basketball. Then I'd have starred in college. Then I'd have turned pro. Then the movie makers would have seen me and I'd have become a movie star. If all that had happened I would have never become me and I'd have never known how others felt who struggle.

## Heavenly Father Doesn't Care Who Wins The Game, But He Cares About The Players

When we lived in Kentucky, my son played junior varsity basketball. Most of the crowd who attended one game were Baptists, and they were almost all cheering for my son's opponents. The game ended in a tie. The first overtime also ended in a tie. By this time most of the fans were in a bit of a frenzy. The second overtime came down to its final agonizing seconds and still the score was tied. With just two seconds to go, my son got the ball and shot. The shot missed, but the whistle blew—he had been fouled.

As he went to the foul line to shoot the deciding shot the opposing coach called time out. In the few seconds of the time out I had time to pull myself together and to do some nearly logical thinking. I decided to pray, and then I thought, "But the Lord doesn't care whether or not he makes it, nor does he care who wins. Besides," I thought, "all the Baptists in here are praying that he'll miss, and it's hard to outpray a Baptist."

So I decided I wouldn't pray about it. The whistle blew and the boys took their places for the foul shot. My son stepped to the foul line. My heart pounded. As the referee handed him the ball, I lost control of my rational reasoning and found myself silently begging the Lord, "Please let him make it! Please!" Sometimes we get to the point that we don't know what else we can do but pray.

The shot went up and in. The other team quickly took the ball and threw it in bounds, but the game was over. I came down out of the stands and hugged my son. He didn't even seem embarrassed.

I'm still quite sure that in most cases the Lord doesn't care who wins a ball game. He knows that we learn lessons in both victory and defeat. But I do know that he does care about many things—he cares very much.

## What Is Winning Anyway?

A little league team manager in Huntsville, Utah told his friend that he had a boy on his team who had never played any kind of sport. He had no idea of the fundamentals of the game. He knew so little that when the game ended he didn't even know who had won.

He excitedly came to the manager and eagerly asked, "Did we win? Did we win?"

The manager, who had been a little disappointed at the final score, looked into the enthusiastic face of the new recruit and asked, "Did you get to play?"

The boy replied, "I sure did."

The manager asked, "Did you have fun?"

Again the boy shouted, "I really had fun."

The manager put his hand on the boy's shoulder and said, "Then I guess we won."

## When You Find Another Member Of The Church You Feel At Home

The assistants and I were driving north toward Nashville after having spent two days in Chattanooga. A carload of young men came up behind us rather rapidly and pulled alongside us. They looked over at us. We were dressed in our white shirts and ties. They were dressed differently. We thought at first that they were determined to cause us some trouble. But then they held up a book for us to see. We read the title *Mormon Doctrine*. Excitement filled both cars as we realized the great kinship that exists among Mormons.

Oh, it's great to be a Mormon! I don't believe any club or any group or any religion binds people together like our glorious Church. Go into a community as a stranger, meet another Mormon, and it's almost as if you're home again.

## My Little Girl's Prayers Made It, So I Was Not Scared Anymore

My family traveling in Yellowstone park had seen several bears during the day. That evening as we rented a little one-room log cabin surrounded by the dark forest. One small electric bulb dangled from the ceiling and gave but a dim light. I could tell that our children were a bit fearful. After preparing for bed I asked our five year old daughter, Kathryn to lead us in our evening prayer.

With deep sincerity in her voice she softly said, "Heavenly Father, bless the doors and bless the windows. Help them stay closed real tight so that no bears can get in. In the name of Jesus Christ. Amen."

When she finished I held her close to me because now I was no longer afraid.

## Flying In Makes You More Credible

I was walking this morning thinking about a talk I had to give to large group of people. As I walked I saw a group of policemen with their sirens on leading a car into town from the airport. And I thought, "Gee! If that was me in that car, I'll bet when I arrive the people would really listen to me." It gives a speaker more credibility if he or she flies in from out of town.

When I was made a Regional Representative, I hoped that I would be assigned somewhere where I could fly in. I was living in Provo and they assigned me to Orem. So the people weren't too impressed when I got off my bicycle and came into conference.

## We Did Not Know Our Brother Was That Smart

I've never seen my son Dwight happier than he was at a certain family home evening. He was five years old at the time, and a bit rowdy as I talked to the family. I was upset with him and said in a somewhat harsh voice, "Dwight! Come over here by me."

I believe he sensed that he might be in trouble. As he came closer I felt a bit of inspiration. "Dwight," I said, "you are a pretty smart boy so I've something for you to do. It will be hard, but I believe you can do it."

I then continued as all the family listened intently. "White Crow (that is what we call Dwight), I'm going to ask you to do some difficult things. I want you to go up those stairs. Go in my bedroom. Open the drawer where I keep my stockings. Get a pair of the stockings. Put them on the bed. Close the drawer. Go in the upstairs bathroom. Turn on the cold water.

Turn it off. Come down the stairs. Go in the kitchen. Get a drink of water. Turn off the water. Come back in this room. Go up three stairs and back down. Come into this room and go around that chair right there. Then come over in front of me and say, 'Dad, I did it.'"

White Crow's eyes were opened wide with excitement as I asked, "Can you do it?"

Before he could answer, his older brothers and sisters tried to help by saying, "Dad, White Crow can't do all that."

His expression indicated a feeling of excited confidence and I said, "Take off."

The house was silent except for the sounds made by little White Crow. We heard his footsteps go up the stairs. The drawer was opened and closed. Then into the bathroom. The water on, then off. Down the stairs, past where we sat as he rushed into the kitchen, the water on, and then off. Back into the room and up three stairs and back down. Around the chair. And then, with his mission completed, he stood in front of me. He caught his breath and proudly announced, "Dad, I did it."

His brothers and sisters were amazed and said, "Wow! White Crow, we didn't know you were that smart."

I asked him to come over to my side. I put my arm around his shoulders and pulled him close to me. I then said, "White Crow, you are really something. I'm proud of you. I'm so glad to be your dad. You are so smart." Marilyn beamed her approval as she looked adoringly at her young son.

He beamed until he almost glowed. I believe he'll never have another moment like that. Even if he were to someday stand on top of the winner's stand as an Olympic champion, he'd not feel as special as he felt in that room on the night with his family, and especially his father, singing his praises.

I believe that although he didn't realize it, he really felt as he stood before me, "I can do things. People love me. I have great worth. I am a child of God."

For years after, White Crow would sometimes quietly say to me, "Dad, remember the night I did all those things? Can I do that again tonight?"

## Stop Your Meeting On Time

I was once asked by a General Authority, "Are you as a ward leader punctual in conducting your meetings?"

I said, "Yes, I always start meetings on time."

He said, "But are you punctual?"

I answered again the same way, "We start on time."

He asked me the same question again, and as I sat looking perplexed he said, "I know that you begin your meetings on time, but do you end them on time?" He added, "End the meeting at the appointed time and let people go home to their families. Those who neglect the appointed quitting time are as much unpunctual as are those who neglect the beginning time."

## How To Make a Father Happy

My friend with his vast influence he was able to get me a blind date with a girl from Salt Lake City who was his girlfriend's friend. When I went into her house to get her I got talking to her dad who was a plumber. He and I hit it off pretty good because even though he was from Salt Lake City he was more like an American Forker. I could tell that he was pleased that I was going on a date with his daughter. As she and I were going out the door he told me how glad he was that he knew he could trust me with his daughter because she was the joy of his life.

His words had a profound effect upon me. That night I treated that girl like a queen. Her dad waited up for her to come home and I went right in to tell him that I had treated his daughter just the way he wanted her to be treated. My words caused him to be choked up with emotion. Treating her that way made that the best date I had ever had up until that time.

## What Is Greatness Anyway?

I saw the great horse, Man of War, as a statue in Kentucky. It was a great big heroic-size statue of the world's greatest race horse. I said to one of my missionaries who knew much about horses, "He's a great horse. But I think Secretariat, this year's winner of the Triple Crown, is greater."

He said, "Oh, you can't say that, President. You don't how great a horse is until you see how well his children and their children do."

## How Long Has It Been Since You Told Your Wife That You Love Her?

As a Regional Representative, I went to a stake conference in a big stake. It was to be divided into two. The old stake presidency was going to be released. Two new stake presidencies were to be called. I went there with one of the great leaders of the church—Elder Theodore M. Burton. He wanted to do it right so we started interviews on Friday night and spent all Saturday morning. We interviewed a large number of the men in the stake.

The first man came in and the first question Elder Burton asked each man was, "When was the last time you told your wife you loved her?" The man answered nervously, "Well, I think it was about a week ago."

"Oh," replied Elder Burton quite firmly, "That isn't good enough. When are you going to repent? Don't you know that telling your wife that you love her is the most important thing you could ever do?"

The man shuffled his feet and said, "Well, I think I'll repent right away. I'll tell her that I love her as soon as I get home."

Then, at the conclusion of the interview Elder Burton stood up and stood close to the man, took him by the hand and said with great tenderness, "I testify to you that I know Jesus is the Christ and that this is His Church." He then added, "I love you, my dear brother. Now go home and tell your wife that you love her. From now on, tell her that each time you leave the house." The man began to gently weep in the face of such a testimony and challenge.

Elder Burton repeated this procedure with each man. The testimony he bore to each varied, but the challenge to each to express love to his wife each day was always the same. It wasn't long until the men waiting to come to be interviewed had heard from those already interviewed the question being asked. Those waiting their turn were lined up at the telephone—waiting to call home to tell their wife, "Hey, honey, I love you."

Soon the word spread to those who were still at home waiting to come to their interview. The last thing each man did before he left home was to tell his wife that he loved her. It was marvelous to watch and to feel what was happening. Each was able to report that the last thing he had done before leaving home was to express his love to his wife. A spirit of love was building in the stake as each man tenderly told his wife of his love for her.

Needless to say the conference sessions were like heaven on earth. Even now, all these years later, when I think about it tears come to my eyes. What a joy comes into our lives when we take the time to say to our wife, "I love you." If you can't say it, write it with some soap on the mirror. Put a note on the refrigerator. There are so many benefits that come from that. You can do it. If Moses could part the Red Sea, you can part your lips and say, "I love you."

## What Is In A Name?

I didn't use to like the name George. I wanted to be called Don, which is my middle name. If I had been called Don in high school, I would have been popular. All the guys named Don were popular at my school. The girls would see a Don and say with deep and respectful tones, "Hello Don!" But to me they'd blend sarcasm with humor by saying, "Hello, Ge-orge."

It wasn't until I was out of high school that my mother told me how I got the name George. She told me I'd been named after her older brother. She said he was the grandest person who had ever lived. He died just before I was born. She promised the Lord that if I turned out to be a boy that she'd name me after her wonderful brother, whose name was George. She told me stories of how good he always was to her—how he gave her two gold pieces to buy her a new dress to wear when she graduated from school.

When she told me that story, I softly said to myself, "George."

"I like it," I said to mom. "I like it a lot." *George!* It sort of begins and ends the same way. Say it softly to yourself. It's a fun name to say. People don't name their little boys George anymore. We need to get back to good names like George.

## Be A Number One Christian

World War II, combined with other world events, in an indirect way opened the door for increased interest in Christianity in South Korea. During the period following the

Korean War, I was there as a member of the United States Army.

Shortly after arriving in this land, I observed that some people were excited about Christ and his teachings. At the same time, the Koreans were confused because the good they had read and heard about Christianity was quite different from the questionable conduct observed in the soldiers who supposedly were Christians.

Korean civilians came into our camp each day to perform the menial tasks that were undesirable to us, such as K.P. They, in turn, were paid, and the arrangements made both groups happy. As they went about our camp from building to building they, like us, used the dirt paths that wound there way between the weeds and rocks. When American soldiers and Koreans met on the paths, the Koreans jumped aside into the weeds while the soldiers proudly passed by.

Observing this situation, it occurred to me that this was not the way things should be. This was their land, and we, if anyone, should move off the paths. Therefore, I made it a practice to move aside and let the Koreans pass by on the path. This amazed them and as they passed by me I would smile and sort of bow and say to them, "Ahnyong hash imikka." As they went on they would look back with grateful expressions. They seemed amazed but also pleased at my actions. As time went by I learned many of their names, and as they passed I greeted them by name.

The American soldiers had created a system to communicate with the Koreans. One part of this was to call that which was very good "number one" and that which was very bad "number ten." For example, if we were talking to a Korean about our good jeep, we would say, "This is a number one jeep." Or if it were a wreck, we would say, "This is a number ten jeep."

It was a rule at our camp that if a soldier held the rank of a corporal or higher, he would enter the mess hall and go to a table where a Korean worker would bring him his meal. All who had lesser rank went through the line for their own food.

One day I entered the hall, noticed the line was long, and sat down at a table with five of my friends who were eating while I waited for the line to get shorter. As I talked to the others at the table, I felt someone at my elbow. I looked up, and standing at my side with a tray of food was one of the Korean workers. I realized that he was about to put the tray before me. To stop him from doing so, I said, "You can't serve me. I'm just a private!" All my friends at the table fixed their eyes on him.

He looked down at me with moistened eyes and quietly said, "I serve you. You a number one Christian!"

What that wonderful Korean man called me was not true of me then nor now, but I long for it to one day be true. Sometimes I think I hover around four or five, but my dream is that someday I can stand before my fellow men and before God as a number one Christian.

I know why the Korean worker judged me as he did. It was because of the little things I'd done. It's the little things that make a "number one" Christian. It is the little things that, when added together, make up the big thing called "life."

## The Mean Sergeant Could Not Call Me Bad Names

I was in the army, but I was never in a battle. When we'd be marching I'd try very hard to not make any mistakes, because we had a real mean sergeant. If you made a mistake while you were marching and went right when you were supposed to go left, he would call you bad names. I didn't want to be called bad names by the mean sergeant.

Each night when I'd pray, I'd say, "Heavenly Father, please help me to march good so that the mean sergeant won't get angry and call me those bad names that he calls the other soldiers."

Then one Saturday we were standing in formation in front of our barracks, waiting to be dismissed. I was very happy that we would have the afternoon off, and I was thinking about that instead of about marching. The mean sergeant shouted, "Left face!"

I got confused and did a right face, and that made it so everyone else was facing away from the mean sergeant but I was standing face-to-face with him.

My heart pounded with fear, for now I knew that the mean sergeant would call me bad names, just like he called all of the other soldiers bad names when they made mistakes.

But as I looked into the mean sergeant's eyes, he couldn't seem to even talk. Then in a really soft voice he said, "Private Durrant, turn around." Then he said, "Company dismissed!"

Everybody shouted with happiness and ran toward the barracks. But instead of running and shouting, I quietly and slowly walked away. I was very happy that Heavenly Father made it so that the mean sergeant could not call me bad names.

I learned that if you pray, Heavenly Father will protect you against things like the words of the mean sergeant.

## Please Send An Angel

Angels are those who see someone with a great need and they go to their aid. Melissa was such an angel. This is the story of Melissa the angel.

Our family had lived in Kentucky for three years. Now we had moved back to Utah. It was our daughter Kathryn's senior year in high school.

She was slightly shy and it was not easy for her to make friends at her new school. Each day she would walk home for lunch. I told her that she should stay at school and eat her lunch there. Tears came to her eyes as she said, "I can't eat school lunch."

"Why not?"

"Because I can't go to the lunch room and sit there all my myself." Then she asked, "Have you ever gone to a school lunch room and sat there all by yourself to eat?"

Sensing how she felt, I asked, "Couldn't you sit with one of your friends?"

"I had friends in Kentucky, but I don't have any here. Nobody here even says hello to me. I've never felt so lonely in all of my life," she said.

I decided to do something about this. I'd go over to the school and ask the principal to call a student-body assembly so that I could stand up and tell the students the story of my daughter and her loneliness. I would say, "Students, you ought to be ashamed of yourselves. My daughter has lived in Kentucky for three years. Now we have moved here. She longs to have a friend here but none of you will even say hello to her. How can you care so little about those who have no friends?"

But after I had considered this I decided not to do all that. Instead I went to my room and knelt down and prayed. I asked, "Dear Heavenly Father, my daughter is sad. She needs a friend. Please send someone to be her friend."

The next day I came home for lunch and Kathryn was not there. That night I saw her and she excitedly said, "Father guess what?" Before I could respond, she said, "Today I ate school lunch."

Sensing her happiness, I eagerly asked, "What happened?"

She replied, "As I was walking down the hall of the school to get to the door so I could come home, I saw a girl coming toward me. She said, "Hi, Kathryn. I'm Melissa. You are in my math class. You are new here. Let's go to lunch."

The she added, "Dad as we walked along she introduced me to two boys and one girl. Other people came to our table and she introduced them to me. It was so fun. I have never felt happier in my life. She said that she would like to be my friend and that she wanted me to eat with her again tomorrow."

That night I thanked the Lord for answering my prayers and sending my daughter a friend. A friend she desperately needed.

A week later Melissa came to our home. Kathryn said to me, "Dad, this is Melissa. You know, the one who invited me to sit with her at school lunch." When she said that I felt much gratitude. I knew that when I asked Heavenly Father to send a friend for my daughter he had sent Melissa. Then and each time since when I have seen Melissa, I always know that I am in the presence of an angel.

## Finally The Father Was Comforted

I know a man whose son was one of the most unusual and choice young men who ever lived. He had stored so many scones in his heart that it was a joy to know him. His warm smile and cheerful greeting caused many to love him. He knew how to goof off, but never in such a way that anybody got hurt. He knew how to have fun, but it was always clean fun. As the school years went by, he attracted many friends because of his positive and sincere attitude. In his last year of high school he was elected senior class president. But toward the end of that year, this fine young man, who had never been sick in his life, contracted a rare disease. Within a period of just ten days he had gone from perfect health to death.

This was a heartbreaking experience for all who knew him, but particularly for his father. This father was aware that his son was a most unusual young man, and the two of them, as well as being father and son, had been the dearest of friends. The father didn't know how he could carry on after sustaining the loss of this boy who had been so much the pride and love of his heart.

The night before the funeral, many people called at the mortuary, and one by one they tried to say those words that might bring comfort. But it seemed that the father couldn't be comforted. Finally there came a young man who was regarded by the other students as a social misfit. This boy, who was a loner, had very few friends. He had some problems that he hadn't brought upon himself but which limited him socially. As this awkward young man stood before the father he was not able to use any eloquent words whereby to offer any comfort.

He stood silently on that sacred ground and looked into the father's eyes. Then he began to sob. Amidst his sobs he was able to utter these words, "The only reason I ever came to school was because of your son. Every time I saw him in the hall he smiled, he stopped, and he talked to me. He made me feel that I was really somebody. He's the only one in the school who ever did that. Now that he's gone, I don't know if I can even keep coming to school. He was the only friend I've ever had." These words pierced the very heart of the father, and he and the social misfit fell into one another's arms and wept together. To a greater degree than had been the case in many days, the father was comforted.

# THE SCONES OF SACRIFICE AND SERVICE

## I Finally Got a Trend of Thought For My Upcoming Talk On Service

A little neighbor girl knocked on my door while I was trying to prepare a talk on service. I tolerated her but did not give her my full attention. I needed the time to prepare the talk. Then her parents came and told me that they needed a ride to the school to get their other little girl because their car had broken down. I was glad to help but it sure did break my trend of thought that I hoped would be the substance of my talk on service. But now that I think back. I really did not have a trend of thought about this talk until I got back from helping. Then for some reason I had some ideas on what I could say.

## We Did Not Have A New Couch, But Neither Did We Have Another Debt

I recall once when we went shopping in Ogden. We had driven down from Brigham City where I taught seminary. In a large department store there we stood looking at an early American couch. While looking at it a man came up and stood at our side and said, "Have you got a house?"

We said, "Yes."

He said, "Have you got a fireplace?"

And we said, "Yes."

"How would that couch look by your fireplace?"

We said that the couch would look great by our fireplace.

Then he said, "Why don't you get it?"

We said, "Because."

And he said, "Because why?"

And I said, "Because we don't have any money."

He asked, "What has that got to do with it?"

I asked him what he meant. He said, "You don't have to make any payments for three months on it, and then you'll only have to pay so much a month. You can do that. Now, how would it look by your fireplace?"

I said, "Good."

And he said, "Should we deliver it Wednesday?"

We suddenly wised up and ran the other way. We drove our old car up the highway toward home. As we rode along, we were so happy. We didn't have an early American couch, but more importantly we didn't have any more debts.

The next week we went to Deseret Industries and got an early American couch that was far earlier than the one we had looked at. Marilyn took an upholstery class and I got the shop teacher to make a new arm for it. Pretty soon it was in our little house. It was beautiful by our little fireplace.

## If You Don't Have The Money You Can Say No

If you want to raise good kids, it's good to be sort of poor. Then you can answer their requests for things with the great word "No."

Such as, "Can we have this Dad?"

"No." But you say it with love. You can't always give them things, but you can always give them love.

I often tell the children, "The one who does good gets a prize." They say, "What is the prize? A kiss as usual?"

I reply, "That is correct." I give kisses for prizes in games. That is why none of my children are very competitive.

## I Can Carry More

I recall that the most difficult time of my life was in the early months of my mission in England. I was desperately homesick. I missed my mother and the ease of my life at home. At that time I was going forth to do my duty in the name of the Lord, but I was trying to fight my inward battles on my own.

Deep in my heart I wondered if I had the strength to make it. Feeling discouraged, I prayed at my bedside for guidance. That night as I slept I had a vivid dream. In the dream I was at home and I felt happy to be there. I could see myself doing a chore that I had done during my childhood—bringing in the kindling wood that would be used to start the morning fire.

To complete this task I opened the side door of our big kitchen and walked past the cellar door, through the gate that kept the cow in the backyard, and on to the shed where the kindling was kept.

As I entered I noticed that someone else was there. The person's back was to me, so I could not tell who he was. I hurriedly picked up the kindling, but as I did part of it fell back to the ground. The stranger then, without looking at me, beckoned for me to hold out both arms in a cradle-like manner. When I did so, he picked up the kindling piece by piece and placed them in my arms. Sensing that I had a full load, I turned, left the shed, and started back to the house.

As I passed the gate and then the cellar, I felt happy to be home. When I arrived at the door to the house, I was just about to go in when I looked down at the load I was carrying. I felt that I could carry more, and I decided to go back. I hurriedly returned to the shed. Once inside I saw the person. He was still faced away from me. I said, "I can carry more."

At those words he turned toward me, and I recognized him as my Savior. He smiled in a way that made me glad I had returned. He then heaped my arms with so much kindling that I could scarcely see over it. The size of the load was much greater than it had been, but now it seemed lighter than before. I once again headed back toward the house. I was able to make it back to the kitchen door. But before I could go in, the dream ended.

The next morning I knew that what I had experienced had just been a dream, but to me it was a most wonderful dream. That day was in many ways the first day of my mission. I was ready now to carry my load, for I knew it was a load given to me by the Lord and I knew that I was not carrying it alone.

## The Children Will Make The Same Calculations On Tithing That The Father Made

A missionary I had known some twenty-five years earlier came to see Marilyn and me. With him were his wife and their eight children.

We sat in our front room discussing the memories of the past and the present activities of each of his children. Our discussion turned to his occupation as a farmer. I said, "Figuring your tithing on a farm must be a complicated matter."

He replied, "It isn't that complicated."

His children all wanted to speak at once. It was obvious that this question had come up before in their family. His oldest daughter became the spokesperson. She said, "It isn't complicated for Dad because he pays tithing on everything. Even things that he isn't supposed to pay it on, he pays it anyway." I could tell that all the children shared the view that their dad was paying far more tithing than is required.

As they spoke he first looked down. All were silent as we waited for him to speak. As he lifted his head, we could see that this was a very sensitive matter for him, for his eyes were filled with tears. Finally he spoke almost in humble defense. "I've got so much and I get it all from the Lord, so I just try to be as fair as I can with Him in what I give back."

I could tell that these children and this adoring wife looked upon this great man as a priesthood man. A man they would love, honor and follow all the days of their lives. I sensed that when it came to tithing, each of them would make about the same kind of bookkeeping errors that their father had made.

## Like Unto Tithing

An old Indian father who knew his life's journey would soon end, called his ten sons together in order that he might divide his flock of sheep among them.

In the father's flock there were 100 sheep. Therefore, when he divided the sheep among his ten sons, each son got one-tenth of the sheep, or ten sheep. Each son thanked his father for the sheep he had received, and then each led his ten sheep to his own home.

One week later the skies became very dark. A terrible rainstorm struck the country side. The rain came down as if it were a giant waterfall dropping from heaven. The waters ran across the ground and into the gullies. Soon a large river was formed, and it swept forward, washing away everything in its path.

Now it so happened that the ten sheep of one of the sons were in a gully trying to avoid the rain by standing under some small cedar trees. Suddenly the giant river came like a wall, sweeping away both trees and sheep.

The next day when the father visited the unfortunate son, he learned what had happened. He felt sorry for the son who lost all his sheep. He wished that he had more sheep to give to his son, but he had already given away all that he had.

As the father journeyed home, an idea came into his mind. "Perhaps each of my other sons would be willing to give one sheep of his ten to the son who has lost his sheep," he thought. "Thus they would help their brother, and they would still have nine sheep each." The father was filled with happiness as he hurried to the home of one of his sons.

Upon arriving at the home of the first son, he said, "My son, your brother has lost all his sheep. I have come to ask you to give one sheep to him. If you will do this and if your brothers will do the same, your unfortunate brother will again have a flock of sheep."

The son frowned and said, "I am sorry, Father, but I cannot give you one sheep for my brother. I have bought a new saddle for my horse. I have promised to pay for the saddle with wool. I will need the wool from all ten of my sheep. I cannot help my brother. I need all I have."

The father was saddened and hurried to the home of another son. He was certain this son would return one sheep, but the son replied, "I wish I could help my brother, but I cannot. I have told my wife that we have ten sheep. She is counting on that much wool to weave a rug. I am afraid she would be angry if she had to do without any of the wool that I promised her."

The third son answered, "I cannot return a sheep. I am trying to build up a large herd. If I return one sheep, next year I will have two less lambs. No, I cannot return a sheep or my herd will not grow as fast as I want it to grow."

One by one the father went to eight sons. Each refused to

return a sheep. Finally, tired and discouraged, he arrived at the home of the last son.

As he entered the home, the son and his wife brought him food and drink. The father felt better after eating, but he was still discouraged. He could see no need to ask the son for a sheep, because he was sure the answer would be no. He told his son of the misfortune of his brother.

The son's eyes filled with tears as he listened. When the father had ended his account, the son stood and said, "My father, my brother shall have one-half of my sheep. Come, let us go to the herd and take the five biggest ones to him."

The father could not believe the words he had heard. "My son, the ten sheep are yours. Surely to give away just one sheep is enough."

"The sheep were given to me by the goodness of a loving heart. And I shall give one-half of them away in that same spirit."

Upon arriving at the unfortunate brother's home, they placed the five sheep in his corral. The brother who had received and the brother who had given embraced, and the father who stood nearby wept both for joy and for sadness. His tears of joy were shed for the son who had found happiness through giving and for the son who had needed and had received help. His tears of sadness were for the eight sons who had built corrals of selfishness around their hearts. He knew that the same barrier that would not let giving get out could not let happiness get in.

## A Kiss Is Worth More Than Money

Our children used to get a few A grades on their report cards. They would say, "Do we get five bucks for each A?"

"No," I'd reply.

"Well the other kids in the neighborhood get five bucks an A."

I'd reply with a look of love mixed with mischief, "You can't have five bucks for each A, but come over here and I will give you a big kiss for each one."

"We don't want no kisses," they would reply with a tinge of disgust in their voice.

I guess that reward system is why our children were not too motivated academically. They did not know then, but they do now (as adults) that a kiss from mom or dad is worth a lot more than five bucks.

## When You've Sat On The Bench, You Know How Others Feel

I wanted to be a star basketball player, but I ended up on the bench. Some guys can sit on the bench and laugh and enjoy watching the cheerleaders. But for me, sitting on the bench was pure failure. It was almost more than I could bear. All that saved me was a feeling that would not die, a feeling that someday things would change and I'd be a star. I lived on that little pilot light of hope.

Toward the end of a lopsided game, some of my classmates would mockingly shout, "Coach, put George in." Their words were like water that nearly doused my hope. I'd want to disappear when they'd do that. I would pray that the coach would put me in the game, but the Lord didn't seem to care if our team lost so he wouldn't inspire the coach to call out my name. So I'd sit there.

My prayers remained unanswered. Better said, they weren't answered in the way I wanted. But thinking back, I know the Lord was with me: he let me know how it felt to sit on the bench, to feel like a failure, to want to disappear, and to just barely hang on to a thread of hope. In our town he placed a few people who knew how I felt. One was Mr. Boley who ran the meat market. Mr. Boley would seek me out. He'd say things that would give me hope. He'd say, "George, I don't know why the coach doesn't play you. You are by far the best player on that team." Oh, it's wonderful to hear someone say nice things when you can hardly stand up to face another day. The Lord does so much for our foundation of hope, and to add to that he sends me to you one day to give you hope and then another day he sends you to me to give me hope.

So maybe the Lord did answer my prayers. He taught me that the only thing that even comes close to the good feelings that come when someone gives your hope a boost is to give a boost to the delicate and dim hope of another.

The Lord taught me by letting me sit on the bench that the important thing in life is to find people who are sitting on life's dismal bench and then say to them, "Come on, I'll help you stand up." Perhaps they will say, "Why? What's the use?" And you can reply, "Because I love you. I need you. And so do others. And because you're great. That's why."

## That Thine Alms May Be In Secret

*That thine alms may be in secret: and thy Father which seeth in secret himself shall reward thee openly.*

*—Matthew 6:4*

Most folks in Steelville were just a little bit afraid of Big Sam Edwards. Sam had lost his job when the steel plant had cut back, and he hadn't been able to find work during the past six months. He was a proud man; and now, with Christmas coming, he made a few telephone calls to important people telling them that he didn't want any "do-gooders" trying to help his family at Christmas. He gruffly warned, "I'll be staying up on Christmas Eve, and if anybody comes around trying to leave anything at the door, somebody's going to get hurt."

On Christmas Eve, when his wife, Kathryn, and his children had gone to their beds, Sam sat in his small front room with a shotgun draped across his lap. He became so weary that around two o'clock he fell asleep.

The next morning when he awoke, there in front of him he saw a whole pile of toys, a large ham, a small Christmas tree, and an open Bible. For a few seconds, he felt a surge of joy. But then he became angry. To himself he muttered, "I warned them, and somebody will pay for poking their nose into my business." Just then the children came into the room. Seeing the toys, they shouted, "Look, Daddy! See what Santa left us!"

Sam jumped from his chair and quickly stepped between the children and the toys. "Don't touch those things!" he shouted. "This is not our stuff, and somebody is going to pay for sneaking in here and leaving it. That's breaking and entering, and I'm not going to put up with it."

Sam went quickly to the telephone and called his longtime friend Sheriff Walt Durrant. After several rings the sleepy sheriff picked up the phone. Sam blurted out, "Sheriff, you get over here. Somebody broke into my house. I want them arrested." He hung up.

Sam looked over to the corner of the room where his children were standing in a huddle, gazing longingly at the pile of toys. "You kids get back to bed," he said. They didn't move, but fixed yearning eyes on their mother, who stood behind them. She didn't know what to do. During the past few discouraging months, she had more or less given up on helping Sam. If she voiced her thoughts, it always started an argument.

Sam sternly repeated, "I said get back to bed. It's too early for you kids to be up anyway."

The children reluctantly retreated. Kathryn went into the kitchen and started cooking some oatmeal. Breakfast might be the best meal they were going to have that day.

Thirty-five minutes later, Sheriff Walt Durrant knocked on the door. "Come in!" Sam shouted. The sheriff opened the door and said cheerfully, "Merry Christmas." Sam's only reply was a look of disgust.

"Now, what's happened here?" asked the sheriff.

Somebody broke in last night and left all of this stuff on the floor, and I want them arrested."

"Well, Sam, that looks like pretty good stuff to me. Did they take anything?"

"No, they didn't take nothing, but I'm fed up with all of the do-gooders in this town. I can take care of myself and my family. I don't need help from nobody. Besides, didn't I tell you to keep those meddlers away from here?"

"Were you gone away last night when they did it?"

"No, I was sitting right there in that chair."

"Well, Sam, you know nobody could have come in here without making a big racket."

Sam, more angry than ever, replied, "They might have made a big racket, but I guess I slept right through it."

"I guess you did," the sheriff drawled. "Funny thing is, when I drove down your lane from the road, I could see that nobody else had been down here since the big snow last night."

"Well, somebody drove or walked in here. Now you find out who it was."

"I told you, there's not a track out there. The snow quit falling last night around nine, and nobody has been in here since then."

"Sheriff, there must be some tracks out there."

"Go see for yourself, if you think you're so smart. See if you can see where anybody came in here."

"I'll show you," said Sam. "I don't know why we pay taxes for a blind sheriff like you anyway."

Together the two men went outside. Sam wandered down the lane searching for some tracks other than those left by the sheriff, but there were none.

He returned to where the sheriff stood. "Let's go around the house," he said. "There will be some tracks out back."

Together they circled the house, but all around it the snow was as smooth as a calm lake. Not a mark on it.

Sam, more irritated than ever, shouted, "Somebody's raked over the tracks."

"Nonsense," said the sheriff, "nobody has been here. I don't know where that stuff came from, but I know this—nobody brought it here."

Sam didn't know what else to say or do. The sheriff spoke as kindly as he could. "Look, Sam, I've got Christmas waiting at home. Why don't you just take the stuff and enjoy it. Forget where it came from. Just be grateful."

Sam's voice was choked with emotion as he replied. "Sheriff, I'm not grateful for nothing, except the stuff I provide for my own family."

The sheriff replied, "I know, Sam. But you'll get work soon. Things will get better." He drove away.

Completely mystified by what had happened, Sam came back into the house and sat in his chair. Kathryn spoke softly. "Sam, what does it matter how it got here? It's here."

Sam's only reply was, "I just can't figure out how somebody came here without leaving no tracks."

Little four-year-old Katie, who was standing nearby with the other children, excitedly said, "Daddy, maybe there's some tracks on top of the house."

"I don't think so, honey," Sam replied gently.

Then it hit him like a light. Some troublemaker had actually rented a helicopter and landed on his roof!

A few minutes later Sam propped his old wooden ladder against the side of the house, and to the amazement of Kathryn and the children he almost ran to the top. Up there he looked carefully around. "Nothing," he muttered. Little Katie called up to him, "Are there any reindeer tracks?"

Sam paused and looked down at her and the other children. Then he winked at Kathryn and said with a chuckle, "Yeah, I think I can see some reindeer tracks over by the chimney."

Suddenly Sam had a feeling that he had not had in years. He shouted out, "Well, what are you kids waiting for? Those toys are for you, you know!"

Soon the ham was cooking in the oven. The children were playing with their toys. The miniature Christmas tree was on the table. Unnoticed by his family, Sam picked up the open Bible. A verse was underlined. He softly read: "That thine alms may be in secret: and thy Father which seeth in secret himself shall reward thee openly." Never before or since has more joy been packed into one little house or into one father's heart than there was at that moment.

From then on and through the years everybody in town knew that Sam had changed. During the next thirty-six years almost everyone had been touched by one of Sam's kindnesses. He'd done everything from helping Arnold Conder build a house to being the chief cook at the annual old folks' dinner. On his sixty-eighth birthday he was honored as the city's most generous citizen. Sheriff Durrant, his closest friend, was appointed to present him the plaque.

Sam wasn't much of a public speaker. As he accepted the award, he awkwardly said, "I don't do no more stuff for others than anybody else around this here town. I just wish I could do like Jesus said in the Bible. I wished I could do something good and do it in secret so nobody would ever know."

As the years went by, in almost every conversation he had with Sheriff Durrant he would say, "You remember, don't you, Sheriff—that Christmas when there was no tracks nowhere? If I could do something good for someone and leave no tracks, that would be the merriest Christmas of all for me." The sheriff would smile and say, "Maybe someday, Sam."

All in the community mourned when Sam's wife died. By now the children were all grown up and married, and had moved to larger cities to get work. They and their children visited Sam as often as they could, but most of the time he was alone.

Now it was once again Christmas Eve. Tomorrow Sam's house would be filled with his children, his grandchildren, and even his two-week-old great-grandson. It was a family tradition for all the family to come home on Christmas afternoon. But tonight he was alone. He would have gone to visit some friends but his eyesight was such that he could no longer drive, and his arthritis made walking a lot less than pleasurable.

At about five o'clock the Gentrys had come over to sing Sam a Christmas carol. They were a young family who during the past summer had moved into the old Conder home across the hayfield from Sam. Their two young children, five-year-old Lexie and three-year-old Ben, had taken a special liking to Sam, and he to them. The family made it a point to give Sam a ride to church every Sunday. The children loved him to tell them stories about when he was little. They and their mom, Marinda Gentry, came to visit him often.

This Christmas Eve tears moistened his cheeks as first Lexie and then Ben hugged him and said, "We love you, Grandpa Sam. Merry Christmas." Just before they left to go home he gave Lexie a doll and Ben a ball. He had wanted to make each of them something, but his hands were not now his servants as they had once been. Sam watched them through his front window as the little family departed down his driveway toward the country road that led the one block to their home. A heavy snowfall had begun.

Sam, who had difficulty in sleeping anyway, had decided to stay up late this night. As he prepared for bed he looked out of the window and saw that the gentle snow had covered all of the fields in the country neighborhood with a soft smooth whiteness. The snow by then had stopped falling. The winter scene reminded him of that mysterious "trackless" night so long ago. As he let his mind wander in a multitude of memories, he was suddenly jolted back to reality. Looking out across the field toward the Gentry house he saw an orange glow. To his horror he realized that the Gentrys' house was on fire. Hurrying from his chair he scooped up a jacket on his way to the back door. He quickly climbed the wire fence that separated his house from the hayfield. His pains forgotten in his fears for his friends' safety, he hurried toward the burning house. There he found a group of people standing together near the mailbox. The firetruck had just arrived, and the hurrying men were unrolling hoses and exchanging shouted instructions.

No one saw Sam approach, all eyes being on the 10 leaping flames. Mrs. Gentry was screaming, "Bennie is still in there!" The boy's father shouted, "I'll try again!" but two men grabbed him and shouted, "You can't go back! It's no use!" Unnoticed by anyone, Sam ran around and entered through the back door. He couldn't see because of the thick smoke but that didn't matter because he knew the layout of the house, since he had helped build it. Flames were everywhere. He could feel the heat biting against him. The smoke choked his lungs. Suddenly he heard a faint cough. He blindly made his way toward the sound and found little Bennie lying on the floor. He scooped the crying child up in his arms and, running through the flames, made his way to the back door. Once outside he held the boy close to his body and looked heavenward. After coughing violently for several seconds the child began to cry. He placed little Bennie down on the snow and told him to go out front to the mailbox to his mother.

Now for the first time Sam could feel the pain. His lungs seemed to be on fire and his skin felt as though he had been immersed in boiling water. He wanted to be home. Home was where he wanted to die. Without consciously knowing what he was doing, Sam, as if carried by the angels, crossed the snow-covered field, climbed the fence, and staggered into his home.

A fireman found Bennie crying and making his way through the snow. Soon the little boy was in the arms of his mother, who embraced him as she wept with love and gratitude. As she held him, Bennie repeated over and over, "Sam, Sam, Sam." Overwhelmed with emotion, the parents didn't register this, but someone else did. The former Sheriff Durrant, now too old to be a regular lawman, but always a volunteer, stood up straight, and a look of wonder crossed his face. "Sam," he said softly to himself, and he walked back a few yards so that he could see across the field. Just as he did, he saw the light go on in Sam's bedroom window.

The sheriff walked back to where he could watch as Doctor Jones looked at the boy. After just a minute the doctor said, "He looks fine, other than his curly hair is mostly gone. But why don't you drive down to the hospital, and I'll come down and we'll have a good look. Then we'll find a good place for you to stay until the house can be rebuilt."

The sheriff tapped the doctor on the shoulder and said, "You rode out on the firetruck. Why don't you let me give you a lift down to the hospital." As the old sheriff and the doctor pulled out of the Gentry lane, the sheriff said, "Let's just stop in and wish old Sam a Merry Christmas. It will only take a minute." The doctor replied, "He'd be sleeping, wouldn't he?" "No, I don't think so," the sheriff replied. "I think he stays too busy to sleep much."

As they pulled down Sam's lane, the sheriff said softly, "No tracks in or out."

"What's that?" asked the doctor.

"Oh, nothing."

The deep new snow on the doorstep was undisturbed. The two men knocked, but there was no response. The door was not locked. The sheriff pushed it open and entered. The doctor said, "Let's go, he's asleep. Let's not wake him."

"Sam," shouted the sheriff, as he moved further into the house. "Let's look back here," he said, as he walked toward the bedroom.

A few seconds later they switched on the light and found Sam lying fully dressed on his bed. He didn't stir as the sheriff said, "Sam! Sam! are you okay?" At the same time, the doctor took Sam's limp wrist in his hand. There was a faint pulse. He put his hand on Sam's forehead. "He looks flushed," he said softly. "Feels like he has the flu that's all over town. He's burning up with fever."

The sheriff moved closer and said, "I can smell smoke, can't you, Doc?"

"Yeah, it must be on our clothes," replied the doctor.

The sheriff spoke again, "Sam, can you hear me?" There was no response. "Sam, have you been over to the Gentrys'?"

"What are you talking about, Sheriff?" the doctor asked. "This man's one of my patients. He can hardly walk."

The sheriff leaned down so his face was only a foot away from his old friend and asked, "Sam, did you go to the Gentrys'?"

"What's wrong with you, Sheriff? I told you he can't walk much, and he's sick, and besides, when we drove in here I noticed that there wasn't a single track out there in the snow."

An almost indistinguishable smile crossed Sam's face. A smile that only someone like the old sheriff could have seen. Then his head fell to the side. Sam Edwards had died. The doctor placed his fingers around Sam's wrist, and after a few seconds he said, "He's gone. The flu didn't do it on its own. My best guess is his old ticker just plain gave out on him."

"Maybe too much strain?" the sheriff asked.

"No, just too much age," the doctor replied.

Near two in the morning, the sheriff had the Gentrys settled in at the local motel. Warren Anderson from the mortuary had come an hour earlier and had taken Sam's body away. Now the sheriff came back to Sam's house. There was something he felt he had to know.

Sheriff Durrant parked his car just in front of the dark and quiet house. In his heart he felt certain that in some miraculous way Sam had gone to the burning house. Soon he would know. Were there tracks out back and across the field? Had Sam saved the boy and brought the greatest joy a family could ever know?

As the old sheriff's boots crunched into the cold snow, he felt for a moment he could hear the angels singing. He paused and looked up at the stars.

He spoke softly as he looked up. "Oh, heck, Sam! You and I both know there ain't no tracks out there. Besides, I need to be home. It's Christmas."

As the sheriff opened his car door, he looked back at Sam's house. He'd miss his old friend. A tear ran down his cheek, and he felt he heard Sam's voice saying, "I finally did it, Sheriff. Merry Christmas."

Already there was a rumor in town that the life of a little child had been saved by a miracle. Sheriff Durrant felt satisfied with that.

# ABOUT THE AUTHOR

George D. Durrant was born and raised in American Fork, Utah. He has served in many capacities with the LDS Church Educational System. For several years he was the director of Priesthood Genealogy for the church.

He served for three years as president of the Missionary Training Center in Provo, Utah, and he has taught religion at Brigham Young University.

He is the author of more than a dozen books, including the best-selling *Love at Home—Starring Father* and *Don't Forget the Star*.

He is married to the former Marilyn Burnham. They are the parents of eight children.

# CEDAR FORT, INCORPORATED
## Order Form

Name:________________________________________________

Address: ______________________________________________

City: ____________________ State: ________ Zip: ____________

Phone: (    ) _____________ Daytime phone: (    ) ____________

***Scones for the Heart***

Quantity: _____________ @ $15.95 each: ___________

plus $3.49 shipping & handling for the first book: ___________

(add 99¢ shipping for each additional book)

Utah residents add 6.25% for state sales tax: ___________

TOTAL: ___________

Mail this form and payment to:

Cedar Fort, Inc.

925 North Main St.

Springville, UT 84663

You can also order on our website **www.cedarfort.com**
or e-mail us at sales@cedarfort.com or call 1-800-SKYBOOK